No Water No Moon

Osho taught philosophy at the University of Jabalpur,
before establishing the commune in Poona, India, which
has become famous as a mecca for seekers from all over
the world wanting to experience meditation and transformation. His teachings have influenced millions of
people of all ages and from all walks of life.

NO WATER NO MOON

Talks on Zen Stories

OSHO

ELEMENT

Shaftesbury, Dorset • Rockport, Massachusetts
Brisbane, Queensland

This edition published in Great Britain in 1994 by
Element Books Limited
Shaftesbury, Dorset SP7 8BP

Published in the USA in 1994 by
Element Books, Inc.
PO Box 830, Rockport, MA 01966

Published in Australia in 1994 by
Element Books Limited for
Jacaranda Wiley Limited
33 Park Road, Milton, Brisbane 4064

Reprinted 1995

Editing by Ma Anand Pratiksho
Design by Ma Dhyan Amiyo
Cover design by Max Fairbrother
Typesetting by Swami Dhyan Vimukta
Photography by Osho Photo Services
Paintings by Ma Anand Meera (Kasué Hashimoto)
B.F.A. (Musashino Art University, Tokyo)
Printed and bound in Great Britain by
Hartnolls, Bodmin, Cornwall

British Library Cataloguing in Publication
data available

Library of Congress Cataloging in Publication
data available

Sixth edition

ISBN 1–85230–490–1

TABLE OF CONTENTS

NO WATER NO MOON...................................... 1

TRADING DIALOGUE FOR SHELTER 29

IS THAT SO? 63

THE DEAD MAN'S ANSWER 87

GUTEI'S FINGER 113

WHY DON'T YOU RETIRE? 137

BLACK-NOSED BUDDHA....................................... 165

THE GIVER SHOULD BE THANKFUL 189

A PHILOSOPHER ASKS BUDDHA........................... 221

NINAKAWA SMILES... 249

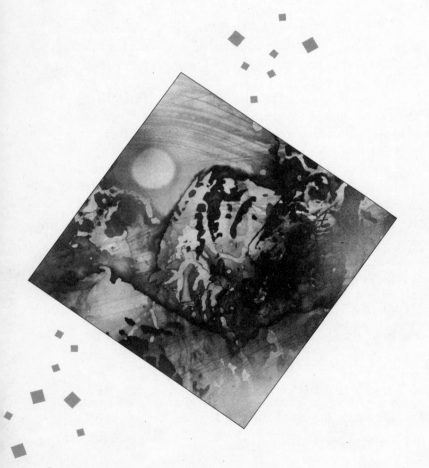

*"...Zen never promises you anything.
It simply gives you* here *and* now.*"

*t*his book is precious; it is a treasure. It can become a dialogue between you and the enlightened master Osho. It can become the rarest of phenomena – a meeting, a sharing of being.

In his compassion Osho reveals the essence of Zen in all its beauty and mystery. You will certainly delight in the absurdities and humor, the unpredictable and sudden surprises in No Water, No Moon. Woven throughout are Zen shocks, Zen knocks and great laughter, which can shake you from everyday sameness into a glimpse of who you really are. Osho pours his unique insight and clarity about life, love, death, meditation and enlightenment in and around the printed word. In the mirror of the silences between you may begin to see yourself.

The discourses based on ten Zen stories can become stepping stones to a deeper understanding of your own life because they are *about* you, they are addressed *to* you, they *are* you! You are the treasure, hiding from yourself.

*"Meditation is opening the eyes.
Meditation is looking."*

This book is precious; it is a treasure. It is a gift from existence to you, calling you to come back home.

Ma Yoga Rabiya

no water
no moon

*The nun Chiyono studied for years, but was
unable to find enlightenment. One night, she was
carrying an old pail filled with water. As she was
walking along, she was watching the full moon
reflected in the pail of water. Suddenly, the
bamboo strips that held the pail together broke,
and the pail fell apart. The water rushed out; the
moon's reflection disappeared – and Chiyono
became enlightened. She wrote this verse:*

*This way and that way I tried to keep the pail
together, hoping the weak bamboo would never
break.*

*Suddenly the bottom fell out. No more water; no
more moon in the water – emptiness in my hand.*

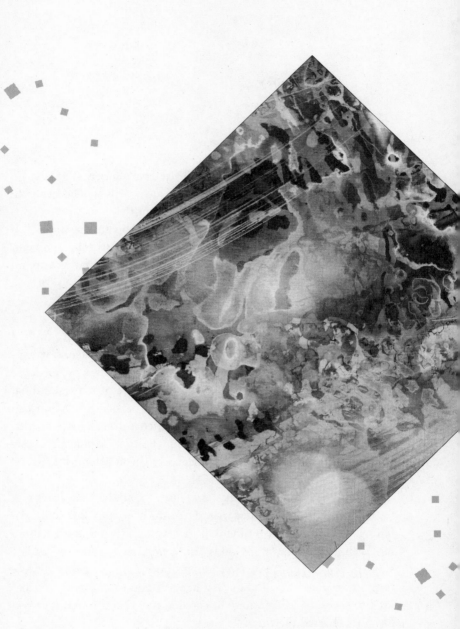

*e*nlightenment is always sudden. There is no gradual progress towards it, because all gradualness belongs to the mind and enlightenment is not of the mind. All degrees belong to the mind and enlightenment is beyond it. So you cannot grow into enlightenment, you simply jump into it. You cannot move step by step; there are no steps. Enlightenment is just like an abyss, either you jump or you don't jump.

You cannot have enlightenment in parts, in fragments. It is a totality – either you are in it or out of it, but there is no gradual progression. Remember this thing as one of the most basic: it happens unfragmented, complete, total. It happens as a whole, and that is the reason why mind is always incapable of understanding. Mind can understand anything which can be divided. Mind can understand anything which can be reached through installments, because mind is analysis, division, fragmentation. Mind can understand parts; the whole always eludes it. So if you listen to the mind you will never attain.

That's what happened: this nun, Chiyono, studied for years and years and nothing happened. Mind can study about God, about enlightenment, about the ultimate. It can even pretend that everything has been understood. But God is not something you have to understand. Even if you know everything about God, you don't know him; knowledge is not 'about'. Whenever you say 'about', you belong to the outside. You may be moving round and round, but you have not entered the circle.

When someone says, "I know about God," he says he doesn't

know anything at all, because how can you know anything about God? God is the center, not the periphery. You can know about matter – because matter has no center in it, it is just the periphery. You cannot know about consciousness: there is no self, there is no one inside. Matter is only the outside; you can know about it. Science is knowledge. The very word science means knowledge – knowledge of the periphery, knowledge about something where the center doesn't exist. Whenever the center is approached through the periphery, you miss it.

You have to become it; that is the only way to know it. Nothing can be known about God. You have to be; only being is knowledge there. With the ultimate, 'about and about' means missing and missing again. You have to enter and become one.

That's why Jesus says, "God is like love" – not loving, but just like love. You cannot know anything about love, or can you? You can study and study, you can become a great scholar, but you have not touched, you have not penetrated. Love can be known only when you become a lover. Not only that: love can be known only when you become love. Even the lover disappears, because that too belongs to the outside. Two persons in love become absent. They are not there. Only love exists, the rhythm of love. There may be two poles of the rhythm but *they* are not there. Something of the beyond has come into being. They have disappeared.

Love exists when you are empty. Knowledge exists when you are filled. Knowledge belongs to the ego, and the ego can never penetrate to the center; it is the periphery. The periphery can know only the periphery. You cannot know something which is of the center through the ego. The ego can study, the ego can make you a great scholar, maybe a religious scholar, a great pundit. You may know all the Vedas, all the Upanishads, all the Bibles and Korans, and still you know nothing – because it is not knowledge from the outside, it is something which happens when you have entered and you have become one.

The nun Chiyono studied for years...

She may have studied for lives. You have been studying for many lives. You have been moving and moving in a circle. But when somebody moves in a circle, a very great illusion is created: you feel you are progressing. You always feel you are moving, and you are still not going anywhere, because you are moving in a circle. You go on repeating. That is why Hindus have called this world *samsara*. Samsara means the wheel, the circular. You move and move and move and never reach anywhere, and you always feel that you are reaching. "Now the goal is nearer because I have walked so much." Just try moving in a big circle. You can never see it as a circle, because you know only part of it. So it is always a road, a way. This is what has been happening for many lives.

Chiyono studied and studied, *but was unable to find enlightenment* – not because enlightenment is difficult, but because when you study it you miss the whole point. You are on the wrong track. It is as if someone is trying to enter this room through the wall. Not that entering this room is difficult, but you have to enter through the door. If you try through the wall it looks difficult, almost impossible. It is not. It is you who are on the wrong track. Many, many people, whenever they start the journey, they start through study, through learning, through knowledge, information, philosophy, systems, theology. They start from the 'about'; then they are knocking against the wall.

Jesus says, "Knock and the door shall be opened unto you." But please remember if it is a door or not. Don't go on knocking on the wall, otherwise no door shall be opened unto you. And, in fact, when you knock at the door, when you really reach near the door, you will find it has always been open. It has always been waiting for you. A door is a waiting, a door is a welcoming, a door is a receptivity. It has been waiting for you, and you have been knocking on the wall. What is the wall? When you start through knowledge and not through being, you are knocking at the wall.

Become, be! Don't gather information. If you want to know love, be a lover. If you want to know God, be meditation. If you want to enter the infinite, be prayer. But be! Don't *know* about prayer. Don't try to accumulate what others have said about it. Learning will not help; rather, unlearning will help. Drop whatsoever you know, so that you can know. Drop all information and all scriptures, forget all Korans and Bibles and Gitas; they are the barriers, they are the wall. And if you go on knocking against that wall, those doors will never open, because there are no doors. And people are knocking against the Koran, knocking against the Vedas, knocking against the Bible, and no door opens. They go on studying and studying, and they go on missing like the nun Chiyono: she *studied for years, but was unable to find enlightenment.*

What is enlightenment? It is becoming aware who you are. It is nothing to do with the outside world. It is nothing to do with what others have said. What others have said is irrelevant. You are there! Why go and consult the Bible and the Koran and the Gita? Close your eyes and you are there in your infinite glory. Close the eyes and the doors are open. Because you are there you need not ask anybody. You ask...then you will miss. The very asking shows that you think you are somewhere else. The very asking shows that you are asking for a map. And for the inner world there is no map – there is no need, because you are not moving to an unknown destination.

Really, you are not moving at all. You are there. You are the goal. You are not the seeker, you are the enlightenment. So what is enlightenment? One state – when you seek without – is unenlightenment; another state – when you seek within – is enlightenment. So the only difference is of a focusing. If you focus out, you are unenlightened. If you focus in, you are enlightened. So the only question is of a turning.

The Christian word conversion is beautiful, but they have used it in a horrible way. Conversion doesn't mean to make a Hindu a Christian or to make a Christian a Hindu. Conversion means a turning. Conversion means a turning to the source, turning within; then you are converted. And your consciousness can flow in two ways, outwards or inwards; these are the two possibilities for the stream of your consciousness to flow. Outwards it can flow for many, many lives – it will never reach to the goal, because the goal is at the source. The goal is not ahead, it is behind. The goal is not somewhere where you will reach. The goal is somewhere where you have already left. The source is the goal. This has to be understood very deeply. If you can go backwards to the first point of your beginning, you reach the goal.

Enlightenment is to go to the source, and the source is within you; life is there flowing, throbbing, continuously beating within you. Why ask others? Studying means asking others. Asking about yourself and asking others? This is foolishness par excellence. This is absolute absurdity – asking about yourself and asking others. That's what study means: looking for the answer. And you are the answer!

> Chiyono studied for years, but was unable to find
> enlightenment.

It is natural, obvious. Nothing was wrong in it. She was looking out, studying.

Another thing to remember: your being is life, and no scripture can be alive. Scriptures are bound to be dead. Scriptures are corpses, and you are asking the dead about your life. This is not possible. Krishna will not be of much help, neither will Jesus – unless you become a Krishna or a Jesus. Life cannot be answered by the dead. And if you think that you will find the answer, you will be more and more burdened by the answers, and the answer will remain unknown. This is what happens to a man who is studying, who is a thinker, who is a philosopher. He goes on being burdened by his own efforts – words and words and words – and is lost. And the answer was always there. Just a turning-in was needed.

No, nobody will answer you. Don't go to anybody, go to yourself. And whenever you reach a master, all that he can do is help you to reach yourself, that's all. No master can give you the answer, no master can give you the key. The master can only help you to look within, that's all. The key is there, the treasure is there, everything is there.

One night, she was carrying an old pail filled with
water. As she was walking along, she was watch-
ing the full moon reflected in the pail of water.
Suddenly, the bamboo strips that held the pail
together broke, and the pail fell apart. The water
rushed out; the moon's reflection disappeared –
and Chiyono became enlightened.

One night she was carrying an old pail filled with water.

You are also carrying a very, very old, ancient pail filled with water. That is your mind, filled with thoughts. It is the most ancient thing that you are carrying, almost dead.

Mind is always old, it is never new. It cannot be, by its very nature, because mind means the memory. How can the memory be new? Mind means the known. How can the known be new? Mind means the past. How can the past be new? Look at your mind: all that it carries is old, dead. The moment you come to know, it is already past. When you recognize something that you have known, it is already gone. It is not here and now, it has moved into the world of the dead.

So mind by its very nature, mind as such, is old. That's why, through mind, nothing original is ever born. Mind cannot be original, mind can only be repetitive. So mind goes on repeating. It may repeat in thousands of ways, it may repeat in new words, but the thing remains the same. Mind cannot know, cannot come to encounter the fresh, the young, the new. Whenever you encounter the fresh, the young, the new, mind has to be put aside, because only then your eyes are not filled with the past, not filled with the dust of the past; then your mirror can mirror that which is here and now.

All that is new is born out of consciousness, not out of mind. Consciousness is your innermost source. Mind is the dust gathered in many of your journeys, as if you have never taken a bath. And you have been journeying and journeying, and everything gets dirty and dust gathers, and you have never taken a bath. Your mind has never taken a bath. You cling to it. It is absolutely dirty. And all methods of meditation are nothing but methods to bathe this mind, to take a bath, the inner bath, so the dust is thrown away and the hidden consciousness comes to the surface and can encounter the reality.

The reality is there, you are there, but the encounter is not there because between you and the reality is the mind. Whatsoever you see, you see through the mind. Whatsoever you hear, you hear through the mind – and then you are almost deaf, almost blind. Jesus goes on saying to his disciples, "If you have ears to hear, hear me. If you have eyes to see, see." They all had eyes like you. They all had ears like you. But Jesus knows, as I know, that you are deaf, you are blind.

Whenever you hear through the mind you are not hearing, because the mind interprets, the mind colors, the mind changes, mixes itself; and anything that reaches to you is now already old. The mind has done its trick. The mind has given its own meaning, the interpretation. The mind has commented.

That's why, unless you become a right listener.... Right listening means the capacity to listen without the mind. Right seer means the capacity to look without the mind, the capacity to look without interpreting, judging, condemning; without evaluation, without saying yes or no. When I speak to you, I can even see your mind nodding yes or no. Even if the nod is invisible, l can see it. You may not be aware, sometimes you say yes – the mind has interpreted. Sometimes you say no – the mind has interpreted, the mind has come in, evaluating. You have missed.

Just listening, not judging, suddenly you become aware that this mind has been the whole trouble. It is old – one thing to remember – and it can never be new. So never think that you have an original mind. No mind can be original, all minds are old, repetitive. That's why mind always likes repetition, and is always against the new. Because the mind has created the society, the society is always against the new. The mind has created the state, the civilization, the morality; they are all against the new.

Whatsoever is created by the mind will always be against the new. You cannot find anything more orthodox than mind.

No revolution is possible with the mind. So if you are a revolutionary through the mind, don't deceive yourself. A communist cannot be a revolutionary, because he has never meditated. His communism is through the mind. He has changed bibles – he doesn't believe in Jesus, he believes in Marx; or he believes in Mao, the latest edition of Marx – but he believes. He is as orthodox as any Hindu, any Catholic, any Mohammedan. The orthodoxy is the same, because orthodoxy doesn't depend on what you believe. The orthodoxy depends on whether you believe through the mind; the orthodoxy depends on the mind. Mind is the most orthodox element in the world, the most conformist.

So whatsoever mind creates can never be new, will always be old, and will always insist against the new; it will be always counter-revolutionary. That's why in the world there is no revolution other than the religious revolution; there cannot be. Only religion can be revolutionary, because religion hits at the very source. It drops the mind, the old pail, and then, suddenly, everything is new, because mind was making everything old through its interpretation. Suddenly you are a child again. Your eyes are fresh and young, you look at things without knowledge, without learning. Suddenly the trees have a freshness. The greenery has changed – it is not dull, it is alive. Suddenly the song of a bird is absolutely different.

This is what is happening to many people through drugs. Aldous Huxley became so fascinated with drugs because of this. All over the world the new generation is so attracted by drugs. The reason is this: because the drug for a moment, or for a few moments, chemically puts the mind aside. You look at the world – now the colors all around are simply miraculous. You had never seen such a thing. An ordinary flower becomes the whole existence, carries the whole glory of the divine. An ordinary leaf becomes so deep, as if the whole truth is revealed through it. Everything and anything immediately changes. The drug cannot change the world; the drug is only chemically putting your mind aside.

But you can become addicted to it – then the mind has absorbed the drug also. Only once, in the beginning, for the first time, or twice or three times, you can deceive the mind chemically. By and by, the mind becomes attuned to the drug, the mind again takes its mastery. The original shock is lost. It becomes addicted to the drug. Then it demands, and now the demand is coming from the mind. Now, by and by, even chemically you will not be able to push the mind aside. It will be there, you will be addicted. Trees will again become old, colors will not be so radiant, things will again become dull. The drug has killed you; it couldn't kill the mind.

The drug can only give you a shock treatment. It is a shock to the whole body chemistry. In that shock, the old adjustment is broken. Gaps are there; through the gaps you can look, but this cannot be made a practice. You cannot practice a drug. Sooner or later it becomes part of the mind; the mind takes over. Then everything is old again.

Only meditation can kill the mind, nothing else. Meditation is mind suicide, mind committing suicide. If you can put the mind aside – without any chemicals, without any physical means – then *you* become the master. And when you are the master, everything is new. It has been always so. From the very beginning to the very end, everything is new, young, fresh. Death has never occurred in this world. It is life eternal.

> *One night, she was carrying an old pail filled with water...*

You are also carrying the old pail filled with water. Mind is the old pail, and thoughts are the water. And because you value thoughts so much, you cannot throw this old pail. Because then what will happen to *your* thoughts? You cling to them as if they are a very deep source of bliss, a deep source of silence; as if through thoughts you are going to achieve life and the hidden treasures of life. You have never achieved anything like that through thoughts. It is simply a hopeless hope.

What have you achieved through thoughts? Nothing but anxiety, tension. But you cling to them in the hope that some day or other, somewhere in the future, through your thinking, you are going to achieve the truth. Up to now, nothing like that has happened, and it is not going to happen any day. It is not going to happen ever, because truth is nothing to be thought. It is there. You just have to look. There is no need to think about it. Thinking is needed if it is not there, if you are groping in the dark. But there is no darkness in existence; existence is absolute light. You need not grope. You are unnecessarily groping with closed eyes, and you think, "If I leave groping, I will be lost." Thinking is groping.

Meditation is opening the eyes. Meditation is looking. That is why Hindus have called it *darshan*. Darshan means looking – looking at, not thinking about. The very looking transforms. But you carry thoughts in this old pail, and you go on patching the pail, caring about it: if it breaks, what will happen to your valuable thoughts? And they are not valuable at all.

One day do this, a little experiment. Close your doors and sit in the room, and just start writing your thoughts – whatsoever comes in your mind. Don't change them, because you need not show this piece of paper to anybody. Just go on writing for ten minutes and then look at them: this is what your thinking is. If you look at them, you will think this is some madman's work. If you show that piece of paper to your most intimate friend, he will also look at you and think, "Have you gone crazy?" And it is the same situation with him also. But we go on hiding the craziness. We have faces, and behind those faces we are madmen.

Why do you value this thinking so much? You have become addicted to it – it is a drug, it is chemical. Remember well, thinking is chemical, it is a drug. Whenever you start thinking, you are in a sort of hypnotic sleep. That's why you have become addicted – just like opium. You can forget the world, the worries, the responsibilities. You just start a different type of world within yourself: dreaming, thinking.

Those who have been working for a long time on the science of sleep, they say that sleep is needed for dreaming. And if you ask them why dreaming is needed, they say it is needed so that you can remain sane, because in dreams you can throw your insanity. The whole night is a catharsis. In your dreaming you are throwing your insanity, and by the morning you can behave sanely. The whole day you can behave in a sane way, because the whole night is there to behave in an insane way. Scientists say that if you are deprived of your dreaming and sleep for a few days you will go mad, because the catharsis will not be there and then madness will start erupting. You will explode.

In the night you dream – that's a catharsis. In the day you think – that is also a catharsis, and it helps you to be sleepy. It is a drug. You need not worry what is happening. You just close yourself within your thoughts. And they are well known to you, you feel cozy, it is your own home; howsoever dirty and old, but you have been living in it for so long that you are accustomed to it. You have become accustomed to your prison. It happens to prisoners: if they are for a long time in the jail, they become afraid of coming out, they become afraid of freedom. There is a fear of freedom, because it will bring new responsibilities. And there is nothing like coming out of the mind – it is absolute freedom. Hindus have called it *moksha*, the absolute freedom. There is nothing like it – the prison is shattered, you are simply under the infinite sky. Fear grips you; you want to go back to your home – your cozy home, walled, fenced.

If the infinite is not there, you are not afraid. The infinite always looks like death. You have become accustomed to the finite, with boundaries clearcut, distinctions clearly made. That's why you cannot throw the thoughts, you cannot throw the pail. Rather, you go on making the pail bigger and bigger and bigger, and it is just like your belly; the more thoughts you put in it, the more it goes on expanding. And the belly may burst if you eat too much, but not the mind.

An ordinary mind can contain all the libraries of the world. In your small head there are seventy million cells, and each cell can carry at least one million pieces of information. No computer has

yet been developed which can be compared to your mind. Within
your small head, you carry the whole world. And it goes on expanding.

Chiyono studied and studied – she put more and more water in
the old pail. She could not find enlightenment. But:

> *One night, she was carrying an old pail filled with*
> *water. As she was walking along, she was watch-*
> *ing the full moon reflected in the pail of water.*

The full moon was there high in the heaven, and in the water, in
the pail, it was reflected, and she was looking at it. That is what is
happening to everyone. This is not a story, this is not an anecdote, it
is a fact – this is happening to you. You have never looked at the
full moon. You cannot. You always look at the moon reflected in
your water, in your thoughts. That's why Hindus – particularly
Shankara – have said: All that you know is *maya*, illusion. It is as if
you are looking at the moon in the water, a reflection, not at the
true moon. And you think this is the moon.

Whatsoever you see, you see through the reflection. Your eyes reflect; your eyes are just mirrors. Your ears reflect – *all* your senses are
just mirrors, they reflect. And then there is the greatest of all mirrors,
your mind; it reflects. It not only reflects, it comments, interprets.
With the reflection it gives a commentary side by side. It distorts.

Have you seen distorting mirrors? No need to go anywhere, you
have that within you – it distorts everything. Whatsoever you have
known up to now has not been the real moon in the sky, because
with this old pail filled with water, how can you look at the real
moon? You go on looking at the reflection, and the reflection is illusory. That is the meaning of maya, illusion. Whatsoever you know
is maya, it is appearance, not the real. The real comes only when
the pail is broken – water flows out, reflection disappears.

> *Suddenly, the bamboo strips that held the pail*
> *together broke, and the pail fell apart.*

It happened suddenly; it is like an accident. Try to understand this phenomenon. Enlightenment is always like an accident because it is unpredictable – because you cannot manage, you cannot arrange so that it happens, you cannot cause it to happen. If you can cause it to happen, it can never be beyond your mind. And if you manage for it to happen, it will be just a trick of the mind. Many people try to manage it. They do this and that, just creating the cause for enlightenment to happen, but it is not a causal thing. If *you* cause it, it cannot be greater than you. If you cause it, it is absolutely useless. It happens, it cannot be caused. It is not a continuity with your mind, it is a discontinuous abyss. Suddenly you are not there and it is there. How can you manage it? If you manage, you will be there.

When Gautam Siddhartha became enlightened, became a Buddha, was he the same man? No! If the same man becomes enlightened…it is impossible. The continuity is broken; the old man has simply disappeared. This is an absolutely new man. Siddhartha Gautam, the prince who had left his palace, wife and child, is there no more. That ego is there no more; that mind is there no more. That old man is dead – the old pail has broken. Now this is absolutely new; this has never been there. That's why we give him a new name, we call him Buddha. We drop the old name, because that old name belonged to some other identity, to some other personality, to somebody else. That old name never belonged to this man.

Enlightenment is a discontinuous phenomenon. It is not continuous, because if it is continuous it can only be at the most a modified past; it cannot be absolutely new, because the past will continue – modified, changed a little bit here and there, painted, polished, but the old will continue. It may be better, but it will still remain the old.

Enlightenment is like an accident. But don't misunderstand me, because when I say enlightenment is just like an accident, I am not saying don't do anything for it. That is not the meaning. If you don't do anything for it, even the accident will not happen. The accident happens only to those who have been doing much for it; but it never happens because of their doing. This is the problem: it never happens because of their doing; it never happens without their doing. That doing is not a cause for it to happen. The doing is just a cause which creates the situation in them so they become accident-prone, that's all.

All your meditations will create just an accident-proneness, that's all. That's why even a Buddha cannot say when your enlightenment is going to happen. People come to me and they ask; I tell them, "Soon." It means nothing. Soon may be the next moment, soon may not come for many lives, because an accident cannot be predicted. If it can be predicted it is not an accident at all, then it is a continuity.

But don't stop doing things. Don't think that if it is going to happen, it will happen; then it will never happen. You have to be ready for it, ready for the accident, ready for the unknown – ready, waiting, receptive. Otherwise the accident may come and may pass you. You may be asleep. The unknown may knock at the door and you may not listen. You may be fast asleep, or you may be talking to someone, or you will interpret that it may be just wind knocking at the door. You can think so many things – everybody is a great thinker.

Be ready for the accident. And remember: all that you do is not a cause for it, all that you do simply creates a situation in you, all that you can do is not a cause, but only an invitation. The difference is great, because if you think it is a cause then you start demanding. If you think it is a cause then you say, "Why is it not happening? Why has it not happened to me up to now?" It creates an inner tension, and if tension is there then it is impossible for it to happen. You have to be caught unawares. You should be waiting, but not anxious – relaxed. You should invite it, but don't be certain that the guest will be coming.

Finally it depends on the guest, not on you. But without the invitation the guest will never come, that is certain. With your invitation it is not certain that he will come; but with your no-invitation it is certain that he will not come. With your invitation he may come, the possibility is there. So wait at the door, but don't be anxious, don't be too certain.

Certainty is of the mind, waiting is of the consciousness. And mind is shallow, all its certainties are shallow. It can happen any moment. Whenever you are ready to see, to look, you will come to know that it has always been happening just by the side. You were not looking at that, you were not looking at that corner.

I have heard: once it happened, Mulla Nasruddin was resting in his chair. His wife was looking at the street and he was looking at the wall. They were sitting back to back, as husbands and wives always sit.

Suddenly the wife said, "Nasruddin, look! The richest man of the town is dead, and thousands of people are going to give him the last send-off."

Nasruddin said, "What a shame I am not facing that way!"

"What a shame I am not facing that way." He will not look – just a turn of the head.... But this is what is happening to you. What a shame. You are not looking that way where the accident is passing, where the unknown is passing.

All meditations will help you only to look towards the unknown, to look towards the unaccustomed, to look at the stranger. They will make you more open, more open for the accident. But you cannot cause it.

Even if you are ready, you may have to wait. You cannot force it; you cannot bring it to you. If you can force it, then religion will be just like science. That's the basic difference between science and religion. Science can force things because it depends on cause, not on invitations. Science can make anything because it finds the cause. Once the cause is known, then anything can be done. Science knows that if you heat water up to one hundred degrees it will evaporate – that's a cause. You can be certain: once it is a hundred degrees, the water starts evaporating. You can force the water to evaporate by heating. You can mix oxygen and hydrogen and you can force them to become water. You can cause. Science tries to know the cause.

Religion is different, basically different. And religion can never become a science in that sense, because it is looking for the un-caused, it is looking for the discontinuous; it is looking for an absolute conversion. A relative conversion can be caused, a partial transformation can be caused. But *absolute?* Nothing of the old and everything new? – then there must be a gap. The link cannot be there. There must be a jump. So suddenly the old goes out of existence and the new comes into existence, and they are not joined together – the gap is there. Siddhartha Gautam simply disappears. Gautam Buddha appears – there is a gap.

This gap has to be remembered. That's why I say enlightenment is just like an accident. But you have to be continuously working for it, that's the paradox. Listening to me, don't become lazy. Listening to me, don't just go to sleep. Listening to me, don't start thinking and reasoning that, "If it is an accident and we cannot cause it, then why meditate? Then why do this and that? Then simply wait." No, your waiting must not be a lazy waiting. Your waiting must be alive. You must wait with absolute energy at your disposal. You should not be waiting like a dead man: you should wait young, fresh, alive, throbbing. Only then that unknown can happen to you. When you are at the best of your life, at the best of your ca-pacity, when you are most alive, when you are at the peak – only then it happens. Only a peak can meet that great peak; only peaks – only the similar can meet the same.

Go on working as much as you can, but don't create any de-mand out of it. Don't say, "I have done this, now it must happen." There is no must about it. It is a stranger. You go on writing invita-tions to it, but it has no address so you cannot post them. You go on throwing your invitations to the winds; they may reach, they may not reach. God is always a 'perhaps'; but it is beautiful when things are 'perhaps'. When things are certain, the beauty is lost.

Have you ever observed that in life only death is certain and everything else is uncertain? Everything is uncertain! Whether love will happen or not, nobody knows. Whether you will be able to sing a song or not, nobody knows. One thing is certain: death. Certainty belongs to death, never to life. And if you are in search of life eternal, then live in the perhaps. Live open, waiting, but remembering continuously you cannot cause it to happen. When it happens, you will disappear.

That is the meaning of this beautiful happening:

> *Suddenly, the bamboo strips that held the pail*
> *together broke...*

Suddenly it happened. But she was working, studying, meditating. She was a great nun. She had lived for at least thirty, forty years with the master, and she had worked tremendously.

I must tell you something about Chiyono. She was a very beautiful woman – rarely beautiful, unique. When she was young, even the emperor and the princes were after her. She refused, because she wanted to be a lover only to the divine, so nobody was up to her expectations, nobody was able to fulfill them.

She went from one monastery to another to take sannyas, to become a nun; but even great masters refused – because she was so beautiful she would create trouble. There were so many monks – and of course monks are repressed people – and she was so beautiful that they will forget God and everything. And she was really beautiful, so everywhere the door was closed.

The master said, "Your search is okay, but I have to look towards my followers also. There are five hundred sannyasins; they will go mad. They will forget their meditations, their scriptures, everything. You will become the god. So Chiyono, don't disturb these poor people, you go."

So what did Chiyono do? Finding no way, she burned her face, scarred her whole face. And then she went to a master; he couldn't even recognize whether she was a woman or a man. Then she was accepted as a nun.

She was so ready. The search was authentic. The accident was worthy, the accident was earned. She studied, meditated for thirty, forty years continuously. Then suddenly, one night, the stranger came to her door.

> *Suddenly, the bamboo strips that held the pail*
> *together broke, and the pail fell apart. The water*
> *rushed out; the moon's reflection disappeared –*
> *and Chiyono became enlightened.*

She was looking at the moon – it was beautiful. Even reflections are beautiful, because they reflect the absolute beauty. The world is also beautiful because it is a reflection of God. So don't say the world is ugly. How can the reflection be ugly when it reflects the divine?

So those who say that the world is ugly and renounce it are absolutely wrong, because if you renounce this world, deep down you are renouncing the creator. Don't renounce. Even a woman's face is beautiful, because it reflects. A man's face is beautiful, the body is beautiful, because they reflect. The trees are beautiful, the birds are beautiful, because they reflect. The reflection is so beautiful – what to say about the original?

So a real seeker is not against the world. A real seeker loves the world so much, he loves the reflection so much that he wants to see the original. He loves this reflection so much that a desire arises to see, to see the full moon in the sky. He leaves this reflection, not because he is against it, he leaves this reflection just in search of that which has been reflected in it. He is not against love, his prayer is not against love. He has known such beauty in love that now he wants to go deeper. Prayer is the deepest 'in-love'. He has known so much in the reflection, it was so beautiful, so fragrant, such music was there, that now a desire has arisen to know the source. And if the reflection is so musical, what harmony must there be in the original source.

A real seeker is never against anything. He is for something, but never against something. He is for God, but never against the world, because finally the world belongs to God. If I see your face in a mirror and it is beautiful, should I be against the mirror? Really, I should be thankful because it reflected you. But I will not focus myself on the mirror; I will be in search of you who was reflected in the mirror. I will have to leave the mirror, but not because I am against it. I will have to turn my face away from the mirror, but not because I was against it. I will be thankful to it because it mirrored something, and in the reflection it was so beautiful – but now I must go to find the original source.

> *The water rushed out; the moon's reflection*
> *disappeared – and Chiyono became enlightened.*

She was looking at the moon reflected in the pail. Suddenly the pail fell down, the water rushed out, and the moon disappeared – and that became the trigger-point.

There is always a trigger-point from where the old disappears and the new starts, from where you are reborn. That became the trigger-point. Suddenly, the water rushed out and there was no moon. So she must have looked up – and the real moon was there. And this became a parable, this became an inner phenomenon. The same was happening inside: everything was seen through the mind – it was a mirror. Suddenly she became awakened to this fact, that everything was a reflection, an illusion, because it was seen through the mind. As the pail broke, the mind inside also broke. It was ready. All that could be done had been done. All that could be possible, she had done it. Nothing was left, she was ready, she had earned it. This ordinary incident became a trigger-point.

But remember: don't follow Chiyono. It will not happen to you that way. Because you know the story you can break the pot, and the water rushes out, and the reflection disappears – and nothing happens within you. It cannot be made a ritual.

But this is how the foolish humanity has been acting for centuries and centuries. Trigger-points are known, but they are always individual and unique. They cannot be repeated, because nobody can be a Chiyono again. The world never repeats. God is so original, he never repeats. Chiyono is born only once, never again – never, never again. So you cannot repeat it, because you are not Chiyono.

But that's what goes on and on, because our mind works as a logical system. If it happened to Chiyono carrying a water-pail, then the water-pail dropping, breaking, water flowing, reflection gone, enlightenment happening – make it a ritual. That is what is being done in churches, mosques, temples – rituals.

How did it happen to Buddha? Sit the same way, plant a *bodhi* tree, sit under it with closed eyes, just Buddha-like – and you are just stupid. You will not become a Buddha, you are simply stupid. You would not have repeated it otherwise. Rituals are repeated by idiots. Because this much understanding...that it is not a question of sitting under a bodhi tree. The long preparation that Buddha underwent, the millions of lives that he passed – he is a unique personality. This is the last trigger-point. It is a concluding thing. Many, many lives of effort, search...and then comes this climax.

This is just accidental that he was sitting under the bodhi tree. It would have happened anyway. If he was not sitting there, then too it would have happened. If there was no tree, then too it would have happened. It was not necessary that he must be sitting – he may have been walking and it would have happened. It is a conclusion. It is just coincidental that he was sitting under the bodhi tree in a particular posture. The posture is not the cause, the tree is not the cause, the way he was sitting is not the cause. If it was a cause, then you could repeat it. Heat it to one hundred degrees and water evaporates. Sit under the bodhi tree exactly in a Buddha posture, even more perfect than him, and enlightenment happens.

No, it is not that way. And don't be stupid, don't follow blindly, and don't make anything a ritual. Understanding is needed, not ritual. It is good to sit in a Buddha posture, but remember well that you are not Buddha and the same trigger-point is not going to work for you – something else. And if you go on following Buddha, absolutely blind, then you may miss your trigger-point; that is the problem, because that will not happen with this repetitive ritual, you have to seek your own. Take the help of all the buddhas, but don't be blind. Understand them as deeply as you can, because they have attained – but there is no path.

The spiritual dimension is just like the sky: no trace is left, you cannot follow. A bird flies, no trace is left. The sky remains empty, no path is created. It is not like the earth. If many people pass, then a footpath is there; you can follow. The spiritual dimension is the dimension of the sky, because it is non-material, it is not earthly, no trace is left. Buddha flies; look at the flight, the beauty of it, the glimpse, the light; enjoy it, understand it, but don't try to follow, don't be blind. Blindness won't help.

Chiyono became enlightened, and this way has never been so with anybody else. Buddha was not carrying a pail of water, neither was Mahavira, nor Krishna, nor Lao Tzu, nor Zarathustra – nobody was carrying a pail of water. And after Chiyono many have carried because it seems so simple. You can manage it, it seems so simple, no difficulty is involved. Fullmoon night comes every month; you can wait and do it again.

Don't be ritualistic. Ritual is not religion. Ritual is the most anti-religious thing in the world. You are unique – remember. And something unique is going to happen to you which has never happened before, which will never happen again. Not only your fingerprints are unique, your soul is unique.

I was just reading a scientific research work which proves that every part of the body is unique – not only fingertips: you have a different liver, a different type of heart, a different type of stomach; nobody else has got that. And in the textbooks where you read and you see the figure of the stomach, you will never find that stomach anywhere; that is just average, imaginary. If you look at the stomachs of real people they will all be different.

'Average' is not the truth; average is just a mathematical approximation, it is not a fact. The fact is always unique. You have a different type of being and it differs in every way. And it is good and it is beautiful that you are different – not a repetition, not like a

Ford car. A million cars can be produced all alike. You are not a machine, you are a man. And what does your manhood, your humanity consist of? Where are you different from a machine? In your uniqueness. Machines are repeatable – they can be repeated – replaceable. You can replace one Ford car with another Ford car; there is no problem. But no man can be replaced, never. It is such a unique flowering, it happens only once.

So don't be ritualistic – understand. Let understanding be the law, the only law that has to be followed.

Chiyono wrote this verse afterwards. She celebrated this phenomenon with a verse, with a song. She wrote:

> *This way and that way*
> *I tried to keep the pail together,*
> *hoping the weak bamboo would never break.*
> *Suddenly the bottom fell out.*
> *No more water; no more moon in the water –*
> *emptiness in my hand.*

This way and that way I tried to keep the pail together.... You have been trying this way and that way to keep the pail together. You have been supporting your mind in every way to remain together. And the mind is the barrier – and you think mind is the friend. Mind is the enemy, and you have been supporting it in every way.

I am saying many things to you which are against mind, and you will take those things into your minds and make them a support. If whatsoever I say becomes knowledge to you, when you leave me and go away from me you are more knowledgeable. Then, even things against mind have been converted into supports. Whatsoever I say, don't make it a learning, don't make it your knowledge. Rather, look at what I am saying and drop all that you know. Don't make it a new addition to your old mind.

This way and that way

> *I tried to keep the pail together,*
> *hoping the weak bamboo would never break.*

Can you find anything weaker than the mind? Can you find anything more filmy than thoughts? Can you find anything more impotent than thoughts? Nothing happens out of them, nothing comes out of them; they just continue. They are made of the same stuff dreams are made of – nonexistential really, just whirlpools in the emptiness of your being.

Suddenly the bottom fell out – and Chiyono says, "It was nothing on my part. Rather, I was doing the contrary; keeping the pail together this way and that way and hoping that *the weak bamboo would never break. Suddenly the bottom fell out* – it was nothing that I have done, it was not my doing."

> *Suddenly the bottom fell out* – it was an accident.
> *No more water; no more moon in the water –*
> *emptiness in my hand.*

"And the water disappeared. And the pail disappeared. And only emptiness in my hand."

And this is what a Buddha is: emptiness in the hand. When you have emptiness in the hand you have all, because emptiness is not a negative thing. Emptiness is the most positive thing, because everything comes out of nothing. This all is born out of emptiness. Emptiness in the hand means *source* in the hand.

A seed is there, so small, and then a big tree is born. From where does this tree come? Look in the seed, break it, and try to find out. If you break the seed you will find emptiness there. From that emptiness comes this big tree, from that emptiness comes this whole universe – from nothing comes being.

Emptiness in my hand means all in my hand – the very source from where everything arises, and to where everything goes back, returns. Emptiness in my hand means all in my hand, everything in my hand.

"And suddenly it happened. I cannot congratulate myself for it. Suddenly it happened. I was doing the contrary."

That is why saints have always said...those who believe, or those who use the terminology of God, they say it happens through his grace. Chiyono or Buddhists don't believe in any God, they don't use that symbology. So Chiyono cannot say, "Out of his grace" – she cannot. Eckhart would say, "Out of his grace – no qualification on my part. I have done nothing for it. I have not caused it." Meera would say, "Krishna's grace." Theresa would say, "Jesus and his grace."

Buddhists don't believe in any personalized God; their approach is absolutely beyond personalized symbols. They are not anthropocentric. So Chiyono cannot say 'grace', she simply says, "Suddenly it happened," but the meaning is the same. "Suddenly it happened. I was doing rather the contrary. Everything disappeared: water flowed out, the moon disappeared – *emptiness in my hand.*"

And this is enlightenment: when emptiness is in your hand, when everything is empty, when there is nobody, not even you – because if you are there, the pail is there, the old pail. If you are not there and the room is totally empty, your being is not filled at all, you have become the source. You have attained to the original face of Zen.

And this is the most blissful moment possible. And this moment becomes eternal – then there is no end to it. This moment becomes eternity. Then you can never be anything otherwise, because you are no more. Who can be sad? Who can be in sorrow? Who can be disappointed? Who can desire and feel frustrated? Emptiness cannot be frustrated. Emptiness cannot desire. Emptiness cannot expect anything, so it remains absolutely in bliss, absolutely bliss.

If you are, you will be in misery. If you are not, there cannot be any misery. So the whole problem is: To be or not to be?

And Chiyono suddenly found that she is not: Emptiness in the hand.

Enough for today.

trading dialogue for shelter

There is an old tradition in some Japanese Zen temples that if a wandering monk can win an argument about Buddhism with one of the resident monks, he can stay the night. If not, he has to move on.

There was such a temple in northern Japan run by two brothers. The elder brother was very learned and the younger brother was rather stupid, and he had only one eye.

One evening a wandering monk came to ask for lodging. The elder brother was very tired as he had been studying for many hours, so he told the younger brother to go and take the debate.

"Request that the dialogue be in silence," said the elder brother.

A little later the traveler came to the elder brother and said, "What a wonderful fellow your brother is. He has won the debate very cleverly, so I must move on. Good night."

"Before you go," said the elder brother, "please relate the dialogue to me."

"Well," said the traveler, "first I held up one finger to represent Buddha. Then your brother held up two fingers to represent Buddha and his teaching. So I held up three fingers to represent Buddha, his teaching, and his followers. Then your clever brother shook his clenched fist in my face to indicate that all three came from one realization."

With that the traveler left.
A little later the younger brother came in looking
very distressed. "I understand you won the
debate," said the elder brother.
"Won nothing," said the younger brother, "that
traveler is a very rude man."
"Oh?" said the elder brother, "Tell me the subject
of the debate.
"Why," said the younger brother, "the moment he
saw me, he held up one finger insulting me by
indicating that I have only one eye. But because
he was a stranger I thought I would be polite, so I
held up two fingers congratulating him on having
two eyes. At this, the impolite wretch held up
three fingers to show that we had but three eyes
between us, so I got mad and threatened to punch
his nose – so he went."
The elder brother laughed.

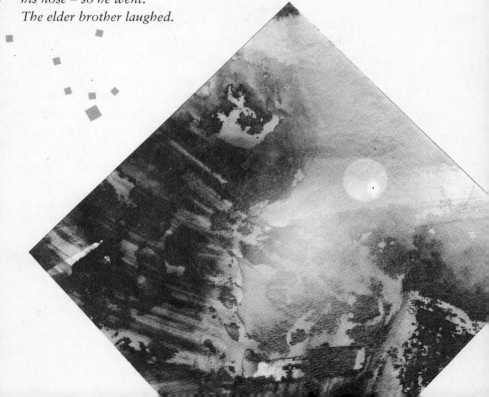

All debates are futile and stupid. Debate as such is foolish, because no one can reach the truth through discussion, through debate. You may get a night's shelter, but that's all. Hence the tradition.

The tradition is beautiful. In any Zen monastery in Japan, for many centuries, if you ask for shelter you have to discuss. If you win the debate, you can stay for the night – this is very symbolic – but only for the night. In the morning you have to move on. This indicates that through debate, logic, reasoning, you can never reach the goal, only a night's shelter. And don't deceive yourself that the night's shelter is the goal. You have to move on. In the morning you have to again be on your feet.

But many have deceived themselves. They think that whatsoever they have attained through logic is the goal. The night's shelter has become the ultimate. They are not moving, and many mornings have passed. Logic can lead to hypothetical conclusions, never to truth. Logic can lead to something which approximates truth, but never to the truth.

And remember, that which approximates the truth is also a lie, because what does it mean? Either something is true or not true; there is no in-between. Either something is true or it is not true. You cannot say that this is a half-truth; there is nothing like that – just like there cannot be a half-circle, because the very word circle means the full. Half-circles don't exist. If it is half, it is not a circle.

Half-truths don't exist. Truth is the whole, you cannot have it in fragments, you cannot have it in parts. Approximate truth is a deception, but logic can lead only to the deception. You may have a shelter for the night, just to retire, relax, but don't make it your home. By the morning you have to move again, the journey cannot end there. Every morning it will begin again and again. Relax in the logic, in the reasoning, but don't remain with it, don't become static with it – and continually remember that you have to move.

The tradition is beautiful. So one thing to be understood about the tradition and the meaning; it is symbolic. Second thing: all discussions are foolish, because through the mood of discussion you can never understand the other. Whatsoever he says is misunderstood. A mind which is bent on winning, conquering, cannot understand. It is impossible, because understanding needs a nonviolent mind. When you are seeking how to be victorious, you are violent.

Debate is violence. You can kill through it, you cannot revive through it. You cannot give life through it, you can murder through it. Truths can be murdered through debate, but they cannot be resurrected. It is violence; the very attitude is violent. Really, you are not asking for the truth, you are asking for the victory. When victory is the goal, truth will be sacrificed. When truth is the goal, you can sacrifice victory also.

And truth should be the goal, not victory, because when victory is the goal you are a politician, not a religious man. You are aggressive, you are trying somehow to overpower the other, you are trying somehow to dominate and domineer. And truth can never become a domination, it can never destroy the other. Truth can never be a victory in the sense that you have overpowered the other. Truth brings humility, humbleness. It is not an ego-trip – but all debates are ego-trips. So debate can never lead to the real; it always leads to the unreal, the untruth, because the very phenomenon that you are after, victory, is stupid. Truth wins, not you, not I. In discussion you win or I win, truth never wins.

Real seekers will allow the truth to win both. Debaters are asking that the victory should belong to me, it should not belong to the other. In truth, there is no other. In truth, we meet and become one.

So who can be the winner and who can be the loser? In truth, no one is defeated. In truth, truth wins and we are lost. But in discussion I am I and you are you; really there is no bridge.

How can you understand the other when you are against him? Understanding is impossible. Understanding needs sympathy, understanding needs a participation. Understanding means listening to the other totally, only then understanding flowers. But if you are discussing something, debating, arguing, reasoning, you are not listening to the other, you only pretend that you are listening. Deep down you are preparing, deep down you have already moved to the next step – when the other stops, what you are going to say. You are getting ready how to refute him. You have not listened to him and you are trying to refute him!

Really, truth is not significant in a discussion, in a debate. So debate is never a communication, and it is impossible through debate to come to a communion. You can argue, and the more you argue...you fall apart. The more you argue, the bigger the gap is, it becomes an abyss; there can be no meeting ground. That's why philosophers never meet, pundits never meet: they are great arguers. An abyss exists. They cannot meet with the other – impossible.

Only lovers can meet, but lovers cannot be in a debate – they can communicate. That's why so much insistence in the East for *shraddha* – trust, faith. If you argue with your master the gap widens. Then it is better to move; then let this master be a night's shelter, but move. Being with him will not lead you anywhere, the gap will widen. If you are argumentative, then the gap cannot be bridged. It is impossible. Trust means sympathy; trust means you are not arguing – you have come to listen, not to argue. You have come to understand, not to debate. You have not come to win; rather, you are ready to lose.

A real disciple is always in search of being defeated by the master. That is the greatest moment in the life of the disciple, when he is completely destroyed and defeated. Not that the master is going to win; he is going to be defeated, the disciple is going to be defeated. And when the disciple is there no more – completely defeated, disappeared – only then the gap is bridged, the abyss is gone, and the master can penetrate you.

Hence, it happened: Jesus was wandering all over his country, but all the disciples that he could gather were simple men, not a single educated person, not a single scholar. Not that there were not scholars; there were great scholars at that time. Jews were at the peak of their glory, that's why they could produce such a son as Jesus. Jesus was the culmination. Jesus could happen – that shows that the Jews touched their peak. Never again would they reach to such a peak. There were great scholars, great debates were arranged. The Jewish synagogue was the seat of learning, a real university. People would travel from all over the country to discuss, to debate, to argue, to find; but it was an argument. Not a single scholar followed Jesus.

Really, all the scholars were unanimously agreed that this man should be destroyed. All the scholars, learned people, were ready to kill this man. Why? – because this man was against argument. He was pulling at their very base; the whole structure would fall down. This man was saying something against reason. He was talking about faith, he was talking about love, he was talking about how to create a bridge between two hearts.

Debate is between two minds, two heads; love, communication, trust, is between two hearts. He was opening a new route – of friendship, of discipleship, of growth. He was thinking in terms of a totally different dimension – the quality was different. He was saying, "Put aside your scriptures. Your bibles are not needed, because they are only words." The scholar, the pundit, couldn't tolerate it. Jesus was crucified.

He could only find simple people: a fisherman, a woodcutter, a shoemaker – simple men. All his disciples, except Judas, were uneducated. Only Judas was really cultured, a refined gentleman, and he sold Jesus for thirty pieces of silver. This cultured, refined Judas betrayed him, and Jesus knew that if anybody can betray him it is Judas. Why? Because the heart can be betrayed only by the head. Love can only be betrayed by logic; nothing else can betray.

So this is the second thing to remember before I enter the story; that through logic, through the head, argumentativeness, you become alien, strangers to each other; the bridge between is lost. How can you attain to the truth when you cannot understand the other, when you are not even capable of listening to him, when your mind goes on and on inside arguing, fighting? You are violent, aggressive. This aggression will not help.

So all debates are futile, they never lead anywhere. Even if you feel that a conclusion is reached, the conclusion is forced; it is not reached through discussion. You can silence the other but conviction never comes out of it, never. And I say it categorically: *never.* If you have some logical tricks, you can silence the other. He may not be able to answer you. You know more than he knows. You know more tricks than he knows. You can put him in a corner through words and reasoning and he is unable to answer. But this is not the way to convince him. Deep down he knows that, "Some day I will find more tricks and put you right in your place. Right now I cannot answer. Okay, I accept defeat." He is defeated, but not won over.

And these are two different things. When you win a heart he is not defeated – he is happy. He is victorious in your victory, he participates. It is not your victory – truth has won, and you both can celebrate. But when you defeat a person, he is never won over; he remains the enemy. Deep down he is waiting for the right moment when he can assert himself.

No debate can become a conviction. And if conviction is not reached, where is the conclusion? The conclusion is forced, it is always premature. It is just like an abortion, it is not a natural birth. You have forced – a dead child is born or a crippled child, who is going to remain crippled, weak and dead his whole life.

Socrates used to say, "I am a midwife, I help natural birth." A master is a midwife. He is not going to force, because a forced birth cannot be a real birth. It is more like death and less like life.

So a master is never argumentative. And if sometimes he appears to be argumentative, he is just playing with you – and playing for a certain reason. Don't become a victim. He is playing for a certain reason; he can be argumentative just to find whether your argumentativeness is aroused or not. If it is aroused, you have missed. If you can listen to his argumentativeness without becoming argumentative, he will not play the game with you. He has to look within you. You may be consciously listening, unconsciously argumentative. Then he has to bring your unconscious up so that you can become aware of it.

Sometimes a master will look as if he is aggressive, as if he is bent upon defeating you. But he is never bent upon your defeat – just to defeat your ego, not you; just to destroy your ego, not you. And remember: the ego is the poison, it is destroying you. Once the poison is destroyed you will be free and alive for the first time. An abundance of light will happen to you for the first time. He is destroying the disease, not you.

Sometimes he may have to be argumentative. There have been masters who were very argumentative. It was impossible to defeat them, impossible to play the game of words with them. But they were just helping to bring your consciousness up, so that you can become aware whether your faith is true or not.

It happened: a Sufi, Junnaid, was living with his master. And the master was so argumentative that whatsoever you said, he would immediately negate it. If you said, "It is day," he would say, "No, it is night" – and it was really not so, it was day.

Whatsoever Junnaid would say, he would always find that the master would negate it. And he would simply bow down his head and say, "Yes, Master, it is night."

One day the master said, "Junnaid, you have won. I couldn't create argumentativeness in you. And I was so obviously false that anybody who had never argued anything would say, 'What foolishness. It is day. There is no need to argue, it is so obvious.' And still you said, 'Yes, Master, it is night.' Your trust is deep. Now I will never be argumentative with you, now I can talk truth, because you are ready."

When the heart says yes totally, then you are ready to listen. And only then the truth can be revealed to you. If even a slight no remains within you, the truth cannot be said to you, because that 'no' will destroy the whole thing. The no, howsoever small, is powerful, very powerful; then the truth will be said but it will not be revealed to you. The no will hide it again.

That's why I say all debates are futile. And that's why I go on repeating again and again that the whole effort of philosophy has been useless. It has not reached any conclusion – it cannot.

I will tell you one story, then I will enter this Zen anecdote.

Once it happened, a great prime minister of a very great emperor died. The prime minister was rare, very intelligent, almost wise, very cunning, shrewd, a great diplomat, and it was very difficult to find a substitute. The whole kingdom was searched. All the ministers were sent to find at least three people; then the final decision will be taken and one of them will be chosen.

For months the search was on. The whole kingdom was searched; every nook and corner was searched. Then three persons were found. One was a great scientist, a great mathematician. He could solve any mathematical problem, and mathematics is really the only positive science – all sciences are its branches – so he was at the root.

Another was a great philosopher, he was a great system-maker: out of nothing he could create all. Just out of words, he could create such beautiful systems – it is a miracle, only philosophers can do it. They have nothing in their hands; they are the greatest magicians. They create God, they create the theory of creation, they create everything – and nothing is there in their hands. But they are clever artisans of words: they join words together in such a way that they give you a feeling of substance – and nothing is there.

And the third one was a religious man, a man of faith, prayer, devotion. And the people who were searching for these three men must have been very wise, because they had found three.

These three represent the three dimensions of consciousness.

These are the only possibilities: a man of science, a man of philosophy and a man of religion – these are the basis. A man of science is concerned with experiments: unless something is proved through experiment, it is not proved. He is empirical, experimental; his truth is the truth of experiment.

A man of philosophy is a man of logic, not of experiments. Experiment is not the question; just through logic he proves, disproves. He is a pure man, purer than the scientist, because the scientist has to bring experiments in, then the laboratory comes in. A man of philosophy works without a lab – just in the mind, with logic, with mathematics. His whole lab is in his mind. He can prove and disprove just through logical arguments. He can solve any riddle or he can create any type of riddle.

And the third is the religious dimension. This man does not look at life as a problem. Life is not a problem for a religious man. It is nothing to be solved, it is something to be lived.

The religious man is the man of experience, the scientist is the man of experiment, the philosopher is the man of thinking. The religious is the man of experience, he looks at life as something to be lived. If there is any solution, it will come through experience, it will come through living. Nothing can be decided beforehand through logic, because life is greater than logic. Logic is just a bubble in the vast ocean of life, so it cannot explain all. And experiments can be done only when you are detached, experiments can be done only with objects.

Life is not an object, it is the very core of subjectivity. When you experiment you are different; when you live you are one. So the religious man says, "Unless you are one with life, you can never know it." How can you know it from the outside? You may go about and about, around and around, but you will never hit the target. So neither experiment, nor thinking, but experience; simple, trusting – a man of faith.

They searched and they found these three men, and then they were called to the capital for the final judgment. The king said, "For three days you rest and get ready. On the morning of the fourth day will be the examination, the final. One of you will be chosen and he will become my prime minister – the one who is proved to be the most wise."

They started working in their own ways. Three days were not enough! The scientist had to think of many experiments, and work it out – who knows what type of examination there is going to be? So he couldn't sleep for three days, there was no time: and there was his whole life to sleep once he was chosen, so why bother about sleep? He would not sleep, he would not eat – there was not time enough, and many things were to be done before the examination.

The philosopher started thinking, many problems were to be solved: "Who knows what type of problem is going to be asked?" Only the religious man was at ease. He ate, and ate well. Only a religious man can eat well, because eating is an offering, it is something sacred. He slept well. He would pray, sit outside, go for a walk, look at the trees, and be thankful to God; because for a religious man there is no future and there is no final examination. Every moment is the examination, so how can you prepare for it? If something is in the future you can prepare; but if something is right now, here, how can you prepare for it? You have to face it. And there was no future.

Sometimes the scientist said, "What are you doing? Wasting time – eating, sleeping, prayer. You can do your prayers later on." But he would laugh and he would not argue, he was not a man of argument.

The philosopher would say, "You go on sleeping, you go on sitting outside in the garden, you go on looking at the trees. This is not going to help. Examination is not a child's play, you have to be ready for it." But he would laugh. He believed more in laughter than in logic.

And on the morning of the fourth day, when they started for the palace for the final examination, the scientist was not even in a position to walk. He was so tired with his experiments, as if his whole life had oozed out. He was dead tired, as if any moment he would fall and go to sleep. His eyes were sleepy and his mind was troubled. He was almost crazy.

And the philosopher? He was not so tired, but he was more uncertain than ever, because he had thought and thought and argued and argued, and no argument can become the conclusion. He was muddled, in a mess, he was a chaos. The day he had arrived he could have answered many things, but now, no. Even his certain answers had become uncertain. The more you think, the more philosophy becomes useless. Only fools can believe in certainties. The more you think, the more intelligence comes to you, you can see these are all just words, there is no substance. Many times he wanted to go back because this was not going to be of any use. He was not in the right shape. But the scientist said, "Come on! Let us try. What are we going to lose? If we win, it is okay. If we don't win, it is okay. But let us try. Don't be so discouraged."

Only the religious man was walking happily, singing. He could hear the birds in the trees, he could see the sun rising, he could see the sunrays on the dewdrops. The whole life was such a miracle. He was not worried because there was no examination – he would go and face the thing, he would simply go and see what happens. And he was not asking for anything, he was not expecting, he was fresh, young, alive – and that's all. That's how one should approach God; not with readymade formulas, not with readymade theories, not with many experimental research works, not with many PhD's. No, it is not going to help. This is the way one should go – singing and dancing to the temple. And if you are alive, then whatsoever comes you can respond to it, because response is through life, it is through the heart, and the heart is ready when it is singing, when it is dancing.

They arrived. The emperor had made a very special device. They were taken into a room where he had fixed a lock, a mathematical puzzle. Many figures were on the lock, but there was no key. Those figures were to be fixed in a certain way: the secret was there, but one had to search for it and find it. If those figures were fixed in a certain way the door would open. The emperor took them in and said, "This is a mathematical puzzle, one of the greatest ever known. Now you have to find the clue – there is no key. If you can find the clue, the answer to this mathematical problem, the lock will open. And the person who comes out of this room first will be chosen. So now start." He closed the door and went out.

Immediately the scientist started working out many experiments, many things, many problems on paper. He looked – observed the figures on the lock. There was no time to lose, it was a question of life and death. The philosopher closed his eyes, started thinking in mathematical terms what to do, how this puzzle can be solved. The puzzle was absolutely new.

That is the problem with the mind: if something is old the answer can be found, but if something is absolutely new, how can you work it out through the mind? The mind is quite efficient with the old, the known, the routine. Mind is absolutely inefficient when the unknown faces it.

The religious man never went to the lock, because what can he do? He does not know any mathematics, he does not know any experimental science. What can he do? He just sat in a corner. He sang a little, prayed to God, closed his eyes. Those two others were thinking that he is not a competitor at all. "In a way it is good, because the thing has to be decided between us two." Then suddenly they became aware that he had left the room, he was not there. The door was open.

The emperor came in and he said, "What are you doing now? It is finished. The third man is out."

But they asked, "How?...because he never did anything."

So they asked the religious man. He said, "I was just sitting. I prayed and I was just sitting and a voice said within me, 'You fool. Just go and see. The door is not locked.' And I just went to the door; it was not locked. There was no problem at all to be solved, so I went out."

Life is not a problem. If you are trying to solve it you will miss it. The door is open, it has never been locked. If the door was locked, then scientists would find the solution. If the door was locked, then philosophers may find a system to open it. But the door is not locked, so only faith can go – without any solution, without any readymade answer. Push the door open and get out.

Life is not a riddle to be solved, it is a mystery to be lived. It is a deep mystery, so trust and allow yourself to enter into it. No debate can be of any help – with somebody else, or with yourself inside the mind – no debate. All debates are futile and stupid.

Now we will enter this beautiful story:

> There is an old tradition in some Japanese Zen
> temples that if a wandering monk can win an
> argument about Buddhism with one of the
> resident monks, he can stay the night. If not,
> he has to move on.

Arguments can give you this much – a night's shelter, but that's all.

> There was such a temple in northern Japan run by
> two brothers. The elder brother was very learned
> and the younger brother was rather stupid, and he
> had only one eye.

Two types of people are needed to run a temple: a learned person and a very stupid one. And this is how all temples are run – two types of people: the learned who have become the priests, and the stupid who follow them. This is how every temple is run.

So these stories are not just stories, they are indications to particular facts. If stupid people disappear from the earth there will be no temples. If learned people disappear from the temples there will be no temples. A duality is needed for a temple to exist. That's why you cannot find God in a temple – because you cannot find him in a duality.

These temples are inventions of the clever people to exploit the stupid. All temples are inventions – clever people exploiting…they have become the priests. Priests are the most clever people, they are the greatest exploiters, and they exploit in such a way that you cannot even revolt against them. They exploit you for your own sake, they exploit you for your own good. Priests are the most clever because they spin theories out of nothing: all the theologies, all that they have created – tremendous! Cleverness is needed to create religious theories. And they go on creating such big edifices that it is almost impossible for an ordinary man to enter those edifices. And they use such jargon, they use such technical terms, that you cannot understand what they are talking about. And when you cannot understand you think they are very profound. Whenever you cannot understand a thing you think it is very profound – "It is beyond me."

Remember this: Buddha speaks in a very ordinary language which can be understood by anybody. It is not the language of a priest. Jesus speaks in small parables – any uneducated man can understand it – he never uses any religious jargon. Mahavira talks, gives his teachings, in the language of the most ordinary and common people.

Mahavira and Buddha never used Sanskrit, never, because Sanskrit was the language of the priest, the *brahmin*. Sanskrit is the most difficult language. Priests have made it so difficult – they have polished and polished and polished. The very word *sanskrit* means polishing, refining. They have refined it to such a pitch that only if you are very very learned can you understand what they are saying, otherwise it is beyond.

Buddha used the language of the people, Pali. Pali was the language of the people, of the villagers. Mahavira used Prakrit. Prakrit is the unrefined form of Sanskrit; Prakrit is the natural form of Sanskrit – no grammar, not much. The scholar has not entered yet, he has not refined the words so they become beyond common people. But the priests have been using Sanskrit, they still use it. Nobody understands Sanskrit now, but they go on using Sanskrit because their whole profession depends on creating a gap, not a bridge – in creating a gap. If the common people cannot understand, only then the priests can survive. If the common people understand what they are saying they are lost, because they are saying nothing.

Once Mulla Nasruddin went to a doctor – and doctors have learned the trick from the priests: they write in Latin and Greek, and they write in such a way that even if they have to read it again it is difficult. Nobody should understand what they are writing. So Mulla Nasruddin went to a doctor and he said, "Listen, be plain. Just tell me the facts. Don't use Latin and Greek."

The doctor said, "If you insist, and if you allow me to be frank, you are not ill at all. You are just plain lazy."

Nasruddin said, "Okay, thank you. Now write it in Greek and Latin so I can show it to my family."

The clever have always been exploiting the common people. That's why Buddha, Jesus and Mahavira were never respected by brahmins, scholars, clever ones, because they were destructive, they were destroying their whole business. If the people understand, then there is no need for the priest. Why? – because the priest is a mediator. He understands the language of God. He understands your language. He translates your language into the language of God. That's why they say Sanskrit is *dev-bhasha*, the language of God: "You don't know Sanskrit? – I know, so I become the intermediate link, I become the interpreter. You tell me what you want and I will say it in Sanskrit to God, because he understands only Sanskrit." And of course you have to pay for it.

These are the two types which are needed for a temple.

> *There was such a temple...run by two brothers.*
> *The elder brother was very learned and the*
> *younger brother was rather stupid, and he had*
> *only one eye.*

What is the symbolism of one eye in this story? A stupid person is always one-pointed: he never hesitates, he is always certain. And a learned person is always dual: he hesitates, he continuously divides himself into two. He is always arguing within, a dialogue continues inside; he knows both the sides.

A learned man is a duality – two eyes. A stupid man is one-eyed – he is always certain, he has no arguments, he is not divided. That's why, if you look at a stupid person, a stupid person looks more like a saint than a learned man. If you look at a saint he will have something similar in him also – of the stupid, of the fool. The quality differs, but something is the same; the label differs. The fool is just on the first rung and the saint is on the last rung, but both are at the ends of the ladder. The fool does not know, that's why he is simple, one-eyed. The saint knows, that's why he is simple. He is also one-eyed; he calls it the third eye. The two eyes have disappeared into the third. He is also one-eyed – one. He is a unity, and a fool is also a unity. But what is the difference?

Ignorance also has an innocence about it, just like wisdom has an innocence about it. The learned is just in between: he is ignorant and thinks he is wise. This is the division of the learned man: he is ignorant and *thinks* he is wise. He is neither at this level nor at that, he hangs in between. That's why he is always in tension. An ignorant man is relaxed, a wise man is relaxed. The ignorant man has not started his travels, he is at home. The wise man has reached the goal, he is at home. The learned is in between, seeking shelter in some monastery – even for one night, it is okay – he is a wanderer.

Buddhist *bhikkhus* have been wanderers, and Buddha has said, "Be a wanderer until you attain. Be a wanderer. Not only inside but outside also, be a wanderer until you attain. Don't stop before it." When you have attained, when you have become a *siddha,* a Buddha, then you are allowed to sit.

Ignorance and wisdom have a quality about them which is similar – that is innocence; neither is cunning. So sometimes it has happened that a man of God has been known as a foolish man, a fool – God's fool. Saint Francis is known as God's fool. He was! But to be God's fool is the greatest wisdom possible, because the ego is lost. You don't say that you know, so you are a fool because you don't claim knowledge. If you don't claim, who is going to accept that you are a knower? Even if you do claim, nobody accepts. You have to hammer it on others' heads. You have to make them silent, argue it. When they cannot say anything, then, with a grudging heart, they accept that maybe, maybe you are. But they will always say, "Maybe." They will keep the possibility open that some day they can deny it.

And if you don't claim, who is going to accept you? And if you yourself say, "I am ignorant, I know nothing," who is going to think that you are a knower? People will accept immediately if you say, "I don't know." They will accept it immediately; they will say, "We knew it before. We accept it, we totally agree with you that you don't know."

God's fool! If you read one of the great novels of Dostoevsky, then you will feel what this God's fool means. Dostoevsky always has, in his many novels, one character who is the God's fool. In Brothers Karamazov he is there. He is innocent, you can exploit him. Even if you exploit him, he will trust you. You can destroy him, but you cannot destroy his trust – that is the beauty.

What happens to you? If one man deceives you, the whole of humanity becomes the deceiver. If one man deceives you, you have lost your trust in man – not with this man, but with the whole of humanity. If two or three persons deceive you, you make the judgment that there is no man worth believing. All trust is gone.

It seems that you wanted not to trust from the very beginning and these two or three people have given you the excuse. Otherwise you will say, "This man is not trustworthy...but the whole of humanity? – I don't know, so I must trust unless the contrary is proved." And if you really are a trusting man, you will say, "Not only is this man totally untrustworthy this moment, this man was untrustworthy...but the next moment who knows? Because saints can become sinners, sinners can become saints."

Life is a movement. Nothing is static. At this moment the man was weak, but in the next moment he may gain control and will not deceive again. So the next day, if he comes, you will believe him again because this day is different, this man is different; the Ganges has flowed so much, it is not the same river.

Once it happened: one man came to Mulla Nasruddin and asked for some money. Nasruddin knew this man, knew well that this money was not going to be returned, but it was such a small sum that he thought, "Let him take it; even if he is not going to return it, nothing is lost. So why say no for such a small sum?" So he gave him the money.

After three days the man returned. Nasruddin was surprised. It seemed impossible, it was a miracle, that this man had returned. After two or three days the man came again and asked for a big sum. Nasruddin said, "Now! Last time you deceived me." He said, "Last time you deceived me – now I am not going to allow it again."

The man said, "What are you saying? Last time I returned the money."

He said, "Okay, you returned it, but you deceived me – because I never believed that you would return it. But this time, no. Enough is enough. Last time you behaved contrary to my expectations. But enough; now I am not going to give it to you."

This is how the cunning mind works.

One was ignorant in this temple – a simple man, one-eyed, certain. One was a learned man, and the learned man is always tired because he is working so hard over nothing. So busy without business, he is always tired.

One evening a wandering monk came to ask for lodging. The elder brother was very tired as he had been studying for many hours...

You cannot find a learned man *not* tired. Go and look! Go to the pundits of Kashi and look. Always tired, always tired, working so hard – with words. Remember, even a laborer is not so tired because he is working with life. When you are working only with words, futile words, just with the head, you get tired. Life is invigorating! Life rejuvenates! If you go in the garden and work, you perspire but you are gaining more energy, you are not losing. You go for a walk and you gain more energy, because you are living in the moment. If you just close yourself in your study with words, with words you go on thinking and thinking and thinking – it is such a dead process, you will be tired. A learned man is always tired. A fool is always fresh, a saint is also always fresh. They have many similar qualities.

> *...so he told the younger brother to go and take*
> *the debate. "Request that the dialogue be in*
> *silence," said the elder brother.*

...Because he knew that his brother was stupid. So silence is golden if you are stupid, and silence is golden if you are a saint also. If you know something, you will remain silent. If you don't know, it is better to remain silent.

A wise man becomes silent because he knows, and whatsoever he knows cannot be said. A fool has to be silent, because whatsoever he says he will be caught. A fool can deceive if he is silent but he cannot deceive if he speaks, because whatsoever comes out of him will bring his foolishness. This learned brother knew well that this younger brother was not a man of words, was a simple man, innocent, ignorant, so he said, *"Request that the dialogue be in silence."*

> *A little later the traveler came to the elder*
> *brother and said, "What a wonderful fellow your*
> *brother is."*

This other man must have also been a learned man, and if a fool is silent he can defeat a learned man. If you speak you will be caught, because then you enter into the world of the learned man. With words, you cannot win.

This other man was also a learned man, a man of words. It would have been very difficult for him to remain silent and debate. How to discuss? If you are not allowed to speak, just use gestures, the whole thing becomes dumb and your whole cleverness is lost, because if you are not allowed to speak.... That was your only efficiency. So if a learned man is to remain silent he can be defeated by a fool also, because his whole efficiency is lost – it belonged to words.

In silence he is a fool – this is the meaning. That's why scholars will never be silent, they are always chattering. If nobody is there, they are chattering with themselves, but they are chattering. They go on talking and talking and talking, within and without, because through this talking their efficiency grows greater and greater, they become more and more proficient. But if they encounter silence, suddenly all their art is gone. They are more stupid than a stupid man. Even a stupid man can defeat them. They are out of their professional world, they are simply switched off. He must have been in very great difficulty.

> He said, *"What a wonderful fellow your brother*
> *is. He has won the debate very cleverly, so I must*
> *move on. Good night."*

If you encounter a learned man, remain silent. Face him with gestures. You will defeat him because he knows nothing about gestures, he knows nothing about silence. Really, it is very difficult for him to remain without words. The traveler immediately thought he had been defeated – he must move on and reach another monastery before it is too late, and find a fellow who can debate with him in words, intellectually.

Gestures are alive; when you move your hand, your whole being moves it. When you look with your eyes, your whole being pours through them. When you walk, you walk as a whole man. Your legs cannot walk by themselves, but your head can go on spinning and spinning by itself. The head can become autonomous. No other part of the body can become autonomous. So if you want to study a man, don't listen to what he says. Rather, look how he behaves, how he comes in the room, how he sits, how he walks, how he looks. Look at his gestures, they will reveal the truth.

Words are deceivers. We talk not to reveal but to hide. So be silent and look at a person – how he stands, how he sits, how he looks, what gestures he is making. Body language is truer than your head language. And body language is very, very natural; it comes from the very source, so it is very difficult to deceive through it. You may be saying something, but your face goes on saying something else. You may be saying, "I am right," but your eyes, your very manner, the way you are standing, says that you know you are wrong. You may be showing through your words that you are confident, but your whole body gives a tremble and shows that you are not.

When a thief enters, he enters in a different way. When a liar appears, he appears in a different way. When a man of truth walks, he walks differently. He has nothing to hide, he has no reason to deceive. He is true, his walk is innocent. Just do something that you have to hide, then watch yourself – your body will say everything is different. Even while walking you are hiding something. Your stomach is strained, you are alert, your eyes are looking everywhere to see if somebody is looking or not, whether you are caught or not. Your eyes are sly, they are not pools of innocence – cunning. Watch your body movements, they will give you a truer picture of yourself. Don't listen to words.

This I have to do continuously. People come to me with all sorts of deceptions. I have to look at their gestures, not at what they say. They may be touching my feet but their whole gesture is showing ego, so that the touching of feet is useless. They are manipulating it. They are not only deceiving me, they are deceiving themselves. Their whole gesture says, "Ego!" and whatsoever they say through words is humbleness.

You cannot deceive through the body; your body is truer than your mind. And all the religions which have been invented by the

priests say to you, "Be against the body and be with the mind" –
because a priest lives in the mind, exploits through the mind. With
the body it is impossible to exploit; the body is authentic. Even
centuries of inauthentic living have not been able to destroy the
authenticity of the body. The body remains authentic, it shows
clearly who you are.

> *"He has won the debate very cleverly, so I must*
> *move on. Good night."*
> *"Before you go," said the elder brother, "please*
> *relate the dialogue to me."*

He must have been puzzled. How could this stupid brother of his
be clever? What has happened? He is a perfect fool – how could he
discuss, how could he debate, how could he have won? So he
asked,

> *"Before you go, please relate the dialogue to me."*
> *"Well," said the traveler, "first I held up one*
> *finger to represent Buddha."*

…Because a man of learning, even while he is making a gesture,
uses the gesture as words, because he knows only one language. If
he kisses his beloved, inside he will say the word kiss. This is foolishness; you are kissing, there is no need to repeat 'kiss' inside, but
he will. You watch yourself: while making love, you will say inside,
"I am making love." What nonsense! Nobody is asking you.
Nobody is there to be told. Why do you go on repeating?
Whenever you do something, why do you verbalize it? Because
without verbalizing you are not at ease. You are at ease only with
words. With God you cannot be at ease. With the word god it is
okay – that's why a man of learning will go to the temple, to the
mosque, to the church; there too he goes on chattering. He will
chatter with God – but words.

Søren Kierkegaard has said, "When I first entered the church, I used to talk. I used to say things, complain, pray. But then, by and by, it felt foolish. I am talking to him and I am not giving him any chance, any opportunity for him to talk to me. It is better to listen; when you are before God, it is better to listen." So he dropped talking. By and by, he dropped all prayer. He would just go into the church and sit silently, but in his silence there were also words inside. He was not using them outside, but inside they were revolving.

So, by and by, he also had to drop the words inside – then only listening becomes possible. Then you enter a totally different dimension – of listening, of passivity, of receptivity. You become a womb. Then you can receive the truth – then you are not talking, then you are not aggressive. Then only God is working and you are allowing him to work. Then he became absolutely silent; then he stopped going to church.

Somebody asked, "Why? Why have you stopped going to church?"

He said, "Now I have learned what church means; it only means to be silent and to be listening. That can be done anywhere, and it is better to do it somewhere else because many other people go there, to the church, chattering. They disturb me. It is better under a tree. It is better under the sky."

The church is greater there, more natural. And if you have to be silent, then God is everywhere. If you have to talk, then go to the temple. But if you have to be silent, why go anywhere? He is everywhere, but you cannot be silent. You do something and you repeat it inside. You feel hunger and you say, "I am hungry." Is it not enough to feel hunger? Unless you say it, you are not at ease; you have become addicted to words.

This man...a learned man he must have been, really a perfectly learned man:

> "Well," he said, "first I held up one finger to
> represent Buddha. Then your brother held up two
> fingers to represent Buddha and his teaching"
> – the dhamma.

A man who cannot use a gesture without words will interpret the other's gestures also in words. Now look at the link. What is happening? And you will also link the other's gesture to the same way you interpret your own words.

He was thinking, "This finger, one finger represents...." A finger represents nobody. A finger is enough unto itself. A finger is just a finger. Why make it a representative? It is not representative of anybody. And the finger is so beautiful, why should it represent anything? But the mind always loves secondhand things. The finger is not enough, it must represent somebody.

If you look at a flower, you cannot look at the flower directly; immediately it must represent something. So you say, "Looks just like my wife's face." Even the moon, you say, "Looks like my beloved's face." What nonsense. The moon is the moon. And this man, when he looks at his beloved's face, will say, "Looks like the moon." Neither the moon is enough unto itself, nor the beloved's face is enough unto itself. And everything *is* enough unto itself. Nobody is representing anybody.

Everybody is representing only himself. Everyone is original, unique. No one is a carbon copy. And when you say the finger represents Buddha, Buddha has become the original, the finger has become the carbon copy. No! This Buddha cannot allow it. I cannot allow it! The finger is so beautiful not representing anybody. But if you think your finger represents Buddha, then the other's two fingers will represent Buddha and his dhamma – his teaching. Because the way you understand the other is not by listening to the other, you understand the other by listening to your own mind. You interpret the other. When I say something, never believe that you have heard the same. When I say something you hear something, but that is not related to me; it is linked with your own thought process.

His thought process was, "This finger represents Buddha." Then when the other put up two fingers he was blissfully unaware what he meant. You cannot understand the other if you have words inside, because then everything links with your word, with your thinking process, and then it is colored. The traveler thought he is saying two things are there, not one: Buddha and his dhamma – his teaching, his law.

"So I held up three fingers" – look at the link inside.

You are not communicating with the other at all. You are communicating with yourself. This is what madness means. Madness means not relating to the other, just going inside and linking your new moment with the past, the new experience with the past – interpreting, coloring it.

"So I held up three fingers" – because if he says, "Buddha, dhamma," I will say, "Buddha, dhamma, *sangha* – Buddha, his teaching and his followers."

There are three – these are the three Buddhist shelters. When a bhikkhu wants to be initiated, becomes a bhikkhu, he says, *"Buddham sharanam gachchhami* – I go, I take shelter in Buddha. *Dhammam sharanam gachchhami,* I take shelter in the teaching. *Sangham sharanam gachchhami,* I take shelter in the sangha, in the followers of Buddha." These are the three shelters, the three jewels of Buddhism.

But this man is not looking at what the other man is doing – totally unrelated! – so he raised three fingers.

> *"So I held up three fingers to represent Buddha,*
> *his teaching and his followers. Then your clever*
> *brother shook his clenched fist in my face to*
> *indicate that all these come from one realization."*
> *With that the traveler left.*
> *A little later the younger brother came in looking*
> *very distressed.*
> *"I understand you won the debate," said the elder*
> *brother.*
> *"Won nothing," said the younger, "that traveler is*
> *a very rude man!"*
> *"Oh!" said the elder brother, "Tell me the subject*
> *of the debate."*

"Why," said the younger brother, "the moment he
saw me he held up one finger insulting me by
indicating that I have only one eye."

You understand according to yourself: you read a book, you understand only that which you already know. And you listen, but you interpret with the past, your past comes in. A man with one eye is always aware of the wound. He is carrying a wound; everywhere he is looking for the insult. Nobody is worried about you, but if you have a feeling of inferiority then you are looking for somebody who is going to insult you. You are certain about that, and then you will interpret. The other may be saying, "Buddha"; you will see he is showing that you have only one eye. Nobody is bothered with your eyes, but we interpret according to our understanding.

One man reached Bayazid, a Sufi mystic, and asked him a question. He said, "Come back after one year, because right now you are ill. Your inside is in a turmoil and I cannot utter the truth because you will not understand it – you will *mis*understand it. So for one year try to be healthy, silent, meditative and then come back. If I then feel that you can listen, I will tell. Otherwise, go to somebody else."

The man listened, went away. For one year he made every effort to be healthy, silent, peaceful – but never came back again.

So Bayazid inquired, "What happened to that seeker?"

Somebody said, "We asked him, 'Why are you not coming?' He said, 'Now there is no need to come, because I can understand from here, where I am, what Bayazid can say.'"

This is the paradox: when you are not ready you ask, but then nothing can be said to you. When you are ready you don't ask, but only then something can be said to you.

If you are one-eyed you are always looking for insults, and if you are looking for insults you will find them – this is the problem. If you are looking for something, this is the misfortune: you will find it. Not that anybody is insulting you; you will find it. So don't look for such things, otherwise you will find them everywhere.

Somebody will laugh – not at you, because who are you? Why do you think yourself to be the center of the world? This is an egoist trend. You are passing down a street and somebody laughs, and you think they are laughing at you. Why at you? Who are you? Why do you take it for granted that you are the center of the whole world? Somebody laughs – laughs at *you;* somebody insults – insults *you;* somebody is angry – angry against *you.*

In my whole life, I have not met a single person who was angry at me. Many people were angry but nobody was angry at me, because I am not the center of the world. Why should they be angry at me? They are angry – that is something linked with their own being, not with me. I have come across people who were even violent to me, but they were not violent to *me.* This violence was coming out of their past; I was not the cause of its origination. I may be the excuse, but I was not the cause. Just an excuse – if I was not there, somebody else would have done just the same; somebody else would have become the victim. So it is just coincidental that I was there.

When your wife gets mad at you, it is coincidental that you are there. Escape! And don't think too much that she was angry with you. She was angry, you were there, that's all. She would have been angry at the servant, at the child, at the piano, at anything!

Everybody lives through his own past. Only buddhas live in the present. Nobody else lives in the present.

This man thought, "Okay, he is showing that I have only one eye. He is rude. He is insulting me, having only one eye. *But because he was a stranger, I thought I would be polite."*

But the moment you think you should be polite, you are not polite. How can you be? – the idea has entered: if you think the other is rude, you have become rude. There is not a question now, because the very idea "the other is rude" is because your own rudeness has come up. Through your rudeness the other appears rude, you have colored the other. The other is showing his finger representing Buddha, he has not even looked at your eye. He is not concerned, he just wants shelter.

A Buddha...and the interpretation that, "He is showing that I have got only one eye; he is rude." When you think about someone that he is rude, look back: you are rude. That's why you interpret it.

But why are you rude? – because your rudeness is a way of protecting your wound. Those people who are rude are always suffering from feelings of inferiority. If a person is not in any way burdened with a complex of inferiority, he will not be rude. Rudeness is his protection. Through rudeness he protects his wound. He says, "I will not allow you to touch my wound. I will not allow you to hit me."

He protects, but protection becomes projection. He thinks that you are rude, only then can *he* be rude. This is a way to be rude. First you have to prove that the other is rude, and still your ego says, "I will try to be polite."

When you are polite, your politeness is nothing but a façade. Inside, rudeness has entered, and sooner or later it will explode.

"But I thought because he was a stranger I would be polite, so I held up two fingers to congratulate him on having two eyes."

This is just false. How can you congratulate any person if you feel insulted? If you feel you have got one eye and the others have two, how can you congratulate? Deep down you can be jealous, but how can you congratulate? How can congratulation come out of jealousy? But all your congratulations come out that way. It is a polite way, it is culture, etiquette. If you are defeated by someone, even then you congratulate him for his victory. What falseness! If you were really such a person, you would not have fought at all. When you were fighting you were the enemy, and now you are defeated and you go and congratulate him. But deep down there is jealousy, you are boiling, you would like to kill this man. You will try – in the future, you will see!

But society needs etiquette. Why does society need etiquette? – because everybody is so violent. If there were no etiquette, we would be at each other's throats continuously. Society has to create barriers. You should not be allowed to be at each other's throats continuously, otherwise life will be impossible.

But you *are* at each other's throats continuously. Your etiquette, your culture, your civilized ways, manners, are just to hide this fact. They don't allow a real civilization to happen. A false thing – that's why every ten years a great war is needed in which all etiquette, all manners, all morality are thrown away and you can run at each other's throats without any guilt. Then killing becomes the game; the more you murder, the greater you are. The more you are rude, the greater a warrior you are.

And back in your country you will be received as heroes; *Padmabhushan, Mahavirchakra,* the Victoria Cross will be given to you. You will receive medals. For what are these medals given? To become barbarous, to become murderers; and because you have been a great murderer this medal is given to you by your country. And we call these countries civilized – and murderers are recognized, murderers are appreciated.... But only mass-murderers; individual murder and you will be in jail, that cannot be allowed. Only sometimes, when the whole society goes mad, that is war; everything is put aside, your real nature is allowed. That's why everybody feels happy when there is a war. It should be otherwise – nobody should feel happy when there is a war. But everybody feels happy because now you are allowed to be animals. You always wanted to be that. Your culture, your etiquette, your manners are just polished ways to hide the animal behind.

> This man said, *"So I held up two fingers to congratulate him on having two eyes. At this, the impolite wretch held up three fingers to show that we had but three eyes between us."*

Whatsoever you do, your wound will come in. The other is

saying, "The three jewels of Buddha," but for you it is just the wound coming back. You tried to be polite, you tried not to be rude, you even tried to congratulate. But you are you, your mind continues.

Now he is showing three fingers. Again your mind comes in and says, "This wretch! He is saying that we have three eyes between the two of us." Again he is showing that you have one eye. Now this is too much. Now it is enough!

*"So I got mad and threatened to punch his nose –
so he went."*

He was mad from the very beginning. Before they had ever met he was mad, because you cannot create madness if it is not already there. You can only create things which are already there, your creation is not out of nothing. It is only that an unmanifested state becomes a manifested state. Anger is there, you need not create it. Somebody becomes the excuse – it comes up. You are not angry at him, he is not the cause. You were carrying the anger – he has become the excuse. Madness is inside; nobody can make you mad if you are not mad already. But we always think that somebody makes us angry, somebody makes us depressed, somebody makes us this and that.

Nobody makes you anything. Even if you are left alone you will be mad, you will be angry. Even if the whole world disappears there will be moments when you will be sad, there will be moments when you will be happy, there will be moments when you will be angry, there will be moments when you will be very forgiving – although there is nobody.

It is your inner story that unfolds. This is what a man of understanding comes to realize – that the whole thing is an unfolding of *me*. You just give me the opportunity, the situation, but the whole thing is an unfoldment of me.

A seed falls on the ground, sprouts, a tree starts growing. The soil, the air, the rains, the sun, they are all just giving the opportunity,

but the tree was hidden in the seed. You carry the whole tree of your
unfoldment; everybody else becomes the opportunity. Whenever
anything happens don't look out, look within, because the thing, as it
is happening, is linked with your past, not with the person here.

> *"I got mad and threatened to punch his nose – so*
> *he went."*
> *The elder brother laughed.*

The elder brother could see both standpoints. He could see that
the learned wanderer never talked to this man, never gestured to
this man. He could see this stupid brother never understood what
was gestured. They remained untouched – an abyss was there, no
bridge. They debated, they concluded. One was defeated, one has
become victorious, and they never met – not for a single moment.
He laughed.

This laughter can become enlightenment. This laughter can become a profound understanding, a transformation. If this laughter
is not about the stupidity of this brother or the stupidity of that
wanderer, if this laughter is about the whole situation: how the
head functions, how two heads can never meet, how two pasts can
never meet, how two minds always remain separate – that there is
no way for them to meet and mingle with each other.... If he
laughs at the whole situation, not at this brother or at that learned
wanderer – because if he laughs at this brother or at that learned
wanderer, this laughter cannot become enlightenment, he will remain the same – but if he laughs at the whole situation: how the
mind functions, how the mind argues, how the mind goes on
within itself, never moving out, how the mind is always closed, it is
never open, how the mind is just an inner dream, a nightmare....

If he understands that, this laughter will become a shattering.
The pail, the whole pail will fall down, the water will flow out – no
water, no moon.

Enough for today.

is that so?

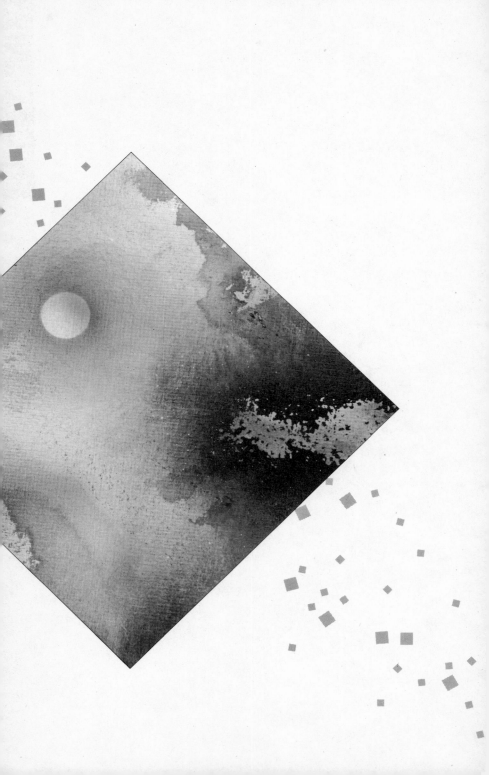

The Zen Master Hakuin was honored by his
neighbors as one who led a pure life.
One day it was discovered that a beautiful girl
who lived near Hakuin was pregnant.
The parents were very angry. At first the girl
would not say who the father was, but after much
harassment she named Hakuin.
In great anger the parents went to Hakuin, but all
he would say was, "Is that so?"
After the child was born it was taken to Hakuin
who had lost his reputation by this time, although
he didn't seem much disturbed by the fact.
Hakuin took great care of the child. He obtained
milk, food, and everything else the child needed
from his neighbors.
A year later the girl-mother could stand it no
longer, so she told her parents the truth – the real
father was a young man who worked in the fish
market. The mother and father of the girl went
round at once to Hakuin to tell him the story,
apologize at great length, ask his forgiveness, and
get the child back.
As the master willingly yielded the child he said,
"Is that so?"

hat is pure life? What do you call purity? Because whatsoever you call purity is not the real purity. Your purity is a calculation, a moral calculation. Your purity is not the purity of a saint – his purity is innocence. Your purity is a sort of cunningness, a shrewdness.

This has to be understood first. If you understand it deeply, only then you can understand what a wise man is, what a saint is, what a man of knowledge is. Because if your measurement is wrong, if your very base of judgment is wrong, everything will go wrong with it.

Real purity is just like a child – innocent; innocent about what is good, what is bad; innocent about any distinction. Real purity does not know what is God and what is the Devil. But your purity is a choice – a choice of God against the Devil, a choice of the good against the bad. You have already made a distinction, you have already divided existence. And a divided existence cannot lead to innocence.

Innocence flowers only when existence is undivided. You accept it as it is. You don't choose, you don't divide, you don't make any distinctions. You don't know, really, what is good and what is bad. If you know, then you will calculate, then purity will be manufactured. It will not be a flowering.

I will tell you one anecdote: Khalil Gibran has written a beautiful story. A priest was going to the temple. Just by the side of the road he saw a man almost at the verge of death – bleeding, dying, as if he had been attacked very severely – wounds all over, blood flowing, soaked in his own blood.

The priest was in a hurry; he had to reach the temple in time, there must be people waiting. But he was a man of morality – I will not say of purity: he was a man of morality. He pondered what to do. He calculated and then he thought, "It is better to help this man who is dying. This is what Jesus has said. It is better to forget the temple, the worshippers; they can wait a little. But this man has to be helped immediately, otherwise he will die."

So he went closer to the man, but the moment he saw his face he was scared. This face looked familiar, very evil-looking. Then he suddenly remembered that in his temple there is a picture of the Devil – and this is the man. This is the Devil, nobody else! So he started running towards the temple.

The Devil called out; he said, "Priest, listen! If I die you will repent forever. Because if I die, if evil dies, where will your God be? If the bad dies, how will you know what is good? You exist because of me. Think it over!"

The priest stopped. The Devil was right: if the Devil dies, there will be no hell. And if there is no fear, who is going to worship God? All prayers are based on fear. You are afraid, your love towards God is based on the fear of the Devil. Your goodness is measured through evil. God needs the Devil.

The Devil said, "God needs me! He cannot be without me. All the temples will fall down and nobody will come to worship. And you will not find a single man who is religious if I am not there. I tempt them; through my temptation they become saints. Have you ever heard about any saint who was not tempted by the Devil? Your Jesus, your Zoroaster, your Buddha – all have been tempted by *me!* It is I who made them saints. So come back!"

The priest hesitated a little, but the Devil was logical – and the Devil is always logical; he is logic personified. You cannot reason with him, you cannot argue. If you argue you are defeated. You cannot win an argument with the Devil.

The priest had to concede and agree. He said, "You seem to be right. Where will we be without you?" So he carried the Devil on his back to the hospital. He waited there until he was certain that now there is no danger and that the Devil will survive – and with the Devil, all the temples, all the priests and all religions survive.

This priest is a moral man, but not a pure man. His life is a mathematical calculation, and if you calculate then you are already defeated by the Devil. You cannot calculate better than he can. If you argue, if you divide life, if it becomes a logical problem, then there is no possibility of your ever winning it. The game is already lost. You are in a losing battle.

A man of innocence does not know who God is and who the Devil is. A man of innocence lives out of his innocence, not out of his calculations. He is not shrewd, he is simple. He lives moment to moment, neither the past nor the future is meaningful to him. This very moment is enough unto itself.

But your morality...your morality is created by the priest, the priest who helped the Devil; because the Devil argued, and he argued rightly. Your morality is not pure. So whenever there is someone who can behave the way you think a pure man should behave, who can manipulate himself, you honor him, you respect him, you call him a saint. Your saints are as bogus as you are, because *you* decide and judge who is a saint. Your morality is just a fear, a hidden fear, and the disguise is so clever that you never become aware of it.

How can a calculation become innocent? And without becoming innocent – innocent like the trees, innocent like the animals, innocent like the babies – how can purity happen to you? It is not something you can control. If you control, it is repression, and the contrary is always present there. If you become a celibate, sex is there hidden in the unconscious waiting for its moment to assert, to rebel. If you become nonviolent, violence is there. The opposite cannot be thrown out. If you choose, the opposite is always repressed – that's all you can do. Only in an innocent mind does the opposite disappear, because nothing has been chosen:

the opposite cannot exist without choice.

Hence Krishnamurti consistently emphasizes not to choose, and to be choiceless – that's the base of innocence. But you can deceive yourself by choosing choicelessness: "Because Krishnamurti says, 'Be choiceless' I will be choiceless." If *you* decide, the will has entered – and the will is cunning. If *you* decide to be choiceless, your choicelessness will be part of a morality, not part of purity.

Just understand, don't choose – don't choose even choicelessness. Simply understand the whole situation: that whatsoever you choose, whatsoever you do, will come out of the calculating mind. It cannot be the real thing. Your mind can only produce dreams, it cannot produce the truth. Truth cannot be produced, nobody can produce it. It is there; it has to be seen. Nothing has to be done, just a look is needed – a look without any prejudice, a look without any choice, a look without any distinctions.

A man of God, if he has suppressed, if he has denied the Devil, is not a real man of God. The Devil will be there by the corner. Once you divide, you are caught in the battle of the opposites – you will be crushed. If you don't decide – you don't know what is good, what is bad – whatsoever happens you simply accept. It is happening, what can you do? Nothing can be done. So you float like a white cloud. You don't know where you are going or why you are going. The wind blows to the north, you go to the north; the wind then drifts towards the south, you drift towards the south. You float with the wind. You don't say, "I am going to the south, I cannot go to the north." You don't fight.

A man of purity is not a soldier, he is a saint. And a man of morality is a soldier, he is not a saint. Of course, the fight is within, not without. Of course, the fight is not with someone else but with oneself – but the fight is there.

You need not be a fighter. And if you fight you will lose the battle. How can you fight the whole? You are just a tiny part, an atomic part. How can you fight the whole? A man of purity neither fights nor surrenders – because surrender also belongs to the soldier. First he fights, then he finds it is impossible to win, then he surrenders. His surrender is also secondhand, it comes through the fight. A man of purity simply exists. He is not a fighter, he need not surrender. There is nothing to surrender, nobody to surrender. Who will surrender and what is to be surrendered? He has never fought.

Understanding leads you to acceptance, and that acceptance gives you purity. But this purity cannot be honored by people, by the neighbors – they cannot understand it. Morality belongs to a country, purity belongs to no country. Morality belongs to an age, purity is nontemporal. Morality belongs to this society or that: there are as many moralities as there are societies. Purity is one – wherever you go it is the same, just like the taste of the sea: wherever you go it is salty.

A Buddha or a Jesus or a Ramakrishna, if you taste them, they are all just like the sea – the same saltiness. But a man of morality is different. A man of morality, if he is a Mohammedan, will be different; if he is a Hindu, he cannot be the same. If he is a Christian, again he will be different. A man of morality has to follow the code, the law of the society. Societies are many, moralities are millions. Societies change, moralities change. Purity is eternal – it transcends time, space. It transcends climate, countries, it transcends tribes. It transcends all that is manmade. Purity is not manmade; moralities are manmade.

Now we should enter this beautiful story – it happened in reality, it is an historic fact.

> *The Zen master Hakuin was honored by his neighbors as one who led a pure life.*

They didn't know, they were not aware that the purity of *their* conceptions cannot be applied to this man. They were not aware. They thought, "He is a moral man," and he was not a moral man. He was a pure man, an innocent one – but not a moral one. He was a religious man – and remember the difference – he belonged to the eternal innocence, he was childlike. But the people honored him because they were not aware yet of the distinction between morality and amoral purity.

They thought that he is a saint, but he was not the saint of their conceptions. He *was* a saint, but he was not a saint who can be measured by you. Your standards won't apply there. You will have to throw out your measurements and look. You will have to throw out your judgments and look; only then the saint, the real saint, is revealed to you.

> *One day it was discovered that a beautiful girl*
> *who lived near Hakuin was pregnant. The parents*
> *were very angry. At first the girl would not say*
> *who the father was, but after much harassment*
> *she named Hakuin.*
> *In great anger the parents went to Hakuin, but all*
> *he would say was, "Is that so?"*

He would not deny, he would not accept. He didn't make any commitment. He didn't say, "I am not responsible." He didn't say, "I am responsible." He simply said a very noncommittal thing; he said, "Is that so?" as if he was not related – so detached, so absolutely out of it. He simply asked, "Is that so, that I am the father of the child?"

What does this mean? It means such a total acceptance that even acceptance is not needed. Because when you say, "I accept," deep down you have denied. When you say yes, then no is implied. He would not even say yes. Who was he to say yes or no? If it had happened, if this was a fact, then he would just be a witness to it. If people had come to think that he was the father, then why unnecessarily disturb them and say something this way or that way? He would not choose. This is what choicelessness is. He would not be this or that, he would not defend himself.

Purity is never on the defense. Morality is always defensive, that's why morality always takes offense very easily. Just look at a moralist, at a puritan, and he feels offended. If you say something, he feels offended; he will immediately deny and defend himself. But this is one of the basic psychological insights of all seekers: that whenever you defend something, it means you are afraid.

If this Hakuin was an ordinary saint he would have defended himself – and he would also have been true in his defense, there was no problem about it: it was proved later on that the child never belonged to him, he was not the father. An ordinary saint, a so-called saint, a man of morality, even if he *was* the father, would have defended himself. And this Hakuin – he was not the father, but he did not defend himself.

Innocence is insecurity, that's why it is innocence. If you defend it and make it secure, it is not innocence – calculation has entered.

What must have happened inside Hakuin? Nothing! He simply listened to the fact that people had come to believe that he was the father, so he asked, "Is that so?" That was all, that is all! He didn't react in any way – this way or that. He would not say yes, he would not say no. He was not defensive, he was open and vulnerable. Innocence *is* vulnerable; it is absolute vulnerability, openness.

Whenever you defend, whenever you say that this is not so, you are afraid. Only fear is defensive. Fearlessness cannot be defensive. Fear always armors itself. If somebody says that you are dishonest, you immediately defend. Why? Why be so worried about it? Why react? – because you know that you are dishonest. That's why it hurts. Truth hurts very much, because the wound is there. You know you are dishonest, and if somebody says you are dishonest, you cannot laugh, you become serious. You have to defend, otherwise the thing will be known. You have to fight, otherwise everybody else will start thinking in those terms.

And if people come to know that you are dishonest, then it will be difficult to be dishonest, because only if people believe that you are honest can you continue to be dishonest. This is the mathematics. People must believe that you are a true man, only then you can lie. If everybody knows that you are a liar – finished! Then how can you lie? Even lies need a sort of trust about you.

You can be a thief only if people believe that you are a saint – then it is very easy to be a thief, because people will not try to protect themselves against you.

An immoral person will always defend his character. He will try to prove that he is a man of character, but this shows that he is characterless. If you are not dishonest and somebody says you are dishonest, you will say, "Is that so? Maybe, perhaps, who knows!" You will say, "I will look again. I will have a look again within myself. You may be right."

But this is honesty. How can this man be dishonest who says, "I will look, I will try to find out. You may be right"? This is authentic honesty. This man cannot be dishonest. But if you are dishonest and somebody says so, you take offense. All your defenses are because you take offense. You are always prepared and ready to answer. You carry character certificates with you, "I am a man of character."

Fear creates an armor. Now depth psychology has come to realize that all characters are armor. A child is born, he does not know what is good, what is bad. Then he has to be taught to make distinctions. He is punished if he goes on doing something which is thought bad. What happens to the mind of the child? What happens in his consciousness? As far as his innocence is concerned, he cannot see what is bad in it. Why is it bad? But father and mother – and they are powerful – they say, "This is bad, and if you do it you will be punished. If you don't do it you will be appreciated, rewarded."

He has to listen to them because they are powerful, and he has to suppress himself and his own innocence. He creates an armor around himself. He becomes afraid of certain things he should not do, otherwise he will be punished. Certain things he should do because then he is going to be rewarded.

Greed is created, fear is created. And then the child moves through many experiences in which he is punished, in which he is rewarded. By and by, he creates a character around his consciousness. Character means creating habits which society thinks are good, and destroying habits which society thinks are bad – this is character. And this character is an armor, because if you don't create it the society will destroy you. The society won't allow you to exist. To exist, to survive, you have to create a character, otherwise you will be in jail, punished.

Why are you so much against criminals? Why do you punish them so much? Not because their crimes are so great, not because it is needed by justice, no. You are taking revenge. They disobeyed society, they disobeyed you, the structure, the establishment. They are rebellious. You were saying, "This is bad," and they still did it – the society will take revenge. And your courts and your judges are not really men of justice, they are the hangmen. They are the murderers appointed by the society, in the name of justice, to take revenge. They murder, they kill, but in the name of justice.

A man steals, he is a thief. He is sent to prison for five years, seven years, ten years. Is it going to help in any way? When he comes out, is it going to prevent him stealing again? No, on the contrary; he will come out a more perfect thief, because there in the prison he will meet the masters. There he will learn the trade secrets, there he will learn why he has been caught, where he was at fault. Next time it will not be so easy to catch him. He will become more efficient, he will become more alert.

Your punishment never changes anybody. But you go on punishing and you say, "We are punishing to change him." A man murders, then the society murders him "...because," they say, "why did you murder?" But this seems to be foolish. He murdered, he was wrong, and now the society murders him – and the society is right! And how is your killing him going to change him? He will no longer be there.

No! You are taking revenge. And you know deep down that not only is society doing that, you are also doing that. You are a father or a mother – you punish your child. Have you ever observed your mind, why you punish? Look deep inside and you will find the revenging attitude. You will say, "We are teaching him. How will he learn if he is not punished?" But these are just rationalizations. Inside, the father feels hurt because the child has disobeyed, he has become rebellious, he has done something which he was told not to do – the father's ego feels hurt.

If you look in the old scriptures, the Old Testament, the Koran and other scriptures, then you will immediately feel that God is very revengeful. He will send you to hell, not that justice needs it, but because you disobeyed. In the Old Testament it is said: Obedience is virtue, disobedience is sin. It is not a question of what is said to you – obedience is virtue and disobedience is sin.

If obedience is forced, then a character arises. Then by and by the child starts learning; he learns, becomes calculating – what to do, what not to do. The innocence is poisoned. The innocence is no longer there, now calculation has come in. And now he knows how to influence you, how to manipulate you, how to be a good child so he is rewarded, and how not to be a bad child.

And this character armor works in a double way. He protects himself from the society; but deep inside, the consciousness does not know what is good, what is bad. So he has to fight with himself continuously. This character becomes a double-edged thing: on the outside it is a protection from society, on the inside it is a constant fight.

You fall in love with a woman and she is not your wife. What to do? The society has taught you that this is immoral. But even your consciousness has fallen in love, because the consciousness does not know what is immoral and what is moral. Something happens, you cannot do anything about it. Your character starts fighting and says, "This is immoral, prevent it, control it. Don't move on this path, this is wrong." Then you start fighting. This fight creates anxiety, your spontaneity is lost. In the eyes of others you are a man of character; you cannot lose your reputation, because then the ego will be lost.

Inside also you think that you are a man of character. You start feeling guilty, you start punishing yourself. So many monks in so many monasteries are fasting, not as a religious prayer but just as a punishment to themselves. They feel guilty, continuously guilty. And it is very difficult to find a monk who is not feeling guilty, very difficult, because everything is wrong: to look at a beautiful woman is wrong, to eat food with taste is wrong, to feel comfortable is wrong – everything is wrong. Continuous guilt, so what to do now?

Only one thing remains…. And he is not a criminal because he has not done anything, so the society cannot punish him. And you all give your respect to him. So what can he do? He has to punish himself. He will go on a fast. He will go on a continuous vigilance for seven days. He will not allow himself to sleep, he will not allow himself to be comfortable, he will not eat with taste, he will not look at anything beautiful – he will not enjoy anything. That is how he will punish himself, and the more he punishes himself the more honorable he becomes in your eyes. And he is just an ill man, perverted.

He is pathological, he is a case. He has to be studied, not respected. Something has gone wrong within him. His mind is not at ease – divided, fragmented, he is continuously against himself. This is what anxiety means: when you are against yourself, you are in anxiety. Continuously fighting with yourself will create tension.

And you cannot allow anything, because you are always afraid that if you allow then all that you have suppressed will come up. You cannot relax. Your so-called saints cannot relax. Even in sleep they cannot relax, because they are afraid of relaxation. If they relax, then what will happen? Then the body will say, "Be comfortable." Then the mind will say, "Find taste in food, find tasteful food." Then the body will desire: "Find a woman, find a beautiful body to hug. Find someone with whom you can merge and melt." If you relax, then all that you have suppressed will also relax. So your saints cannot relax, they are afraid of relaxation. They are tense, continuously tense, you can feel that tenseness. If you go near a saint, all around him there is a field of tenseness. You will also become tense if you go near a saint.

But with a real saint, a sage, who is a man of purity not a man of morality, he is continuously relaxed…if you go near him you will feel relaxed. But then you may feel afraid, because if you feel relaxed your own repressions will start coming up.

Many people come to me and they say, "This is dangerous,

because when we meditate and relax, many things that have not been bothering us before start bothering us."

A married man with six children came to me just a few days ago, and he said, "Never in my life have I looked at other women, never. But what is happening? I am meditating and for the first time – and I am now forty-eight with six children, a wife, and everything is okay – suddenly women have become very attractive. What to do?" He is afraid now. He must have been repressing this continuously for forty-eight years. Now, suddenly, he has learned how to relax. But when you relax, you relax totally, so all that has been repressed also relaxes.

For the first time he is becoming young again. "Really," I told him, "you have never been young. Now you are becoming young again, so women have become attractive. But don't be afraid, everything is going to become attractive now: the trees will look different, the flowers will look different – and why not a woman? Everything is going to become different. And if you are afraid of this then existence can never become beautiful to you.

"And when the whole of existence has become beautiful, then you have come to the door of the divine, never before. And you are afraid of a woman – what will happen when God comes? He will be so beautiful you will forget your wife completely. What will you do? You are afraid of a tiny woman – what will happen to you when a tremendous beauty explodes all over the world, everywhere? So don't close...."

But he said, "You may be right, but what will happen with my family? I have got children."

These are the fears. With a repressed mind, relaxation is the most dangerous thing. You come to me and you ask, "How to relax?" You don't know what you are asking – because your society has trained you not to relax, your society has taught you how to control, and here I am teaching you how to relax. It is absolutely antisocial. But God is antisocial. The beyond is antisocial. Your society is created by pathological minds just like you. They have made rules and regulations – and pathological people are always very efficient in making rules and regulations. They themselves are repressed and in misery; they want others also to be repressed and in misery. They cannot allow you to be so happy.

Look at a schoolmaster in a primary school, with a staff in his hand, killing small children who are still happy. The society has not destroyed them – they are still spontaneous. Look at this schoolmaster: sad, angry, always angry, always killing the natural, the Tao, the spontaneous. He will be happy only when all these children become old and dead. Then he will be at ease, he has done his job.

Psychologists say that people who are attracted towards schools, to become teachers, are people who are sadists. And there is nothing like a school if you are a sadist, because children are so weak, so helpless, you can do anything with them. You beat them and they cannot rebel. You do something and they cannot reply, they will have to suffer. And you are doing this for their own good, so you are beyond reproach. You are helping them to grow.

Pascal has said that the whole society is mad and that children fall into the hands of so many madmen. They come innocent, but immediately we take charge and turn them into madmen. Some of them escape from the back door: they are criminals. And some of them escape from the front door: they are sages.

Sages and criminals have one similar quality, and that is rebelliousness. But the criminal has gone wrong in his rebelliousness. His rebelliousness is destructive, not creative. And the saint has taken a route of rebelliousness – but creative.

> *The parents were very angry. At first the girl*
> *would not say who the father was, but after much*
> *harassment she named Hakuin.*
> *In great anger the parents went to Hakuin, but all*
> *he would say was, "Is that so?"*
> *After the child was born it was taken to Hakuin –*
> *who had lost his reputation by this time, although*
> *he didn't seem much disturbed by the fact.*

Whether you honor or whether you dishonor him cannot make any difference to a sage, to a man of purity. What you think about him is really irrelevant.

Why is it so relevant to you what others think? Why are others' opinions so relevant to you? Why do you care so much? Because you don't know who you are. You depend on their opinions about yourself. That's your only self-knowledge. If they say you are good, you are good. If they say you are bad, you are bad. You have nothing inside which can say, "Their opinions are *their* opinions. If I am good, I am good; whatsoever they say makes no difference. If I am bad, I am bad. The whole world may respect me like a saint, but if I am bad, I know I am bad, and this reputation cannot become a substitute – it is useless. And if I am good, the whole world may say that I am not good, bad, evil, the very devil incarnate – how does it make any difference?"

One who knows himself is never disturbed by what you think about him. But one who doesn't know himself – he is always disturbed, because his whole knowledge consists of your opinions. His whole knowledge is just a file he has gathered about what people think about him. This is not knowledge, not self-knowledge. This is self-ignorance, which you hide, disguise, by others' opinions. Your whole identity, your whole image, is made by others. You are bound to remain in constant anxiety because others go on changing their opinions.

Opinions are like the climate: it is never the same. In the morning it was cloudy and now the clouds have gone. Now it is sunny, and the next moment it is raining. Opinions are just like clouds, just like the climate. What can you do about it? Look at Richard Nixon: just a moment before he was everything, and just a moment later, nothing. The opinion has changed, the people who were for him are against him – and the same people!

This is the beauty of it: the same people who will push you towards the throne will pull you down. There is a dynamic, an inner law, that the people who respect you, deep down also disrespect you. The people who love you also hate you, because they are divided. They are not one. So after they help you to reach to the throne, one part of them is finished – the love part. Now what will happen to the hate part? Immediately the hate part starts functioning. So once a man becomes respectable the climate is changing already. Once a man has become a president or a prime minister, the voters are already changing. Really, the moment they voted one part is finished – the love part. Now the hate part will come up. So the same people take you to the throne, and the same people bring you down.

Only a sage remains undisturbed. Why? – because he never pays any attention to what you say. What you say is really rubbish. You don't know anything about yourself, and you say something about Mahavira, Buddha, Christ. You don't know anything about yourself, and you are so confident about Jesus, that he is good or bad. It is rubbish. And a person can pay attention to your rubbish only if he is just like you. A sage is not like you, and this is the difference.

> *After the child was born it was taken to Hakuin –*
> *who had lost his reputation by this time.*

Of course, obviously, the same people who thought that he is a sage started thinking that he is a devil. He has committed the greatest sin – because for people, sex is the greatest sin.

You are so much against life that sex has become the greatest sin – because it is the origin of life. You are so dead, that's why sex has become the greatest sin. Sex is the most alive phenomenon in the world. Nothing else is so alive as sex. You come through it, the trees come through it, the birds come through it – everything comes through it. Anything that becomes alive comes through it, it is the original source.

If you can give any parallel to God in this world, it is sex. That's why Hindus have made their symbol *shivalinga*. Hindus are really rare – no comparison anywhere in the world – very courageous people to make shivalinga, the sex organ of Shiva, the symbol of the divine.

Sex is the most divine thing in the world. But why do you call it a sin? – because from the very beginning you have been taught that it is sin. You have completely forgotten that you have come out of it. And you have completely disguised the fact that when the sex energy is finished in you, you will die. It is sex energy throbbing in you which is life.

That's why a young man is more alive, and an old man is less alive. What is the difference between a young man and an old man? In young men the sex energy is in flood. In the old man the supply has disappeared, now the flood is disappearing. It has become just like a dripping stream. The moment sex energy has disappeared, you are dead.

Sex is life – and we have made it the greatest sin.

Deep down we are against life.

So when you come to know that a saint has been in a sexual relationship, all his reputation immediately disappears. If he was a thief it would not be so bad, you could have forgiven him. If he was accumulating money – your saints *are* accumulating – then you would have forgiven him; it was not a big problem, greed is not a big problem. Whatsoever he was doing you could have forgiven him, but sex? – impossible!

We have become so deadly against it that Christians say that Jesus was born without sex. Because how can Jesus be born out of sex, the original sin? How can Jesus be born out of sex? Everyone else is born out of sex – not Jesus. Just because sex is such a dangerous thing, they said that Jesus was born from the Holy Ghost. There is no father to Jesus, there has been no sexual intercourse. He was born out of the womb without any meeting with the other sex.

Why this nonsense? But leave Jesus aside, and the Christians. You! If you even think that your father, some time or other, must be making love to your mother, you will feel guilty. How were you born? You are not a bastard. But just to think of your father making love to your mother...the whole thing seems ugly. The whole thing seems so ugly that you cannot conceive of your father doing that – others may be doing it, but *your* father? Impossible! You are born out of a *brahmachari* father, a celibate; that's what Christians are saying about Jesus.

And when you come to be sure that a saint, a great sage like Hakuin, has made a girl pregnant – obviously not only respect is gone. He must have been insulted as much as possible. It would have become impossible for him to go around the town to beg. People must have been throwing stones at him, the same people who were bringing garlands and flowers and who were bowing down at his feet – the same people. But Hakuin was not disturbed.

> *Hakuin took great care of the child. He obtained*
> *milk, food, and everything else the child needed*
> *from his neighbors.*
> *A year later, the girl-mother could stand it no*
> *longer, so she told her parents the truth...*

It must have been too heavy on her, seeing Hakuin's respect going down and down, seeing the insults being thrown at Hakuin, seeing that the whole town is against him, seeing him begging for the child, for the milk, for the food, and doors being closed in his face. It must have been really heavy.

> *...so she told her parents the truth – the real father*
> *was a young man who worked in the fish market.*

They always work in the fish market – the real fathers.

> *The mother and father of the girl went around at*
> *once to Hakuin to tell him the story, apologize at*
> *great length, ask his forgiveness, and get the child*
> *back.*
> *As the master willingly yielded the child he said,*
> *"Is that so?"*

In misery, in happiness, the sage remains the same. Respected,

insulted, the sage remains the same. In life, in death, the sage remains the same. He again simply said the same three words: "Is
that so?" Again noncommittal, again not committing himself to
anything, not saying anything, simply accepting a fact: "If that is
so, okay."

This is the consciousness of purity. Whatsoever life brings, welcome it. If it brings misery and insult – accept it, welcome it. If it
brings honor, happiness – welcome it, accept it. And don't make
any distinction between the two. If you differentiate, your balance is
lost, and the balance is the purity.

When you are balanced, you are a sage. When the balance is
lost, you are lost, you have become a sinner. Sin is not something
that you do, sin is something that happens within you when the
balance is lost. It is not an act, it is an inner balance. It is what
Mahavira has called *samyaktva* – inner balance; neither this nor
that, what the Upanishads have called *neti, neti* – not this, not that.
Just in between – neither moving to this, nor moving to that, because if you move, even a slight movement which nobody can
detect except you…. Remember this: nobody can detect your
inner balance. Only you can detect it, it is so subtle! But even a
slight movement and you are no more at peace, you are no more at
home, you have lost the divine. Because what does a slight leaning
mean? It means you have chosen. It means a distinction is made. It
means you have said this is good, that is bad. It means expectation
has come in. It means desire has sprouted. It means now you are
motivated.

Had Hakuin said, "Right! So you have come to know the
truth?" that would mean he was no sage at all, because that would
mean for the whole year he was waiting for this moment, he was
not in the present, he was thinking for the future, "Some day or
other the truth must be known. The people will respect me again.
When they come to know that the child doesn't belong to me, they
will respect me again: my respect will be back." Then he would
have waited, but the balance is lost….

If Hakuin was not a sage he would have thought and prayed to

God, that God reveal the truth to people. But why? If it happens that a child has happened to you, and people think that it is your child – if life has brought a child to you, what difference does it make who the real father is? No difference! Hakuin took every care of the child, just like a father. The child needs a father, that is the thing. And Hakuin fathered the child as lovingly as no father could. Even if the child was your own, it would have been difficult to take such care as he took.

It was no sin of the child. He was not against the child. If you had been in Hakuin's place, you would have killed the child because he was the cause of your misery. You would have thrown the child and moved to another village where people can respect you again, because they don't know you. You would have done something to defend your respect – your whole prestige was shattered. And Hakuin was just caring about the child, not worried about the village. What people say is not the question, it is irrelevant. The child needed a father, so Hakuin became the father. He was not disturbed, he didn't react.

And then, after one year...when you take care of a child so lovingly, attachment arises – bound to be so. Even if the child is not yours, the child becomes yours. To live with a child for one year and to suffer so much for the child, to sacrifice so much for the child – a deep bond, a deep relationship arises. One becomes attached. But when the parents came again and they told the whole story, asked his forgiveness and got the child back, *as the master willingly yielded the child* there was not a single trembling of attachment. He simply yielded the child – *He said, "Is that so?"* – as if nothing has happened. This whole year has been a dream. Only the dream is broken, and you are awake.

A sage lives in this world amidst you as if he is living in a dream. You are shadows. He lives amidst you just as if he is enacting a part, he is not involved. He is there, but not in it – he remains an outsider. And if you can remain an outsider, then sooner or later you will come to realize: no water, no moon. Because when you get involved, water is created; then you live with the reflection, then you cannot move to the real, then you live with the unreal.

Your attachment creates the delusion. The delusion is not there outside you, the *maya* is not there outside you. It is within you, in your attitudes: attached, choosing, for this, against that, making distinctions, like and dislike. It is in you. You create your illusion and then you live in it, then you are clouded by it. In that clouded state you can see only the reflection, you can never see the real moon.

This Hakuin remained balanced. Whatsoever happened outside didn't affect the inside at all. The inside remained balanced – no waves, no vibrations of the outside entered. He remained silent as if it was a dream. And whatsoever came, he accepted it. He didn't become a doer, a *karta,* he remained a witness.

These three words, "Is that so?" belong to the witnessing soul; not making any judgment, simply saying, "Is that so?" And this is all that was inside him, "Is that so? If it is so, okay."

A sage okays everything that happens, he has no choice. And when there is no choice, there is no water. No water – reflection disappears, maya disappears – no moon.

Enough for today.

the dead man's answer

Mamiya later became a well-known teacher, but
while he was studying under a master he was
asked to explain the sound of one hand clapping.
Although Mamiya worked hard at it his master
said to him one day, "You are not working hard
enough. You are too attached to food, wealth,
things – and that sound. It would be better if you
died."
The next time Mamiya came before the master, he
was again asked what he had to show regarding
the sound of one hand clapping. Mamiya at once
fell over as if he was dead.
"You are dead all right," said the master, "but
how about that sound?"
Looking up Mamiya replied, "Oh, I haven't
solved that one yet."
"What?" roared the master, "Dead men don't
speak. Get out!"

*t*he absurd is needed to bring you out of your mind, because mind is reasoning. Through reasoning you cannot come out of it. Through reasoning you will move and move, but you will move in a circle.

That is what you have been doing for many lives. One thing leads to another, but the 'another' is as much a part of the circle as the first. You feel that you are moving because there is change, but you are following a circle. You go on moving about and about, around and around – you cannot get out of it. The more you reason how to get out, the more you create systems, techniques, methods how to get out, the more you become entangled into it. Because the basic problem is: reasoning cannot bring you out because reasoning is the very phenomenon that you are in.

Something irrational is needed. Something beyond reason is needed. Something absurd, something mad – only that can bring you out. All great masters have been devising things – their devices are absurd. If you think about them you will miss. You have to follow their line without any reasoning. That's why philosophy is not of much use. Only religion can be of help – religion is absolute madness.

Tertullian has said, "I believe in God because God is absurd." There is no reason to believe in it – is there any reason to believe in God? Has anyone ever been capable of proving that God exists? There is no reasoning which can support it – hence faith. Faith means the absurd. Faith means no reason to believe and you believe. Faith means no arguments, no proofs to prove, and you put your whole life at stake. Nobody can prove that God is, and you take the jump into the abyss. Anyone who is reasonable will feel that you have gone mad, and that's how all rationalists have always been feeling. A Buddha, a Krishna, a Jesus – they have gone mad, they are talking nonsense.

There is a whole school in the West which proves that all of religion is nonsense. And I am a religious man and I say they are right – for the wrong reasons they are right. They think that if you prove that religion is nonsense, that you have discounted religion, refuted it. No!

Religious men have always been saying, "We are absurd! We belong not to the world which is of sense, we belong to something which is beyond." And the beyond is bound to be nonsense. What sense can you make out of religion? If you can make any sense out of religion, you have missed. Then you are in the world of theology, philosophy, systems, but you can never touch that purity which is always beyond reason.

Tertullian is right, he is true. He says, "I believe because God is absurd." Belief means belief in the absurd. You need not believe in this world that surrounds you – it is there; nobody needs to believe in it. How can you disbelieve it? It is *so* much there, so present; everything proves it is there. Somebody can throw a stone at you and it is proved, because you will be bleeding. You have been hit; the stone is there.

But God cannot hit you like a stone. You cannot even touch him. There is no way. How to smell him? How to see him? And still you believe. Belief means always believing in the absurd.

But what happens when somebody is capable of believing in the absurd? He is out of his reason. Suddenly the circle stops, the wheel stops, because you are not feeding it any more. Argument stops, thinking stops. Suddenly you are out of it, as if you have been awakened out of your sleep. And the greatest sleep is of reason, because reason creates such beautiful dreams, and so real that everyone is deceived by them.

Once you are awake and out of the vicious circle, God is there, nothing else exists. Then there is no need to believe. Then you know. But before that knowing happens, faith will be needed. And all those philosophers who have been trying for centuries to prove that God is, they are not religious, they are not serving God; they are doing a great disservice. Because when you give proof, you make God also a part of the mind. And when somebody believes because God is a proved fact, he cannot get out of the reason.

So all religious people, all the masters, have devised ways to bring you out of the reason. Zen has its own particular technique, and that technique is known as a *koan*. A koan is an absurd puzzle. You cannot solve it. Howsoever you try, your effort is irrelevant. "Harder and harder," the master will go on saying, "you are not trying hard enough." And he is deceiving you, because whatsoever you do will never be hard enough to solve the problem – because the problem is unsolvable! It doesn't depend whether you work hard at it or not. But if you do it with your totality, suddenly you will become aware of the absurdity – never before. Suddenly you will start laughing. The whole thing was nonsense. And if you can laugh the mad laugh that comes when reason is not functioning....

Have you seen a madman laughing? His laughter is totally different from your laughter. Your laughter is reasoned out, there is a reason for it. Somebody has told a joke, somebody has fallen on the street, slipped on a banana peel, and you laugh. There is a reason, something ridiculous has happened. Why do you laugh when a man falls in the street, slipping on a banana peel? Why? What is humorous in it? There is something: the ego is the most ridiculous thing in man, and when a man falls on a banana peel, then even the banana peel is stronger than you. The whole absurdity of the ego is proved, that man is nothing – even a banana peel can throw you off balance.

The whole civilization of man is ego-centered. Whole cultures, nations, all dreams of greatness have come to man because he is the only animal who stands erect on two feet – that's why man goes on thinking that he is not an animal, he is different, he is unique, he doesn't belong to the animal world. But when you slip on a banana peel suddenly the erect posture is gone. Suddenly you fall into the animal world, you are a helpless animal, nothing else. That's why it is ridiculous, seeing a man fall.

And think – if a beggar falls on a banana peel, you will not laugh so much; but if a prime minister falls, you will laugh more. Why? – because a beggar is a beggar; he was already a part of the animal world, nothing much. But this prime minister, the president, the king, the queen – you could never believe that the queen of England could fall just like other human beings. Impossible! They have created a false impression around them that they are infallible. And just a banana peel cracks the whole thing. You are exposed, that you are just a helpless human being. And not only a helpless human being, just an animal – on all fours, not on two legs.

It is ridiculous. You laugh, but there is a reason. Watch a madman laughing – there is no reason in it. That's why you call him mad. You ask him, "Why are you laughing?" If he can answer the why, then he is not mad. If he cannot answer the why, you say he has gone out of his reason.

When a koan is understood for the first time...not solved, because a koan cannot be solved, a koan is unsolvable, it cannot be solved. There is no way to solve it, it is an impossibility, it is an impasse for the mind – you cannot move any more. Suddenly you are stuck, and the master goes on saying, "Work hard! You are not working hard enough." And the more you work hard, the more you are stuck, moving nowhere: you cannot go back, you cannot go ahead – stuck. And the master goes on hammering you, "Fast, fast, harder. Work hard!" A moment comes when you are not holding any part of your being, your whole being is involved, and still you are stuck.

Suddenly, when the whole energy is involved, you become aware. And this happens only when you are totally involved, when you have put in everything that you can. Only at that peak, at that climax of energy, do you become aware that this problem is absurd – it cannot be solved. A laughter spreads all over your being, it is a mad laughter. And with that laughter everything changes, is transformed. This is the first thing.

The second thing – then we can enter into the story – the second thing: you are all great imitators. It is easier to imitate than to be authentic, because imitation is just on the surface. Authenticity needs your center, needs you in your totality. That is too much. You get involved just on the surface, deep down you remain out.

Imitation is very easy, and the whole culture and society depends on imitation. Everybody is telling you how to behave, and whatsoever they are teaching you is nothing but imitation. Religious people – the so-called religious people, the priests, the theologians – they are also teaching you, "Be like Jesus, be like Buddha, be like Krishna." Nobody ever tells you, "Just be yourself" – nobody. Everybody is against you, it seems. Nobody allows you to be yourself, nobody gives you any freedom. You can be in this world, but you must imitate somebody.

The whole thing is ridiculous, because these same things were said to Buddha. They were saying to Buddha: "Be like Rama, be like Krishna." He didn't follow them, that's how he became a buddha. He became enlightened because he never became a victim of imitation. Nobody can imitate. If you imitate, you will remain false.

I have heard: a lion and a rabbit entered a restaurant. Suddenly everybody became alert, they couldn't believe their eyes. Then the rabbit said to the waiter, "Bring a lettuce for me – and no dressing."

The waiter was scared, but still he asked, "And what about your friend? What should I bring for him?"

The rabbit said, "Nothing."

The waiter asked, "Is he not feeling hungry?"

The rabbit stared at the waiter and said, "If he was a real lion, do you think I would be sitting here? He is an actor."

The whole world has become unreal and acting, nobody is real. It is very difficult to find a real man. If you can find a real man, don't leave him, just be near him; his reality will become infectious. Just being near him will be enough transformation for you. No need to do anything. This is what we have been calling *satsang*:

being near a true man, a real man, an authentic man. Nothing else is needed. Just being near him and watching and feeling the way he is – that's enough.

But the society has made you imitators, actors. You are not real, you are false. You have never been allowed to be yourself, and that is the only thing you can be, you can be nothing else. You can try, imitate, but it will remain just on the surface: deep down you will remain yourself...and that's how it should be. The falseness that you put upon yourself cannot become your being. How can it be? It can be at the most a dress, a posture, a superficial gesture.

The whole world helps you to be imitators. So when you come to a monastery, near a master, again you try the old methods you have been doing in the world. You start imitating there also. There they will not be of any help, they will be the barriers. In the world it is okay, because the whole world is of imitators. If you are real there you will be in trouble; if you are false, you will be accepted. This so-called world only wants you to be a shadow, not a real man, because a real man is dangerous.

Only shadows can be subdued, shadows can be obedient, shadows can follow; whatsoever they are told to do, they will do. A real man will not always say yes; sometimes he will say no, and when he says no, he means no! You cannot subdue him, you cannot suppress him.

So from the very beginning we train children to be false. And this is what we call 'character'. If they become really false, unreal, we appreciate them, we reward them with medals, we say they are real. This falsity is called real, ideal. And if a child rebels, tries to be himself, he is a 'problem child'. He has to be psychoanalyzed, or he has to be sent to some institution where they can put him right – something is wrong with him. And there is nothing wrong, he is simply asserting himself. He is saying, "Let me be myself."

A small child, Tommy, was attending his first wedding ceremony. Somebody asked – a guest – "Tommy, to whom would you like to be married and when?"

Tommy said, "Never. I don't want to get married."

The man was surprised and said, "Why?"

He said, "I have lived too much with married people, and they are so false." And his father and mother were present there. "I don't want to get married because I want to be myself."

The wife will not allow the husband to be himself. The husband will not allow the wife to be herself. Nobody allows anybody to be himself or herself, because this is thought to be dangerous.

Suppress! And this *has* suppressed society: if it is sad, it is bound to be so, it is natural. False people cannot be happy. They can be, at the most, sad; at the most, at their peak, they can be sad, depressed. Freud has said that for humanity there is no possibility, no hope for bliss. And he is right; the way humanity has been moving, if it goes on moving that way, only sadness, depression, a hopeless state is possible. Just carrying oneself somehow, like a burden – no dance, no energy bubbling, no vitality, singing, nothing, no flowers – just dragging along.

False people can only be of that sort. But when these false people get too bored, fed up with the so-called society, they go to a master in search of truth. There also they try their old techniques, but then they will miss there. It is okay to be false with false people, because it will be difficult to be real with them. But when you are in search of truth, when you come to a master and the urge has happened to you to know what reality is, you are not allowed to imitate. If you imitate you have carried your old pattern, your mode of existence, and that mode of existence will become the barrier.

In religion no imitation is allowed. But see religious people; you will see churches, temples, mosques, and you will find there the greatest imitators. That means there is no religion left – churches, temples, mosques are dead tombs now. With Jesus one had to be real, but with the pope of the Vatican you have to be imitators. Now the Christianity of the Vatican is part of the society.

Jesus was never a part of the society. He remained a stranger. All real religious people have remained strangers, they are outsiders.

When they die, then a church is raised on their dead bodies; that church is part of the society, it is managed by the society, controlled by the society.

Society has many cunning devices. If you escape from the market you will be caught in the church, because the church is just the extension of the market. The market feeds the church, the market controls the church, the market is really the owner of the church. And a priest does not represent the divine, he represents the market.

The priest represents the economics of the society. And Marx is right when he says that religion has been playing into the hands of the capitalists, or the feudalists, or those who exploit and are powerful. Religion has been played just like an instrument of exploitation. And Marx is right as far as the religion of the Vatican is concerned, or the religion of Puri Shankaracharya is concerned, or the religion of Mecca and Medina is concerned. But it is not true about Mohammed, it is not true about the original Shankaracharya, it is not true about Jesus. He is wrong – because they existed not as part of the society, they existed in the wilderness, they existed as strangers, they existed against the society and imitation. They existed as divine messengers. That is the meaning of *avatar,* that is the meaning of the son of God, that is the meaning of a prophet, a *paigamber* – they existed as messengers of the beyond.

Remember these two things, then we will enter this story.

Mamiya later became a well-known teacher...

And remember, only one who has been a real disciple can become a teacher. One who has never been a disciple, one who has never known what discipleship is, one who has never been a learner, can never be a teacher. Before you can teach you must learn. But everybody wants to be a teacher without being a learner, your ego wants to be the master and not the disciple – then you will become a false master. And then not only are you in danger, you will lead many others into danger. A blind man leading other blind men – they are bound to fall in a pit.

Remember this, because ego wants to teach. It is so beautiful for the ego to give advice, to teach. Sometimes, catch hold of this ego in you, because you are also doing that. You cannot lose an opportunity to teach. You have been losing thousands of opportunities to learn, but you cannot lose an opportunity.... Somebody is talking, you will poke your nose in. Somebody asks a question – you don't know what the question means, you don't know what the answer is, but you will give the answer, because ego feels very good when you appear to be knowledgeable. You know, and the other is ignorant; that's why there is so much attraction in becoming a teacher. Teach – then you are the knower, and the other becomes the ignorant.

This is the old trick: you have the riches and the other is poor; you have a position and the other is nobody; you are the knower and the other is ignorant. Whenever you can feel that the other has been thrown deep down, you are at the peak. This is exploitation: that's why there are so many teachers in the world but very few real masters. But this will always be so, this has been always so.

When Mahavira was born...he was a real master, and the Jainas in India were waiting for a *tirthankara* for many, many years. The twenty-fourth was to come, the twenty-fourth was awaited. Jainas have a mathematics that in every *kalpa* – one creation – twenty-four great masters are born. So twenty-three had already been born and the twenty-fourth was awaited. There was much waiting for the twenty-fourth, but how to know who is the twenty-fourth? When Mahavira came, he *was* the twenty-fourth, but eight others also claimed that they are the real – and those eight others led many astray.

They were great teachers, but not masters. They could talk, they could preach, they could argue; they were argumentative, debaters, and they influenced many people – because you are influenced by argument. You are not influenced by *being*, because to see the being you have to raise your consciousness higher and higher. Only then you can see the peaks. If you exist in the valley, how can you see the peak? You have to raise yourself higher.

To see Mahavira was difficult; but there was Goshalak, there was Prabuddha Katyayan, there was Poorn Kashyap and there were others. They were ordinary, but extraordinary minds. Ordinary in the sense that they had no evolved consciousness, they were not enlightened. But they were great scholars, greater than Mahavira, they were great arguers – they could silence anybody – logic-choppers, hair-splitters. And when *they* claimed many heard them, and Mahavira remained absolutely silent for twelve years.

Who will go to him? He was chased out of every village. Wherever he went people would chase him out, because he was silent – one thing – and you are always suspicious of a silent man, he may be from the CID, the FBI. So every village was suspicious of Mahavira because this man wouldn't speak, he would not even look at anybody. And he was naked! That created more problems, because people would ask, "Why are you naked?" And he would remain silent. So either he was a criminal hiding, or some madman who is naked, because only the mad are naked. Why should he be naked? Must be someone immoral, because moving naked in society is the most immoral thing.

And then not answering! "Either he is stupid, cannot answer, or he is suspicious – maybe he is an agent of some foreign country," or something or other. They would chase him out of the town; he was chased for twelve years. And we say people were waiting for him.

But just to wait is not enough. You need eyes to see. Jews waited for Jesus for thousands of years. They are still waiting, and Jesus has already happened. What to do with the human mind? The Jews are still waiting for the messiah to come, and he has already come. Twenty centuries have passed. He came to them, he knocked at their door, they refused to believe him – because he was not talking the way they expected. And how can the divine messenger talk the way you expect? He is not part of you, he comes from the beyond, he cannot speak your language. Whatsoever he says will be destructive of you, he will destroy you. As you are, you have to be destroyed, only then the new is born. But the Jews refused to believe and they are still waiting.

And know well: if he gathers courage again.... I think Jesus is not going to gather courage again, because the way you behaved with him – it is enough! If he gathers courage again, if he forgets what happened twenty centuries ago, how you crucified him, how you insulted him, how you misbehaved; if he forgets it and comes again and knocks at the doors of the Jews – who have been again waiting – they will refuse him again.

They can accept ordinary people with extraordinary minds, but they cannot accept people with extraordinary states of being. Because to see that being you have to transform yourself. As you are you cannot see, as you are you cannot understand Jesus.

Remember well, that the ego would like to become a messiah, the ego would like to become a tirthankara, the ego would like to claim something which is not there. Ego is a great claimer; it possesses nothing, but it claims – goes on claiming. There are many teachers – be alert, otherwise you can become a victim.

Remember well: don't give any advice to anybody unless you have learned, unless you have passed through the process of discipleship. And discipleship is difficult, because you have to surrender. You have to drop your ego, you have to become a no-self. And this is the paradox: unless you become a no-self, you will never become a self. The false has to be dropped, only then the real arises. The false coin has to be thrown, only then the search begins for the real and the authentic.

> *Mamiya later became a well-known teacher, but*
> *while he was studying under a master he was*
> *asked to explain the sound of one hand clapping.*

He became a great teacher later on, but he had to pass through discipleship under a master. And he was given a problem to explain.

One of the most famous of Zen koans is, "Find out what is the sound of one hand clapping." Immediately the mind will say, "Useless! The search is useless, futile, because how can one hand clap? Clapping always needs the other. How is sound possible with one hand clapping? – because sound is created by two things clashing. All sounds are created by two things clashing, so how with one hand?" So if you are a good logician you will immediately move away from this master because he is talking nonsense. It is not possible, and whatsoever you do you will never succeed – this is simple logic, simple reasoning. But you miss the point. That is the point!

Many times in your past lives you have gone away from a master because he demanded something impossible. But a master will always demand the impossible; only then you can change. With the possible you will remain the same. Whatsoever your mind thinks is possible, is within it. Whatsoever your mind says is impossible, is beyond it. Try for the impossible. Religion is the effort to reach the impossible. Religion is the effort to make happen that which cannot happen.

...he was asked to explain the sound of one hand clapping.

If he was an argumentative man, he would have left immediately. But Mamiya remained with the master, knowing well that this is impossible. "But when the master says it, there must be something in it. It may be impossible, it may look absurd to me, but when the master is demanding it, there must be something which I cannot see now." This is faith. This is trust.

If you say, "I cannot see. Unless you explain it to me first, I am not going to make any effort...." The master cannot explain it to you, because there is nothing to explain, the explanation is not there. Only your change of consciousness will give you the eyes with which you will be able to know and laugh with the master; then too there will be no explanation.

The master demands the impossible because he demands trust. If he demands the possible – no need for trust. You can reason it out, you can figure it out; then you trust your mind when you have figured it out. But when you cannot figure it out, when your mind feels unable to do anything about it, simply refuses to do anything and still you remain, this is trust. Mamiya remained – he trusted the master.

> *Although Mamiya worked hard at it...*and he started working.

There are only two possibilities: either you refuse the master or you refuse your mind. The fight is not between you and the master, the fight is between your mind and the master. When the mind is defeated, there is no barrier between you and the master – you become one. The disciple becomes the master, the master becomes the disciple, all the barriers are broken. The barrier is the mind, and the mind will say this and that and will try..."This master is mad: he is asking something impossible – nobody can do it. Don't waste time. Find someone who is reasonable."

But Mamiya tried, he worked hard at it. He refused the mind – refusal of the mind is trust. And mind is reasonable, so trust is unreasonable.

> *His master said to him one day, "You are not working hard enough."*

And he *was* working hard. But masters are impossible, you can never satisfy them. They will go on hammering you, hard and hard and hard – because you don't know how much you can do. You don't know anything about you.

When you say, "I am working hard," the master knows that only a part of you is functioning. Psychologists say that even a very talented man, even a genius, never uses more than fifteen percent of his energy; even an Einstein never uses more than fifteen percent of his energy. What about ordinary men? They use nearabout three percent, five percent at the most. Ninety-five percent of your life energy is simply wasted. So when you say, "I am working hard," you don't know what you are saying. Your one fragment which you have been using may be working hard, but this is only one-tenth, the nine other parts are asleep. The master would like you to be total in it, because when you are total...only then the transformation.

> *"You are not working hard enough. You are too attached to food, wealth, things – and that sound. It would be better if you died."*

What did this master mean? These are the ordinary attachments of the world. Food is an attachment, and it becomes a greater attachment when somebody renounces sex.

In a monastery, in a Buddhist monastery, you renounce sex, you live the life of a celibate. When you renounce sex, your whole energy becomes more and more attached to food. This is a problem to be understood, because sex and food are the two deepest things in you.

If you are too much in sex, you will not bother much about food. But if you are not after sex, then the whole energy begins flowing towards food. Hence, all your *sadhus* – those who have renounced sex – will always be after food. Look at Hindu sadhus, Hindu *sannyasins* with big bellies. What has happened? Why these big-bellied Hindu sannyasins? They go on eating and eating and eating – but this is a natural phenomenon; it has to be understood why this happens. They have renounced sex, so the energy that was moving towards sex, where can it move now?

And food and sex are basic. Food is more basic than sex, because you can live without sex but you cannot live without food. Living without sex is not a problem at all. And really, those who have lived with sex will find that it is easier to live without sex, because the other gets involved, and then the other also creates problems. You are enough problem to yourself, and the other creates more. And when two persons live in a sexual life, it is not that the problems are doubled – no, they are multiplied. It is not a simple addition, it is a multiplication.

So those who have lived with sex know well that sex creates more problems than it solves. But by the time you know, you are so much in it you cannot get out. This is the problem: experience comes through experience – but then it is of no use, because you are already in it. And if you say this to somebody who is still out of it, he is not going to listen because he will say that it is very difficult to be alone, somebody else is needed to share. He does not know what is going to happen when he starts sharing. Because then you will start sharing the problems – there is nothing else to share.

Food is more basic than sex. Food is needed from the first moment a child is born – not sex. The child can live for fourteen years without any sex. But on the first day, the first moment, the first scream comes for food, because food is the base of your biological existence. Sex is not the base of your biological existence, sex is the base of the biological existence of the society – not you. Without sex the society will disappear; you can live, but without sex you cannot reproduce, children will not be born, the society will disappear.

If all become *brahmacharis,* celibates, which is impossible, then there will be world peace, real peace, because there will be nobody left. It will be global suicide. But you can exist without sex, that is not much of a problem.

So whenever your energy which is moving towards sex is stopped, the same energy starts moving towards food. These are the basic things. Hindu sannyasins or others, they go on eating too much. So in every scripture – Jaina, Buddhist, Hindu – they have made rules for sannyasins not to eat too much. Why? – because they have stopped sex, now they know that they will eat too much. So many rules have to be made to protect the sannyasin, otherwise he will become a food addict, he will be mad – eating and eating and eating.

Eating can give you sexual pleasure, because the sex center and the mouth are both joined together. That's why a kiss is such a sexual thing. Otherwise, why...? And if you are passionately kissing somebody, immediately you will feel sex energy arising. Why?

...Because mouth and sex are so far apart! They are not, they are joined; they are the two poles of one energy.

So whenever you starve the sex pole the whole energy moves to the mouth, so you will have to eat more, chew gum, *pan* or something. Or, if nothing else, you will have to talk continuously, because by talking the mouth moves. That's why people go on talking continuously the whole day. Even the day is not enough; if you sit by their side during the night you will see they are talking.

Mulla Nasruddin went to a doctor and said, "Do something! It is getting on my nerves. My wife talks too much in the night."

So the doctor said, "Where is your wife? Bring her, I will do something."

Mulla Nasruddin said, "You don't understand me. Nothing is to be done to her. Do something to me so I can remain awake, it is so interesting. I fall asleep...and she is talking, and it is so interesting. She says such beautiful things and reveals such beautiful things; she never talks that way when she is awake. When she is awake she is talking rubbish. So give me something so I can remain alert and listen."

If you watch people, the whole night they are talking – continuously. Their mouth is moving, they are making sounds and doing all sorts of things. If one pole of energy is stopped, then the other starts because the energy has to be released somehow. You cannot contain it. It is just like if you eat and stop defecation – what will happen? You will have to vomit, there is no other way, because if you eat then the things have to be thrown out. If you eat, sex energy is created, then it has to be thrown out. If you don't use sex as an outlet, then some other outlet has to be found.

This Mamiya must have become too much addicted to food. The master says: "*You are too attached to food, wealth, things – and that sound.*"

When a man is patterned, when a man is conditioned for attachment, he may leave the world, but that doesn't make any difference.

He may leave all things but the attachment remains, it starts working in new directions. You may leave the palace: then you have nothing but three robes, but you become attached to the three robes. The whole attachment, the whole energy that was attached to the palace, is now attached to three robes. It doesn't make any difference. You can go on dropping things, but the attachment remains the same.

This Mamiya had come to the monastery, he had left his life, he was a Buddhist monk; now there were no things. A Buddhist monk is not allowed many things: one bowl for food, water, three robes, one mat to sleep on – that's all, nothing much to bother about. He can put it on his back and move, because a Buddhist monk has to be a wanderer and he has to carry all his things himself. Nobody else can carry things for him: Buddha made it a rule so that you don't go on gathering things. If somebody else is allowed to carry them then you may go on gathering things.

Very few things – but the attachment! The master said: "*You are still attached to food, wealth...*" He has no wealth now, but attachments can remain without wealth. Because it is not a question of objective things, it is a question of subjective feelings. *...and that sound* – and that too becomes a problem. If you are too attached to meditation, meditation becomes your world. If you are too attached to your prayer, prayer becomes the barrier.

There is a beautiful anecdote in Hassid literature. Hassids are some of the most beautiful people in the world – Jewish rebels. They have a tradition, a valuable tradition, and the tradition is that whatsoever your mind demands, don't give that thing to the mind – wait. If you want to give, only give when the urge has left. If the mind says, "I am hungry," don't give food – wait. When the urge has left, give food; but don't give it when the mind demands, don't follow the mind, you remain the master.

Once it happened: one of the disciples of Baal Shem was ill, just dying. And when one is dying one has to do the prayer, the last prayer before one leaves the body; the last thanksgiving and prayer. He was just on the death bed, changing sides, much troubled. So

Baal Shem asked – he had come to see him and give the last farewell – he said, "Is there some problem?"

He said, "Yes, because the mind says, 'Do the prayer,' and I cannot do it unless the urge leaves. When the urge leaves I will do the prayer, but I don't know whether I will be alive or dead. So I am changing my position again and again, so that I can remain alive and the urge goes."

Baal Shem said to his other disciples who were gathered there, "Look! This man knows what prayer is."

If the attachment is there and you are praying, the prayer has become of this world, because attachment changes everything to the material. Even prayer is a sin when you do it as an attachment. When you pray, not as an attachment, not as a mind-urge, only then the prayer succeeds.

So the master says, "And that sound also has become an attachment. You are continuously thinking how to solve it. Don't be attached. Solve it, all right, but don't be attached. Don't become mad. Work hard, but don't become mad – *It would be better if you died.*"

But Mamiya misunderstood, as ordinarily all disciples misunderstand. The master said: "*It would be better if you died.*" To whom was the master saying, "*better if you died*"? It was the mind, not Mamiya, because Mamiya cannot die, Mamiya is deathless. It is the mind, the ego, which is also trying to solve this problem which cannot be solved by the mind.

The problem will be solved only when the mind is dead, when the mind has done everything that it can do and then falls helpless and says, "No more is possible, I retire." When the mind retires and you are left alone for the first time without mind – consciousness is there, witnessing is there, but thinking is not there – the problem is solved, you have heard the sound of one hand clapping.

There is a sound, Hindus have called it *omkar,* aum – this is the sound. If you are completely silent you will hear it. And it is not created by any clash of two things. It is not created by two hands clapping, it is not through conflict. It is the universal music, it is the very sound of existence. It is not created, it is there.

Hindus say the contrary: because of this sound the universe is created. This universe is just a transformation of that sound, that beginningless, endless...the base of all. And the same is the experience of Buddhists, Jainas, Sufis, Hassids, all those who have known, the experience is the same; that there is a sound, a melody – continuous. If you become silent and the mind is not there, you will hear it for the first time. It is everywhere. It is the very core of existence. And this whole existence is just a transformation of that sound.

These mystics have said that even matter is nothing but condensed omkar, a rock is nothing but condensed aum. Just as the scientists of today say that matter is nothing but condensed electricity, just electric vibrations, mystics have said that matter is nothing but condensed sound, just vibrations of sound.

There is a possibility now to make a bridge between science and these mystics. If you ask scientists, they say sound is nothing but vibrations of electricity. If you ask mystics, they say electricity is nothing but vibrations of sound. That's why Hindus have stories that through music you can create fire; a particular soundwave and fire can be created – and now it is a scientific truth also.

Continuously creating a particular sound can produce so much heat – and there, you can try it yourself. The night is cold, you stand outside and simply do omkar. Vibrate aum within you as much as you can, so from your very toes to the head the aum sound vibrates. Suddenly you will feel the coldness has disappeared, the body is hot. And if you continue it, soon, in a very, very cold, freezing night, you will start perspiring. That's how Mahavira lived naked. That's how in Tibet, where coldness is below zero, Buddhist monks have lived naked. They sit the whole night under the sky, snow falling, and they are perspiring. They go on creating a particular sound.

But that sound also is not omkar that you create, because that is created; that, again, is the clapping of two hands. There is a sound uncreated, or, the very creation comes out of that sound. That's why aum has become the universal symbol of the ultimate reality. Aum is not a word, it is a sound symbol. Everything is condensed in it, or everything is manifested through it.

Mamiya's master said, "It would be better if you died, rather than being attached to food, wealth, things...*and that sound. It would be better if you died.*" Mamiya misunderstood it. He thought this is going to be a technique. He thought, "So, I can manipulate death, so I will die." But how can you manipulate death? If the mind is the manipulator, you are alive. You can imitate, but you will be alive.

Even suicide is not suicide; because you have manipulated it you will be somewhere. But you cannot commit suicide, suicide is impossible. You go and you hang yourself – you are doing it, the mind is there. This mind will lead you to a new life, to a new womb. You cannot commit suicide – there is only one suicide known and that is *samadhi,* but then the mind is not the manipulator. That's why Buddha dies and simply dies, and is never born again. That's why we say when a man has achieved samadhi, the final enlightenment, he is born no more. Because the mind is gone, who can lead into a new desire, who can lead into a new motivation, who can lead into the new body? The mind has left.

There is only one death and that is the death of the mind. But mind cannot do it, because if you do it through the mind, the mind remains the doer and survives.

The next time Mamiya came before the master, he was again asked what he had to show...

Because these questions are not something you can answer; you have to show the answer through your eyes, through your very being, your face. The answer must be shown through you; you must become the answer. You cannot give the answer, because if you give, the mind will give – you can *be* the answer.

So...he was again asked what he had to show

regarding the sound of one hand clapping.
Mamiya at once fell over as if he was dead.

He imitated. He thought: "Master has said, 'Die!' – better die."
So he thought, this is very good, so he fell down. But the mind is
working; it is mind who has concluded to do this.

"You are dead all right," said the master, "but
how about that sound?"
Looking up, Mamiya replied, "Oh, I haven't
solved that one yet."

This is beautiful, because the master is saying, "If you are dead,
then the problem is solved. What about that sound? You must have
heard it." Because when the mind is not, it is bound to be heard.
Then there is no possibility that you have not heard it if the mind is
not there. When the mind is not there, it is always there. It is because of the mind, the turmoil of the mind, that you cannot hear it.
It is always there, the rhythm is always there. If the mind retires
even for a single moment it is there, you can know it – you can
never miss it.

So the master says, *"You are dead all right, but*
how about that sound?"
Looking up, Mamiya replied, "Ah-ah-ah...
I haven't solved that one yet."
"What?" roared the master, "Dead men don't
speak. Get out."

Only mind speaks. If Mamiya had remained silent... But how
can he remain silent?...because he was only imitating, he was not
really silent. You cannot deceive a master even if you die. Imitation
cannot deceive.
The master said, "Dead men can't speak."
When the mind disappears and the master asks, "What about

that sound?" no answer comes. The whole being is the answer. The disciple remains silent, he is showing himself. Now there is no need, and the master will see...no answer is required really. If you answer, all answers are wrong.

It has happened many times with the same koan – the sound of one hand clapping. It happened with Rinzai; he was given the same koan to work with. And then he worked and worked and worked harder and harder, and the master continued pushing him, ahead and ahead. And one day it happened – the mind disappeared, the sound was heard.

Rinzai came and the master asked, "What about that sound?" Rinzai hit the master. And the master said, "All right, so you have heard!" – because the question is foolish! And the master said, "I was waiting for when you will relieve me of hitting you. Now you can hit me. Now there is no trouble, now I need not hit you – finished! Now you go and teach others the sound of one hand clapping."

No answer is required; you have to show through your whole being. But this can happen only when the mind has disappeared – no water, no moon.

Enough for today.

gutei's
finger

GUTEI'S FINGER

The Zen Master Gutei made a practice of raising his finger whenever he explained a question about Zen.

A very young disciple began to imitate him, and whenever anyone asked the disciple what his master had been preaching about, the boy would raise his finger.

Gutei got to hear about this, and when he came upon the boy as he was doing it one day, he seized the boy, whipped out a knife, cut off his finger, and threw it away.

As the boy ran off howling Gutei shouted, "Stop!"

The boy stopped, turned round, and looked at his master through his tears. Gutei was holding up his own finger.

The boy went to hold up his finger, and when he realized it wasn't there he bowed.

In that instant he became enlightened.

*t*his is a very strange story, and there is every possibility that you will misunderstand it, because the most difficult thing to understand in life is the behavior of an enlightened person.

You have your own values, and you always look through those values. An enlightened person is in a totally different dimension, where he lives without values, where he lives without any criteria, where he lives without any morality, where he simply lives without the ego, because all values belong to the ego. An enlightened person simply lives. He is not manipulating his life, he is a white cloud floating. He has nowhere to go, nothing to achieve. Nothing is good for him and nothing is bad. He does not know any God, he does not know any Devil. He knows only life, and life in its totality is beautiful.

God is also ugly because it is a part, not the whole. The Devil is also ugly because that too is again a part and not the whole. God is not alive, the Devil is also dead, because life exists as a rhythm between the two – the good and the bad, God and the Devil. Life exists between these two poles. Life cannot exist with one polarity. These are the two banks between which the river of life flows.

An enlightened person has come to know this. He is neither against anything nor for anything. He responds moment to moment, without any judgment on his part. That's why it is very difficult. An enlightened person always appears more or less like a madman. So the first thing to be understood is: don't evaluate an enlightened person through your values – very difficult, because what else can you do?

I have heard that once a very great painter asked a doctor friend to come and look at one of the paintings he had just finished. The painter was thinking that this was the greatest creation he had ever attempted, this was the peak of his whole art. So, naturally, he wanted his doctor friend to come and look at it.

The doctor observed very minutely, looked from this side and that. Ten minutes passed. The artist became a little apprehensive, then he asked the doctor, "What is the matter? What do you think about this painting?"

The doctor said, "It appears to me double pneumonia!"

This is happening to everybody, because a doctor has his own attitudes, ways of looking at things. He looked at the painting – he cannot look at anything except in his own fixed ways; without them he cannot look – he diagnosed. The painting doesn't need any diagnosis; he missed. The beautiful thing turned into pneumonia.

This is how mind functions. When you look at a thing, you bring in your mind to color it. Don't do that with an enlightened person, because that is not going to make any difference to the enlightened person, but you will miss the opportunity to see the beauty of it.

Second thing: an enlightened person behaves from a center, never from the periphery. You always behave from the periphery, you live on the periphery, the circumference. To you, the circumference is the most important thing. You have killed your soul and saved your body. The enlightened person can sacrifice his body, but cannot allow his soul to be lost. He is ready to die – any moment he is ready to die, that's not a problem – but he is not ready to lose his center, the very core of his being.

To an enlightened person the body is just a means. So if it is needed, then even an enlightened person will tell you to, "Leave the body, but don't leave your inner being." This is how all *tapascharya,* all austerity, is born. The circumference is to be sacrificed for the center. Even if the head needs to be cut – if that is going to help you, if with your head your ego can fall – an enlightened person will tell you to drop the head, to cut it off:

"Don't carry this head if it helps the ego, because for nothing you are losing all."

This has to be remembered: when you live from the center, the outlook is totally different. Then nobody dies, nobody can die – death is impossible. If you live from the periphery then everybody dies, death is the final end of everybody; eternal life exists nowhere.

Krishna talking to Arjuna in the Gita is really the center talking to the periphery. Arjuna lives on the periphery: he thinks of the body, he does not know anything about the soul. And Krishna talks from the center, and he says, "Don't bother about these bodies. They have died many times and they will die many times. Death is nothing but a transformation, as if someone leaves his clothes, leaves his old house, and enters into a new house. This body is nothing, Arjuna, so don't be bothered about it. Look within." But how can Arjuna look within others if he has not looked within himself?

Remember this: this Zen Master Gutei, he is the Krishna. He lives from the center and behaves accordingly. And this incident happens to a disciple who is on the periphery. But Gutei would not have cut *your* finger, remember. The disciple was worthy of it, he had earned it – only then will a master go to such an extent. To go to such an extent the disciple must have learned, must have earned it, otherwise Gutei would not go that far. Even Arjuna was not so worthy as this disciple of Gutei, because Krishna *talked* to him – Gutei *did* something.

Remember the difference. A master only comes to do certain things to you when you have earned it; otherwise he will talk to you. Doing can be only when you are ready, when the moment is so near that it cannot be missed; nothing can be said, only something can be done. Because if you speak, time is needed; if you speak, then the other has to understand it. Something has to be done immediately, instantly. A master will do something only when he sees that you are just on the brink: now talking won't help, now he has to push you. Now you are just at the door; a single moment gone and you may miss the door, and for many lives you may not be able to come to the door again.

Life is very complex. Rarely are you near the door. And if the master says, "Look, the door is here!" and starts explaining to you, by the time you have understood, the door is no more there. Life is constant movement. The master has to *do* something. Even if he thinks killing you will help, he will kill you. That's why surrender is needed.

Surrender is not easy, because surrender means saying to a master, "From now on, my life and my death are yours." Surrender means "I am ready. If you say, 'Die!' I will die. I will not ask why." If you ask why, there is no surrender, there is no trust. And in the ancient days, many people could become enlightened because they could surrender. Trust was in the very atmosphere, faith was all around, trust was flowering everywhere. You couldn't pass a day without coming across a man who was a man of trust. And the moment you saw a man of trust, you felt jealous – he was such a beautiful person.

But nowadays it has become almost impossible to come across a man of trust. That beauty has disappeared. You come across doubters, skeptics, no-sayers; they are ugly but they are all around. And, by and by, you are also fed on doubt. From the very first day your mother gives you milk you are fed on doubt. The whole scientific device depends on doubt. You have to be skeptical, doubting; only then can science work.

Religion works in totally the opposite way. You have to be trusting, to be deeply a yes-sayer, then surrender is possible. This disciple of Gutei was a surrendered one, that's why this incident became enlightenment for him.

Now we will enter this strange story. Each word is significant.

The Zen Master Gutei made a practice of raising his finger whenever he explained a question about Zen.

Masters never do anything unnecessarily, not even raising a finger. The unnecessary has disappeared. Only the essential exists with a master. He will not do a single movement, a single gesture, if it is not essential. The nonessential exists with ignorance; then, whatsoever you do is trivial, nonessential – if you leave it, nothing is lost.

Look at your life, whatsoever you are doing – if you leave it, what is lost? Nothing is gained through it – trivial things from the morning to the evening. And then you are tired of it, then you go to sleep, and in the morning you are again ready to do the same nonessentials. It is a vicious circle, one nonessential runs into another nonessential, they are linked with each other.

But you are so afraid to look at this triviality of life that you are always keeping your back towards it, because looking at the triviality of life makes you feel so depressed, "What am I doing?" And if you see that everything you are doing is absolutely useless, your ego is lost; because the ego can feel significant only when you are doing something significant. So you create significance in trivial things, and you feel you are doing great duties to the nation, to the family, to humanity – as if without you the existence will simply drop. Nothing is important, whatsoever you are doing – but you have to give significance to it, because through significance the ego is fed, strengthened.

In ignorance, everything is nonessential. Whatsoever you do, even your meditation, your prayer, your going to the temple – all is trivial. Even when you pray, it cannot be deeper than when you read your newspaper. Because it is not a question of prayer, it is a question of you. If you have depth, then whenever you move, whatsoever you do, the act will have depth. If you don't have depth, even if you go to the temple it makes no difference; you enter the temple the same way as you enter a hotel. You are the same, temple and hotel can't make much difference.

Give a child a very costly toy made of diamonds, and he will do the same with that costly toy as he was doing with ordinary toys, because he is a child. He will play with it for a few moments, then throw it in the corner and go away.

Your depth brings depth to your actions. Even when an enlightened master raises his finger, it is meaningful, it is very significant.

Why did this Gutei used to raise his finger...*whenever he explained a question about Zen?* Not always – whenever he explained a question about Zen he would raise a finger. Why? – because he was explaining and he was also showing, because whatsoever you ask about religion, one raised finger is the answer.

All your problems arise because you are not one. All your problems arise because you are fragmented. All your problems arise because you are a disunity, a chaos – not a harmony. And what is Zen, and what is yoga, and what is meditation? Nothing but coming to a unity. The very word yoga means unity, to be one, total, whole.

So Gutei was explaining about Zen: that explanation was secondary, the raised finger was the primary thing. He was saying something and he was also showing it. This is how an enlightened person lives: he says and he shows. His very being, his gestures, his movements, show what religion is.

If you cannot see, if you are blind or if you have lost that dimension of understanding, of looking, then you hear only the words. But if you know how to look, no words are needed. Words are useless, they can be dropped, they are secondary. But the raised finger cannot be dropped; that is primary, that is the only answer. All those who have known, anywhere in the world, they have all raised a finger. They are talking about the one and you are living in the many.

When you live in the many, problems are created, because living in the many, moving in many directions simultaneously, you become split into parts, then you are not together. Then one desire leads to the south, another desire leads to the north. Then one part of the mind loves, and another part of the mind hates. Then one part of the mind wants to accumulate wealth, and another says, "This is useless. Renounce!" Then one of the minds wants to meditate, become deep, become silent, and another mind says, "Why are you wasting your time?"

I have heard: Once it happened a man renounced the world

while he was very young and went to the Himalayas. For almost twenty years he meditated there. Now he was forty. He was sitting and meditating, sitting and meditating, not doing anything at all. Even birds, wild animals, by and by lost their fear with him. He was there, and a very peace-loving man, simply sitting. Animals would come and sit, and when they would have to go hunting they would leave their children near him to be taken care of. His hair became very long, and birds would nest in his hair and put their eggs there, and he would have to take care of them.

After twenty years he got fed up with the whole thing. He said, "If I am to take care of others' children – animals, birds – why shouldn't I go and marry a woman and take care of my own children? This is absurd, and I am reaching nowhere. These twenty years are lost. Now there is no more time to lose because I am forty, and soon life will have ebbed!"

What was the problem? He was really meditating. What was the problem? Twenty years is a long time but the mind was continuously fragmented. One part was meditating, another was continuously saying, "Useless! Why are you wasting your time? Others are enjoying. Go back down to the plains. People are happy there – dancing, drinking, eating, lovemaking. The world is in ecstasy and you are sitting here like a fool." Continuously hearing this other fragment for twenty years, the first fragment by and by became weak.

On the surface he was repeating mantras: Ram, Ram, Ram. But deep down this was the mantra: the other part of the mind continuously saying, "Useless! Sitting like a fool and everybody is enjoying life and now life is ebbing. Soon you will not be able to enjoy anything. You are becoming old." This was the real mantra. On the surface, "Ram, Ram, Ram" – but deep down this was the real mantra.

When your mind is divided you cannot pray, you cannot meditate, because one part is always against it, and sooner or later it will win. Remember this: that the part that is engaged is losing energy every moment. And the part that is not engaged, but which is the critical part, is not losing any energy. Sooner or later it will be more powerful.

You love a woman, and another part hates. You may hide this – everybody is hiding the other part – but unless you become enlightened, the other part is there. This loving part sooner or later will become weak because it is being used, the energy is being applied. The other hidden part, the hate part, will become stronger. So every marriage leads to divorce. Whether you do it or not, that's another thing – but every marriage becomes divorce, unless you are married to an enlightened person: that is very difficult.

This man got fed up one day. He started coming down from the Himalayas. He thought, "From where to start?" – he had completely forgotten the ways of the world, he had been so long out of it. "From where to start? If you want to start in the world you will need a guide, just like when you want to start in the other world you will need a guide. Who can be the right guide for this world?" Then he remembered that in the old days, kings would send their sons and princes to the prostitutes, just to learn how to enter this world.

There is no better guide than a prostitute for this world. She is the world incarnate. Even love has become business for her – this is the last thing in the world – even love has become a profession, a commodity; she sells love. Money has become more important than love. This is the last thing in the world, and this can become the door.

So he went directly to a prostitute. It was evening and the prostitute was getting ready to go to a king. She said, "You are welcome, but I have been invited by a king. He is a miser, I don't hope that we will get much, but still – who knows? Sometimes even misers give. You come with us, come along." So the monk followed.

The whole night the prostitute danced, sang. And the king sat silently, he didn't give anything to her. Then the last part of the night was dissolving, soon there would be light, and the woman was so tired. She said in a song to her husband, who was playing the *tabla,* she said to him, "Now, all that can be done I have done."

She sang it so no one would understand, it was in a code. She said, "All that can be done I have done; now there seems to be no hope. It is better we should leave."

Inside his mind the monk thought, "This was the situation I was in: all that can be done has been done. Nothing more can be done, and I should leave." So he listened very attentively.

The husband said, "All that we could do we have done, but still a little of the night is left. Who knows? We must see the whole business through, so a little more, be patient."

Hearing this, the monk thought, "Now what should I do? Maybe I was just on the brink when I left the Himalayas – a little more patience."

He had only one blanket, he was naked underneath. He became so enthralled that he threw his blanket at the feet of the prostitute and started running out of the palace. The king said to him, "Stop! This is against the convention." This was the convention, that when a rich man is present, he should contribute first; otherwise this is insulting – that a king is present and this man has contributed.

The monk said, "You can kill me if it is against the convention, but she has saved my life. And it was such an ecstatic moment for me, I had to give something. I have nothing else, just that blanket, and I cannot wait for you, I am going to the Himalayas. This woman and this man who is playing the tabla, they have revealed a secret to me: a little more patience." And it is said the man became enlightened then and there. He never went to the Himalayas. Just coming down the steps of the palace he became enlightened.

What happened? For the first time the two parts became one. That is the meaning of patience. Patience means, don't allow the other part to fight; patience means that you are ready to wait for infinity. If you are ready to wait for infinity, there is no possibility for the other part to say, "It has not happened yet." There is no sense in saying, "Why are you wasting your life?" If you are ready to wait for infinity then nothing is wasted. And if your waiting is eternal, infinite, then the other part cannot have its say.

Oneness is needed – when the other is not in a constant fight. That's why Gutei would always use his one finger whenever he was explaining Zen. He was saying, "Be one! – and all your problems will be solved."

There are many religions, many paths, many methods, but the essential point is the same: become one. Whatsoever you choose, become one. If you can be infinitely patient you will become one. If you can surrender totally you will become one. If you become completely silent you will become one. If there are no thoughts and you are in meditation you will become one. If you pray to God and the prayer becomes so intense that even the person who is doing it is no longer there, the person who is saying the prayer has become dissolved in the prayer, one has remained – that will do.

Digging in the garden, if you can dig in such a way, so totally absorbed that nobody is left there who is the digger – you have become the digging, the actor has become the action, the observer has become the observation, the meditator has become the meditation – suddenly all the waves of *maya* disappear, all illusions drop. You are raised to a different layer, a different plane of being. You have come to the one.

When *you* are one, you reach the one. When you are many, you are in the world. The world is many and God is one. But to know that one you will first have to become one, otherwise you cannot know it. Only when you become like it will you be able to know it.

The Zen Master Gutei made a practice of raising his finger whenever he explained a question about Zen.

Zen is from a Sanskrit term, it comes from *dhyan*. It is the Japanese form of dhyan. When Bodhidharma took the teachings of Buddha to China, dhyan, in Chinese, became *ch'an*. When ch'an was taken to Japan, it became zen. But the original term is dhyan. Whenever Gutei would talk about dhyan, meditation, he would raise his one finger. Oneness is dhyan, oneness is all that has to be achieved – that is the end.

A very young disciple began to imitate him...

Of course he must have been very young, because only children imitate. The more mature you are, the less you imitate; the more immature, the more imitation. If you are still imitating you are juvenile, you have not gained maturity, you have not yet become grown-up. What is 'grown-upness'? If you ask me I will say, the realization that you have to be yourself and not an imitator, this is what maturity is.

If you look within yourself you will not find this maturity. You have been imitating others. Somebody has got a new car – suddenly you start imitating, you need a new car. Somebody has got a bigger house, you need a bigger house. The neighbors are constantly on your nerves. They are getting this and that, and you have to imitate. And when you imitate you are just like monkeys. Don't imitate. Be mature. Because imitation cannot lead you anywhere. Why? What is imitation, and what is being true and authentic?

Imitation means the ideal comes from without, it is not *your* desire. It is not something happening within you, it is not your nature flowering in it. Somebody else has given you the ideal and you go after it. If you don't achieve it, you will be in misery because you have not achieved the ideal. If you achieve it, you will be in misery because this was never *your* ideal. You never wanted it, because it never happened to your inner being.

That's why so much misery exists in the world: people imitating others. If they fail, they are in misery because they think they have not attained. If they succeed, they are in misery. Remember, nothing fails like success – if it is an imitation, nothing fails like success. You may reach the goal after a long strenuous journey, effort, wastage of time and energy, and then suddenly you find, "I never wanted it – it was somebody else. I borrowed the ideal." Don't borrow the ideal, this is childish.

A very young disciple began to imitate him...

He must have been very young, juvenile, childish. He started imitating him.

> *...and whenever anyone asked the disciple what*
> *his master had been preaching about, the boy*
> *would raise his finger...*

The same way, the same gesture as the master used to do. People must have enjoyed it, they must have laughed. The boy was a perfect imitator; he would make the same face, he would raise the same finger, he would try to look the same way. He acted it well.

Howsoever efficient you become in acting, you will remain immature. Be true to yourself, even if you are not so efficient there. But be true to yourself, because your own truth can lead you to the ultimate truth. Nobody else's truth can be your truth.

You have a seed within you. Only if that seed sprouts and becomes a tree will you have a flowering; then you will have an ecstasy, a benediction. But if you are following others that seed will remain dead. And you may accumulate all the ideals in the world and become successful, but you will feel empty, because nothing else can fill you – only your seed, when it becomes a tree, will fill you. You will feel fulfillment only when your truth has come to flower, never before.

And people may appreciate your success in imitation – they always appreciate it. This boy must have been appreciated in the monastery because he was acting just like the master. He must have become famous. Imitators become famous, but they don't know they are committing suicide. But you can commit suicide if people appreciate you.

I have heard about an actor who died. His funeral attracted many, many people, many thousands. His wife was beating her chest and crying and screaming. And when she saw thousands of

people had come she said, "If he had known this – that so many
people will come – he would have died sooner."

You can commit suicide if you are appreciated. You all have
committed suicide, because imitators are always appreciated.
Authentic people are never appreciated, because an authentic person is a rebel. He will not imitate anybody. He will say, "I am not
going to be a Buddha, I am not going to be a Krishna or a Jesus.
One is enough! One Jesus is enough, why imitate?" And the second
Jesus, howsoever beautiful, will be just a carbon copy – nothing
worthwhile. Why imitate Jesus? And God is not going to ask you in
the end why you didn't become a Jesus. He will ask why you didn't
become yourself.

I have heard about one Hassid mystic: he was a very poor man,
Magid was his name. Nobody knew much about him, but he was a
real, authentic man. He was dying, and somebody said, "Magid,
have you prayed to God to make you like Moses?"

Magid opened his eyes and said, "Stop! Don't say such things
while I am dying. Because God is not going to ask me, 'Why didn't
you become a Moses?' He will ask, 'Magid, why didn't you become
a real Magid?'"

The others didn't follow it, they couldn't understand, because
this seems insulting to Moses. It is not. It is not insulting to Moses.
Moses became Moses, that is *his* beauty. Magid has to become
Magid, that is his beauty. And only beauty can be offered, only a
flowered being can be offered to God. How can God ask a rose,
"Why didn't you become a lotus?" How can God be so foolish as to
ask a rose, "Why didn't you become a lotus?" No! He is not so
foolish as you think. He will ask the rose, "Why didn't you flower
totally? Why have you come like a bud and not like a flower?"

Flowering is the thing. Whether you are a lotus or a rose, or
some unknown, unspecified flower makes no difference. Who you
are is not the point. Whether you come to the divine door as a
flower, flowered, open, or you have come still closed....

A very young disciple began to imitate him...

And whenever you go to a master, that is the possibility – the first possibility: you will start to imitate him. Remember, this is not going to help, this is dangerous. You are committing suicide. Understand a master, drink his presence, eat his presence as much as you can, but don't become an imitator. Don't become false.

> *Gutei got to hear about this, and when he came*
> *upon the boy as he was doing it one day, he seized*
> *the boy, whipped out a knife, cut off his finger,*
> *and threw it away.*

Seems to be a very hard master, very cruel. Masters *are* cruel, otherwise they cannot be of any help to you. They are cruel because they have such a deep compassion. Why did the master cut the finger? Any less hard and he won't be a help to this boy. Something very severe is needed, something is needed which goes to the very heart. This has to be understood.

You listen to me. If you have come just as a curious person it cannot go very deep. If your curiosity is just intellectual, to know what I am saying, it cannot go very deep; you will not be able to understand what I am saying at all. If life has given you much suffering and you are here because of that suffering, to understand how to transcend it, then what I am saying will go deep. Suffering gives you depth. Suffering leads you towards the center.

If you are in love with me, not an intellectual relationship – which is not a relationship at all – but a love relationship, if you are emotionally in touch with me, then it will go still deeper. Because when you love a person you hear him from the heart, not from the head. And the head is the most rotten thing, rubbish, just a wastepaper basket – nothing much. All that is rubbish, you go on gathering in the head. Rubbish never enters the heart, it accumulates in your head. Only that which is very essential goes in the heart.

So if you are here just as a curious person, just out of curiosity, you will hear me, but just on the surface. It is not going to do much to you. If you are here because you have suffered – if you have come not as a curious person, but as a person who has known life, its suffering, and a maturity has come to you and you want really to be transformed – then you will hear from a deeper depth.

But the depth can go still deeper. If you are in love with me, if you have a trust, then you will be more open – because only trust can be open; otherwise you are always afraid and you are always closed. When you are totally open – you have suffered, life has given you a depth and then you trust, you are totally open – then the thing can go immediately to the very heart. You will never be the same again once you hear it.

Gutei got to hear about this... A master always comes to know who are the imitators. There is no need to...they are so apparent, so obvious. I know very well who are the imitators here. An imitator cannot deceive the one he is imitating. He can deceive anybody else, but he cannot deceive the one he is imitating. His falsity is so patent.

People come to me and they repeat my own words, my gestures, and they think they can deceive me. They can deceive others but they cannot deceive me, because their words are so shallow. You can repeat the same words, there is no problem: the word is not the problem – how much depth you bring to the word, *that* comes from your being. The word can be used by anybody.

You can chant the whole Gita, but those words will not be the same as they were when they came out of Krishna. You can repeat the whole Bible, but when those words were used by Jesus they had a tremendous energy, a transforming force – because Jesus was in those words. In every word his being was moving towards you. You can use the same words.... On every Christian pulpit millions of priests are repeating the same words – the Sermon on the Mount – and the words are so shallow, and they have done such a disservice. It would have been better that they were not repeating, because when you go on repeating certain words, they lose the magic. They become so used, people become so used to hearing them, that they become almost useless, cliches.

Gutei must have come to know about this boy who was imitating him, and...*as he was doing it one day, be seized the boy, whipped out a knife, cut off his finger, and threw it away.*

Too severe! But the man Gutei must have been very, very compassionate. Only out of compassion you can be so hard. Difficult to understand, because we think that cruelty, hardness, is always there where there is no compassion. No – then you will not understand an enlightened person. An enlightened person will not be hard on you if he has no compassion – why bother? But he will be hard on you because he bothers, he is worried about you, he wants to help you. And less than that won't do.

What happened? When he whipped out his knife, took the boy's finger, cut it off and threw it away, what happened? When the boy must have seen that the master had whipped out the knife, what must have happened? If suddenly somebody comes at you with a knife, what will happen? Thinking stops. You cannot think, it is so new, so novel. The old mind simply stops, it cannot work it out, "What is happening?" And nobody could have ever conceived that Gutei will bring a knife.

Can you think of me some day bringing a knife? It was so impossible, incomprehensible. And Gutei whipped out the knife – and the boy must have been in shock: thinking stopped. It was a great shock-treatment. And coming from Gutei, almost impossible. The boy could not have ever dreamed...and then not only taking it out, he cut off the finger.

When Gutei was cutting off the finger, when the finger was severed from the hand, what was happening to the boy inside? For the first time in his life he was attentive without thought. He could not be sleepy in such a moment. Who can be sleepy when somebody is cutting off your finger? You cannot be sleepy. The pain was so intense, the suffering was so intense, that in a sudden moment the boy was transformed. He was no more a child, he became mature.

It can happen in an instant; it may not happen in many lives. The imitation has to be cut severely. The finger is just symbolic. The boy has to be hit severely, and the suffering must go to the very root of his being, and it should be so unknown that he cannot make a theory out of it. He cannot think about it, he cannot philosophize. He was simply shocked. The mind can move nowhere. He must have looked with fresh eyes for the first time, without thoughts floating in them. And the pain was so severe and so sudden that it must have gone to the very heart.

Remember, pleasure never goes so deep as pain. Pleasure never goes so deep. It cannot go, the very nature of pleasure is superficial. So people who live in pleasure always remain superficial, shallow. You cannot find a depth in a rich man – difficult. You may find it in a beggar; you may not look at the beggar, because you think he is a beggar – but don't be too fixed in your ideas. When a beggar passes you, look! He has suffered much, he has lived in much pain, and pain gives depth. A rich man is always shallow, superficial: he has lived in pleasure. Pleasure cannot go very deep.

In this suffering the pain was severe, and so sudden that the mind stopped revolving and the heart was hit.

As the boy ran off howling, Gutei shouted,
"Stop!"

This is what I have been saying to you. But first you must be in deep suffering and howling, only then the 'stop' can be meaningful. The boy ran howling in suffering and pain, and Gutei shouted, "Stop!" If the 'stop' is shouted in the right moment, it works deeply.

Suddenly he stopped! What happened in this stopping? There was no more pain. If you stop suddenly, the whole attention moves towards the sound 'stop'. The body is left behind, you become attentive. And when you are so attentive, the body cannot disturb, the body cannot divert. The finger was not there, blood was flowing – the pain was there, but this 'stop' took his whole attention towards the master.

When attention is not there, there is no pain. Pain exists not in the body but in the attention. If you are ill, lying down on the bed, what do you do? You continuously pay attention to your illness.

You are feeding it. And something has to be done about it, because it has become a very great problem all over the world.

Doctors suggest, whenever you are ill, "Lie down and rest." But what will you do in rest? You will pay attention to the pain, and then you are feeding it. Attention feeds it. Then you are continuously thinking about it; it becomes a mantra, a chanting inside that, "I am ill, I am ill. This and that is wrong." Complaints – and you go all over the body again and again and you try to find what is wrong. And that becomes a brooding, a very pathological thing. And this may become a continuity for the illness. You will get hypnotized by the illness.

If too much attention is paid to illness, you become a hypnotic victim. If you continuously complain about something, it becomes a vicious circle; you complain, then you are inviting it, because every complaint means you are again giving attention, again attention. It becomes a repetitive thing.

I have heard – and many times it has happened: a person was ill, paralyzed; for fifteen years he couldn't walk. Then one night, suddenly, the house caught fire. There was a fire, the house was burning, and everybody ran out of it. The man forgot that he was paralyzed, so he also ran out of the house. Only outside the house, when his family found him running and coming out, they said, "What! You are paralyzed!" – the man fell down.

What happened? In this particular moment of intense accident – the house is on fire – the man forgot for a moment that he was paralyzed. If you can forget your illness, the illness will disappear sooner than any medicine can help. If you cannot forget it, if you continuously brood about it, then you are playing with the wound. The more you play with the wound the deeper it goes.

What happened when Gutei shouted, "Stop!"? The boy looked at Gutei, the howling stopped, the pain disappeared, as if the finger had not been cut off.

The boy stopped, turned around, and looked at
his master through his tears.

The eyes were filled with tears, he was howling and crying and weeping. He stopped! The pain disappeared, but the tears cannot disappear so soon – they were there.

> *Gutei was holding up his own finger. The boy*
> *went to hold up his finger, and when he realized it*
> *was not there, he bowed.*
> *In that instant, he became enlightened.*

Gutei was holding up his own finger – a very intense moment of awareness, a very great device, a situation created by the master. Mind is no longer there, the pain has disappeared, because attention has been called somewhere else...as if the boy will not be able to breathe in this situation. "Stop!" – and the breathing has stopped, and the thinking has stopped, and he has forgotten that he has no finger now. Just out of old habit, when the master raised his finger, he raised his – which was not there. It shows that he has completely forgotten what has happened.

In that moment he was not the body, otherwise how can you forget? – the pain, and your finger has been cut off, and you are bleeding, and your eyes are still filled with tears, and just a moment before he was howling. This "Stop!" caused a miracle.

> *The boy stopped, turned round, and looked at his*
> *master through his tears.*
> *Gutei was holding up his own finger.*

Just out of old habit he always used to hold his finger up whenever the master was teaching his disciples about Zen. He would stand by the side of the chair, or at the back of the chair, and when the master would hold his finger up, he would also do the same. It had become so automatic. Body is an automaton, it is a mechanism, it is mechanical.

> *The boy went to hold up his finger, and when he*

realized it was not there – and then he saw, and
the finger was not there – *he bowed.*

What happened? Why did he became so grateful and bow?
...Because for the first time he realized he is not the body. He is the
attention, not the body; awareness, not the body; consciousness,
not the body. The finger is not there, the pain has disappeared, the
howling is no more. Thinking is not moving around the wound; he
is not brooding about it at all. He is no more a body, he is not em-
bodied. He simply is out of his body. For the first time he realized
he is a soul, a consciousness – the body is just the house.

You are not the body; you are in it, but you are not the body.
If your attention can come to such intensity, you will realize that
you are not the body. And once you realize you are not the body, you
know you are deathless. Who can cut your finger off? How can one
be violent to you? Nobody can destroy you. That's why he bowed to
the master in deep gratitude: "You have given me this opportunity to
know the deepest level of my being, which is immortal."

In that instant he became enlightened.

What is enlightenment? Coming to understand, coming to realize
that you are not the body. You are the light within; not the lamp,
but the flame. You are neither body nor mind. Mind belongs to the
body; mind is not beyond body, it is part of the body – most subtle,
most refined, but it is part of the body. Mind is also atomic, as
body is atomic. You are neither the body nor the mind – then you
come to know who you are. And to know who you are is enlightenment.

When Gutei cut off the finger of the disciple, the pail, the old pail
fell down, broken, the water flowed out – no water, no moon! The
disciple became enlightened.

But Gutei must have waited for the right moment. For many,
many years this young man had been doing that. He waited,
waited. You cannot force the right moment, it comes when it

comes. You grow towards it, you grope towards it, and the master waits. When it comes, when it is there, anything can become the excuse, anything. Even a shout, "Stop!" and the old pail is broken. Suddenly reflections disappear because there is no water. You look at the real moon, you are enlightened.

Enlightened means you have realized who you are.

Enough for today.

why don't you retire?

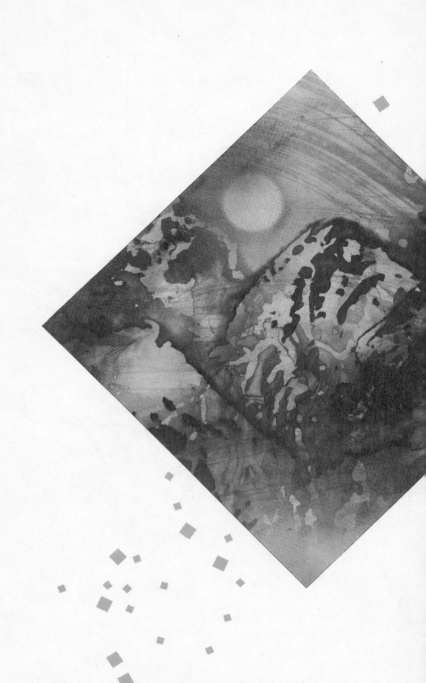

*Tokusan was studying Zen under Ryutan. One
night Tokusan came to Ryutan and asked many
questions.*
*The teacher said, "The night is getting old – why
don't you retire?"*
*So Tokusan bowed, and as he opened the screen
to go out he observed, "It is very dark outside."*
*Ryutan offered Tokusan a lighted candle to find
his way, but just as Tokusan received it, Ryutan
blew it out.*
At that moment the mind of Tokusan was opened.

*t*okusan was studying Zen under
Ryutan. One night Tokusan came
to Ryutan and asked many questions.

The first thing to understand: you cannot study Zen. It is impossible. You can be in it, but you cannot study it – because Zen, or *dhyan*, is not an object of study, it is a way of life. It depends how you live. You cannot get it through scriptures, you cannot get it from anybody. Nobody can teach you, it is not to be taught. It is not knowledge which can be transferred from one hand to another. It is a way of life. You can allow yourself to move into it, you can flow into it, you can be vulnerable to it, open to it – and that's what one has to do with a master.

You cannot study, you can just allow yourself to be infected. It is like an infection; if you are vulnerable, you will catch it. Just living with the master is enough: open, not fighting, just being with the master, there are moments while you are silent...you can learn it.

This story says, *Tokusan was studying Zen....* There he was wrong. No university can offer you a course in religion. They offer, but whatsoever they teach is not religion at all. It may be a history of religion – it is not religion. It may be philosophies of religion – it is not religion. They may help you to learn the Koran, the Bible, the Gita, but it is not religion. They may talk about Jesus, Buddha, Krishna, and you will learn many things, but you will miss the very base, the very core.

So the first thing to be understood is, nobody can explain to you what Zen is, what dhyan is. You can learn it, but nobody can teach you. I have been continuously saying that there are disciples and no masters, because a master cannot do anything positively, directly. He cannot give it to you, he cannot teach it to you. What can he do? If he could teach, he could have given it; then one buddha would be enough to enlighten the whole world. But many buddhas have existed and the world remains as it is. Directly, nothing can be done. The thing is so subtle, so delicate, that if you transfer it, in the very transfer it dies.

I have heard: One Christian priest was sending a Bible as a present to some friend – he had made a beautiful parcel. He came to the post office and the clerk at the window asked, "Is there something breakable in it?"

The priest laughed and said, "Yes, Ten Commandments."

Religion is so delicate, so breakable, no parcel can protect it. The moment you transfer it, it is already dead. It lives with an inner life. It lives in a buddha, in a master. He cannot give it to you, but you can open yourself to it.

It is just like the sun rising in the morning: the sun cannot give life to a flower – no! But the flower opens itself towards it, is enriched through its own opening. If the flower remains closed, the sun cannot do anything. The sun cannot knock at the door, cannot deliver the light, cannot deliver vitality and life – no! The sun will pass unnoticed. A buddha comes – I am here with you, you can open yourself. But if you remain closed nothing can be done. So it is up to you, it is totally dependent on you whether you learn or not – and it is not study.

Study is a dead thing, intellectual. Learning is alive: it is not from the head, it is from the heart. You learn from the heart, you study from the head. When you study you become a great scholar. Go and look at great scholars, all the universities are filled with them, and you will not find people more dead than them. They are almost in their graves – they have already entered! They have never lived; they are so much obsessed with words that they have bypassed life.

They may be talking about love but they have never loved. They cannot afford it – it is so risky; and they are so learned that they cannot take that dangerous step. They have talked about meditation, read about it, but they have never done it. It is dangerous. Nothing can be more dangerous than that. And a scholar is always in search of security; security in words, security in doctrines, security everywhere. He is not a gambler, he cannot stake his life. And unless you stake your life you cannot learn.

This learning is of the heart, it is just like love. That's why Jesus goes on repeating that God is love. It doesn't mean, as Christians have understood or misunderstood it, that God is loving. No! It doesn't mean that God is loving. It simply means if you want to reach God, the method is the same as when you want to enter into love. "God is love" means: the path that leads to the temple of love is the same path that leads to the temple of God. It just indicates the path – it goes through the heart, not through the head.

Tokusan was studying Zen under Ryutan – that's where he was missing. The very first step went wrong, and when the first step goes wrong, then everything else that follows will go wrong. Always remember to take the first step rightly. If the first step is taken rightly, then half the journey is already over, it is almost finished. Because if the first step is right, all that will follow will follow automatically; you will reach the goal. So don't go to a master to study, go to learn. If you go to study, the master will teach you, but the most significant thing cannot be taught. Go to learn.

And what is the difference between the attitudes? Many differences: when you go to study you want more knowledge; when you go to learn you want more being – it is not knowledge. When you learn, your *being* grows. When you study, your memory grows. When you study you know more and more and more; when you learn you become more and more and more – and these are totally different things.

A man may have a great memory, know many things, and deep down in the being he is absolutely a beggar, poor, having nothing there. He may be deceiving himself that he knows so many things, but knowing will not help – unless you *are*, knowing is futile. Only being helps.

If you are dying, what will go with you, your knowledge or your being? Who will be of help? What will be the bridge? What can you carry with you beyond death? Knowledge? The brain is left behind, because the brain is part of the body. Only the being is carried over. And you have never looked at it, it has remained poor, starving – you have never fed it.

Learning is of the being, knowledge is only of the memory, of the mind. Universities can give you knowledge, teachers can give you knowledge, but only an enlightened man can allow you, can help you – and that help is indirect – to gain more being. You can take that help, but that final thing depends on you.

If you go to study, you have missed the first step. And the first step is very significant, because the first eventually becomes the last. The seed is very significant; the seed is the first step and it will become the tree. It may take many years to flower, but if you have planted the wrong seed, then even a million lives will not be of any help. Tokusan was wrong from the very beginning – studying.

Studying, he was more concerned with scripture, not with the master. And what foolishness! When a master is alive you are obsessed with the scripture. When the diamonds are all over, you are clinging to red stones, colored stones! When the master is alive, you are concerned with dead words.

> *One night Tokusan came to Ryutan and asked*
> *many questions.*

A man who is with a master to study is always filled with questions, because this is how one studies. You have to raise questions so you can get answers, and then you can go on collecting the answers and you become more knowledgeable.

A man who is not after study but after learning has only one question, not many. And remember: many cannot be answered, only one can be answered. Many cannot be answered, because if you are that type of man who asks many questions, any answer that is given to you will only create many more questions – nothing else. Every solution will give you many more problems.

You come to me and you ask, "Who created this world?" And if I say "God," then you start asking about God: "Who is this God? And why did he create the world?" And if I say, "Because of this," then you ask…. Every answer will create more and more questions.

But if you have only one question…that is very difficult. Only a very wise man asks the one question. Coming to the one question, you have already become mature – because many questions show your curiosity, one question shows that your being has come to a conclusion. Now this is at stake: if this question is solved, everything is solved. It is a question of life and death.

To ask one question means you have become one-pointed. To ask one question means now you are already a unity. And when you are a unity, the answer can be given to you; otherwise, you are not ready. And no master is going to waste his time and energy on you if you are asking many questions. Ask one question!

First find out what is the one question that is significant. Don't move on the periphery, come to the center! On the periphery there can be many points to be asked, but at the center there is only one point. And when you move on the periphery you go on moving in a circle; one question will lead to another, another will lead to another, and you go on and on *ad infinitum*.

But at the center there is only one question. And that question can be answered even without answering; if you have come to one question, the master can look at you and the question has been answered. The master can touch you and the question has been answered. Because when you are so one-pointed, when you are so intensely alive, your flame is burning so bright, your mind is so clear – not filled with clouds, only one sun, not millions of clouds – you are so unclouded, everything is keen, clear, aflame, just a look may do; just a touch may do. But if you are filled with many questions, even if the master goes on hammering answers on you, nothing is going to happen.

One night Tokusan came to Ryutan and asked
many questions.

These Zen stories are so beautiful, their every word is meaning-ful. *One night* – not in the morning but in the dark. In the morning you come to ask one question, in the night you come to ask many questions. In the morning you are clear, fresh, young. In the night you are old, rotten. In the night means you are in the dark, groping. Even if you come to the door you will not be able to see. Even if the answer is given it will not be understood.

Mind is the darkness of the soul, it is the night of the soul. But you believe in this mind so much – and it has not given you any-thing except promises. It gives you promises, it is wonderful in that – it goes on promising.

I have heard: Once Mulla Nasruddin came back to his home very, very late at night. He knocked, the wife asked, "Nasruddin, what is the time?"

Nasruddin said matter-of-factly, "It is very early, only eleven-fifteen."

The wife said, "Don't you lie to me. I just looked at the alarm clock. It is not eleven-fifteen, it is three-fifteen. The whole night is past."

Nasruddin said, "One minute. You believe in a rotten twenty-rupee alarm clock, rather than believing in your beloved husband? What type of marriage is this? What type of woman are you?"

You always believe in rotten twenty-rupee minds, that you have purchased from an old used-mind shop – it is not even yours! It has been in many hands, thousands of times. What is new in your mind? Everything is old, used. What is fresh in your mind? What is original in it? Everything is borrowed. And when a man purchases an old, old, used car, he thinks millions of times whether to purchase it or not.

You never think about the mind, that it has been used by many.

Your every thought is borrowed, old, rubbish; many have thrown it. But you go on believing in it, because this mind has learned a trick, and that trick is how to promise. It goes on promising: "I will give you everything. You need God? I will give you God, just wait. Do this and that. Make effort, and hope and pray, and you will get it." It always postpones. It says, "Tomorrow it will happen" – and tomorrow never comes. Tomorrow cannot come – all that comes is always today, and all that mind does is to transfer everything for tomorrow. It promises you – in the future. Whether it is heaven, whether it is God, or *moksha,* or nirvana – it always promises you, "In the future."

Meditation, Zen, never promises you anything. It simply gives you here and now. Mind is a postponement, it says, "It will happen. It will happen gradually. Go by and by. Don't be in a hurry, nothing can be done right now." Mind says, "Time is needed. Long is the path. Much has to be done and unless you do it, how can you attain?" Mind always divides ends and means.

In reality, there is no division. Every step is the goal, and every moment is nirvana. The present is all that exists. Future is the most illusory thing, it is a creation of the mind. But you believe in the mind, and it is really wonderful, you don't even get discouraged!

I have heard: One man purchased a used, old car. Then after two weeks he came back to the same shop and asked the salesman, "Are you the same guy who sold me this car?"

The man said, "Yes," a little afraid and apprehensive, because he knew what type of car he had sold.

This man said, "Then tell me again the same things you told me before you sold me this car – I get so discouraged. Give me a little courage; and I will be coming on and off, just to get encouraged."

You don't even get discouraged about the mind. You go on listening to it. And mind is the dark, the dark part of your being where no light enters. It is the night.

So it is right: *One night Tokusan came to Ryutan
and asked many questions. The teacher said...*

He didn't answer. He didn't answer a single question. He simply
listened to the questions.

*The teacher said, "The night is getting old – why
don't you retire?"*

Look! So many questions were asked and the teacher simply
said, "The night is getting old, the darkness is increasing. You are
moving into a darker and darker part of the mind. *The night is getting old – why don't you retire?"*

This is the only answer for so many questions: *"Why don't you
retire?"*

You are the question and the question creator. You – the ego,
the mind – *you* are the disease. Why don't you retire? Many questions were asked – only one answer given, and that too could not be
understood, because a person who asks many questions cannot
understand one answer. His mind cannot understand anything that
belongs to the one. He can only understand the many. 'Many' is
always out, 'one' is always in – because the center is within you,
and the periphery is without.

The master said one of the most beautiful things: *"The night is
getting old – why don't you retire? It is time you should retire."* It
seems irrelevant. He should have answered the questions.... He *has*
answered, because he says, "You please retire."

If you are there, then questions will go on coming. Questions
come to the mind just like leaves come to the trees. And you go on
watering the tree, and then the leaves go on coming. Of course, old
leaves will fall and new will come. So the master can answer a
question: the old will go, but the new will come and it will be replaced again. And a new question is worse, because an old question
– you are already fed up with it. You may throw it. You have lived
enough with it.

A new question is again like a new wife – again you are in love, again the romance starts, again the poetry and again the whole nonsense. A new thought is more dangerous than the old, because with the old you are fed up, you are already getting bored with it, you want to throw it. That's why Buddha, or Ryutan, or persons like that, never answer your questions. They would not like to give you new shelters for the mind. They would not like to give you new substitutes for the old.

Buddha used to say, "Don't ask if you want to be answered. When you don't ask, I will answer. If you ask, the door is closed."

Buddha used to insist with newcomers, "For one year remain with me without asking anything. If you ask, you cannot be allowed to live with me, you will have to move on. For one year simply be silent." And it is not a question of asking visibly – Buddha knows...if you go on asking within, he knows.

One day it happened, Mahakashyapa was sitting there. He had not asked anything. A great disciple of Buddha, but he had come just a few months before and Buddha had told him to remain silent for one year, not asking anything. A few other disciples were sitting there. Suddenly, Buddha asked, "Mahakashyapa, you asked?"

So Mahakashyapa said, "I have not spoken at all."

And others also said, "He has not spoken at all."

Buddha said, "Look within. You have asked. You have broken the promise."

And Mahakashyapa looked, and he bowed down and he said, "Sorry!" He *had* asked. He had not asked so that you could hear, but deep inside the question had been there. Even if you don't ask and the mind is asking, you have asked, because thought is a subtle action. It will become visible sooner or later. The bubble is there, it will come to the surface. You can suppress it, but you cannot deceive a Buddha.

When can you be allowed to ask? When there is no question. This seems paradoxical; if there is no question, then what are you going to ask? Only then you ask the one question, and there is no need to verbalize it. Your whole being becomes one question, one search, one inquiry; then your whole being is an inquiry. And when you stand before a buddha, your whole being transformed into an inquiry, a thirst, a deep hunger, so deep that you are not there, only the hunger is there – then the buddha can feed you, then the answer can be given. Otherwise Buddha, whatsoever he says, will seem irrelevant – and these Zen stories are very irrelevant.

There are millions of Zen stories which are absolutely irrelevant. You ask about A and the master talks about Z – no relationship! We don't know what questions this Tokusan asked. Only one thing we know; the teacher, the master, never replied to them. He simply said, "Tokusan, *the night is getting old – why don't you retire?*" And this is all that Zen is. This is all Zen is about – *retire!*

Are you not tired enough with the mind? Then retire! Has not the mind done enough? Has the mind not created enough chaos in you? Why are you clinging to it? What hope, what promise, makes you cling to it? It has been deceiving you continuously. It said, "There – that goal, in that possession, in that house, in that car, in that woman, in those riches – is everything." And you moved, and when you reached it, nothing came into your hands except frustration. Every expectation led you to frustration. Every desire became in the end a sorry affair, a sadness resulted.

And this mind has been promising you and promising you – no promise has been fulfilled, but you never say to the mind, "You deceiver, stop!" You are afraid of saying that.

Once it happened: Mulla Nasruddin came out of the village tavern and the new priest saw him – he was passing by on the road. The new priest said, "Nasruddin, you are a religious man. What do I see? You are coming out of such a place? My son, drink is of the Devil. And when the Devil invites you again, refuse. Why don't you refuse?"

Nasruddin said, "Reverend, I would like to refuse, but the Devil may get sore and may not invite me again."

That's the problem. You would like to refuse this mind; this mind has never fulfilled anything, but you are afraid – the mind may get sore, will not promise you again. Then…? You cannot live without promises, you cannot live without hope – this is the mechanism.

Unless you are ready to live without hope you cannot become religious. Even your so-called religions are nothing but hopes created by the mind. Are you ready to live without hope? Are you ready to live without the future? Then there is simply no need to retire; the mind retires itself. Then there is no clinging with the mind. But you are afraid – the mind may get sore. And the mind is the Devil and may not offer again, then what will you do?

People come to me, they think their search is religious – their search is still mental. They are still moving in the dark valleys of the mind, they are still listening to the mind, they are hoping. They hope through money and they fail; they hoped through sex – they have failed. They have hoped in many, many ways and they have failed. Now they hope through meditation, now they hope through a master – but the hoping is there. And remember well: if you hope through me you will miss me. I cannot fulfill your hopes.

Why not leave off hoping? Why do you hope? What is the basis of it? Discontent becomes hope; this is the disguise. Because here and now you are in so much discontent, in so much misery, that you need some hope in the future. That hope will help you to move. You can somehow tolerate the present; through hoping, you can tolerate the present…hope is anesthesia. The present is miserable, painful; hope is alcoholic, it is a drug, it makes you unconscious enough so you can tolerate the present.

Hope means here and now there is discontent. But have you ever looked at the whole phenomenon? Why are you discontented here and now in the first place? Why? – because you hoped in the past, that's why here and now you are in discontent. This today was tomorrow yesterday. Yesterday you hoped for today, because it was tomorrow then. Now that hope is not fulfilled, so you are in misery, frustrated. And to hide this misery, to somehow pass today, you are again hoping for the tomorrow.

You are in a rut, and in such a rut that it will be very difficult to come out of it. Tomorrow the same will happen: you will be frustrated, because mind can promise but can never fulfill. Otherwise, there was no need for meditation; then Buddha was a fool, meditating.

If mind can fulfill, then all meditators are foolish, then all enlightened persons are fools. Because mind *cannot* fulfill...when they come to understand the whole mechanism, and the whole misery of it.... This is the mechanism: yesterday mind promised you that something is going to be delivered to you tomorrow. Now the tomorrow has come, it is today, and the mind has not delivered – you are in misery, your expectations are frustrated. Now the mind says, "Tomorrow I am going to deliver." The mind promises again. And what type of stupidity is this, that you again listen to the mind? And tomorrow the same mechanism will be repeated – it is a vicious circle.

You listen to the mind, you become miserable – otherwise, this today is paradise! And there is no other paradise, this today is nirvana. If you had not listened to the mind...just don't listen to the mind, then you are not in misery; because misery cannot exist without expectations and without hopes. And when misery exists you need more hopes for it, to hide it, to live somehow. Live hopelessly – then you are a righteous man, then you are retired.

The words are beautiful. The master said, *"The night is getting old – why don't you retire?* Have you not had enough of this night? Have you not heard and listened to this mind too much already? Drop out of it. Don't listen to it any more. Retire!"

But Tokusan misunderstood him, because a man who is filled with so many questions cannot understand the answer. Out of his compassion Ryutan gave the answer, but the disciple misunderstood – scholars always misunderstand.

What did he think? He thought of the night outside...it was not referred to at all. Masters never talk about outside, they always talk about the inside. The master was talking about the dark night inside, and the disciple thought, "Yes, the night is getting old."

He looked outside – he looked at the periphery. The master was talking about the center. The master was using the language of the within, and the disciple understood in the language of the without. And the language of the within cannot be translated into the language of the without. No, there is no way to translate it. Either you understand or you don't understand – there is no way to translate it for you.

Hindi can be translated into English, English can be translated into Chinese – but religion cannot be translated into any language. The inner cannot be translated into the outer. Why can Chinese be translated into English? Because both are of the without, they both exist on the periphery.

> *"Why don't you retire?"* said the master.
> *So Tokusan bowed, and as he opened the screen*
> *to go out, he observed, "It is very dark outside."*

He understood – he thought he had understood. He bowed: "Yes, it is too late, and the night is getting darker and darker and too old, and it is time to go to sleep."

What the master was meaning, was saying, is, "It is time to awaken." For the man who knows the inner, 'retire' means it is time to come out of your sleep, out of your mind, because mind is the sleep.

You have heard about the sleeping disease? – mind is that disease, it is deep sleep. Even while you are awake it doesn't allow you to be awake; you move in a deep hypnosis, it is a somnambulism. You do things just like a mechanical, automatic machine. You are like an automaton; you eat, you talk, you do things, you are efficient, but don't think that you are awakened. You are not awake.

You have many types of sleep: sometimes you sleep with closed eyes, sometimes you sleep with open eyes. Sometimes you sleep on the bed, sometimes you sleep in the temple, sometimes on the street. Sometimes you are in the shop sleeping. Sometimes you sleep doing things, sometimes you sleep without doing things. Sometimes you sleep with dreams, sometimes you sleep with thoughts – but you continue your sleep.

In the morning you don't become awake. In the morning a new kind of sleep starts with open eyes – dreams float, and thoughts continue, and you do the ritual. Awakening is not needed for the daily ritual. That's why nobody likes new things to happen every day – because if new things are happening, then you will have to awaken. With old things, with a routine, you can move sleepily, there is no need. In a life of seventy years, if you have even been awake for seven moments, it is too much. That's why when Gautam Siddhartha awakened we called him Buddha, the awakened one. Because it is such a rare phenomenon – to be awake.

The master meant, "Retire from the mind, so that you can be awake." And the disciple understood, "Right," he said, "it is very dark outside, I must go to sleep now. I must retire." This is how, whenever the truth is given by a master, it is being distorted in the mind of the disciple.

> So Tokusan bowed...just to thank the master, that
> he has correctly observed that the night is already
> so far passed...and as he opened the screen to go
> out he observed, "It is very dark outside."
> Ryutan offered Tokusan a lighted candle...
> the master offered a lighted candle to the disciple
> ...to find his way. But just as Tokusan received it...
> and he was on the move to go out
> ...Ryutan blew it out.
> At that moment the mind of Tokusan was opened.

What happened? Ryutan offered Tokusan a lighted candle. He said, "Okay, outside it is very dark, so you take this lighted candle to see the path."

For the outside, candles can be offered, not for the inside – because how will you take a candle inside? For the inside, no candle can be offered from without. The master cannot give you the light which will enlighten you inside.

In fact, inside the light has always been burning. It is there, but you go on looking outside. Once you look within, the light is there. It has always been there. You have never missed it for a single moment. You cannot miss it. It is your Tao, your nature, your very self – no need to offer any candle for the inside, and no candle can go inside. But for the outside candles can be offered.

So remember: all those who offer you something for your path, all those candles can be only for the outside. They may light your path in the world, but never in God.

Seeing that the disciple had not understood, the master tried again. He created a situation, a very rare situation: he offered Tokusan a lighted candle.

Tokusan was asking many questions, and he didn't offer a single candle for the inside, he didn't offer a single answer. He simply said, "Retire!" But if darkness is outside, then something can be done, you can be helped. If your body is ill, then you can find a doctor; but if your soul is ill, then no doctor can be of any help – then *you* have to do something. Then the master can only bring you to this point that you have to do something, because inside nobody can penetrate except you. If somebody can penetrate in your inside, it is not inside, because in the interiormost temple of your being how can anybody else enter? There is no space – only you exist there in your total aloneness.

That is why Mahavira has said that even love cannot enter there. You are totally alone. Mahavira used a word for ultimate liberation, for ultimate salvation; that word is *kaivalya*. Kaivalya means absolute loneliness. In your innermost being you are totally alone – nobody can enter there. Not even a master can enter there. If somebody can enter there, then it is outside, then it is not the interiormost core. At the center of a circle only one point can be there, not two. If there are two, it is still not the center. Then still a small periphery is around.

You are alone in your deepest being. The master can help you to become aware of this fact, and once you know it all disease inside disappears. Once you accept your total loneliness you are liberated; then there is no attachment – love can flow. In reality, only *now* can love flow, because now love is not a dependence, you are not dependent on the other. If you are dependent on the other, then you will be against also – because whosoever makes you dependent is the enemy, cannot be the friend. So lovers continuously fight, because the lover is the enemy, the beloved is the enemy. You have become dependent, you cannot live without the other, your freedom is destroyed, and any love that destroys freedom will become hate sooner or later.

Only that love which gives you more freedom will never turn into hate, it will be eternal. So only a Jesus, a Buddha, can love eternally. There is no change of climate, the same harmony continues. Why? – because a Buddha or a Jesus has attained his total loneliness, and has accepted this fact. And this is so beautiful...to be totally alone, like an Everest.

At the very peak, you are alone. At the very core, the innermost being, you are alone. When you have accepted it, now love can flow like the Ganges, now there is no trouble, now you can love without any condition. Now you can love without becoming dependent, or without making anybody dependent on you. Now love can be a freedom.

A master helps you to be aware of your total, ultimate loneliness. The word loneliness is not good, because it carries a sadness about it – because of you, not because of the word. Because of the old associations, you always feel sad when you are lonely.

In Japan it happened once: A Zen master was a great gardener, a lover of gardening. Even the king became jealous of his garden, and one day somebody came to the king and said, "Now you must go and see."

Japanese love the morning-glory flower very much and the man who spoke to the king said, "I have never seen such flowers, millions of them, the whole garden of the Zen master is filled with flowers. And the fragrance – it is so beautiful. Don't miss it. You should go."

It was too much for the king to go to see this poor man's garden. He had a big garden – hundreds of acres of greenery, hundreds of gardeners working there – and he had to go and see?

But the man reported, and he said, "It may not happen again."

So the king said, "You go and inform him that tomorrow morning I am coming."

The master was informed. The next morning the king came with his court, with his generals, queen, princes. The whole capital was stilled, thousands of people gathered around the monastery. And the king came, he looked around and he said, "What! I was informed there were millions of flowers, and I see only one morning-glory flower in the garden."

The Zen master said, "Yes, there were millions, but in the night we removed them all, because we believe in the one. And this is the most beautiful of them all – in a crowd you would have missed this. So we have removed all; only the best, only the most beautiful has been saved for you."

The king became a little sad. He said, "It looks so lonely."

And the Zen master laughed and said, "It is not lonely. It is alone."

Remember this: when you reach to your innermost center you are not lonely, you are alone. And this aloneness is not an emptiness – it is the fulfillment. This aloneness is not empty, it is overflowing. This aloneness is not a void, it is the all.

The master can only make you aware of this fact – which is already there. He cannot give you anything new. He only gives you that which you already have, which you already are, which you have already been carrying within you, but never alert to. He only makes you mindful of the fact that is, of your being. He only makes you aware of the truth: the treasure that is hidden there – and you have not looked at it.

Your being a god is already the case; the master simply makes you aware of this fact. It is not an achievement.

Ryutan offered Tokusan a lighted candle. He said, "Okay. If you cannot look within, and the darkness that you are living in, the darkness of the mind.... I talk about the inside and you look outside – if you are so focused, I will give you a candle."

He gave him...*a lighted candle to find his way, but just as Tokusan received it*...and he was going to move, step down from the temple of the master...*Ryutan blew it out.*

Suddenly, darkness! With the lighted candle there was light. It was not even given and it was immediately blown out, suddenly there was darkness.

At that moment...what happened? ...*the mind of Tokusan was opened* – he became enlightened.

What happened in this moment? Many things happened simultaneously. They happened in a single fragment. No time was lost. Here the candle was blown out; there, immediately, the disciple was enlightened.

What happened? One thing: suddenly he became aware that the master was not talking about the dark night outside. That's why he had blown out the candle – to indicate that this candle won't do. He was talking of the inside, of the dark night within. He was not saying go and retire and fall into sleep. He wanted to make him alert and aware. And when the light suddenly went out, his mind suddenly stopped. He couldn't conceive...it was so unpredictable. The master gave him the candle and then blew it out. It was so absurd! Then why give it?

It was so contradictory, for a moment the mind couldn't think – because the mind cannot think when there is a contradiction. Many times I give you the candle and blow it out immediately. I say a sentence and contradict it immediately, just so that your mind cannot think anything about it, cannot work it out. If your mind can work it out, the opportunity is missed. It was so contradictory: the night was dark and the master offered a candle, and when he was just about to move, he blew it out. What does he mean? So inconsistent!

Enlightened persons are always inconsistent. Consistency is

always of the mind; you can find a consistent thinker, but you cannot find a consistent Buddha. Each moment he behaves in a new way – because he is not behaving out of the past, he responds with the present moment. And it was so accidental that the mind couldn't work it out – and suddenly there was darkness all over.

The disciple understood one thing, that the master was not talking of the outside. He was not talking of the night out there, he was talking of the night here, inside. He offered the candle and then blew it out. He was saying that no help is possible inside. You have to move in your darkness yourself, these candles won't do. Nobody can be a guide there, only indications....

Buddha is reported to have said that buddhas only show the way – *you* have to walk, they cannot go with you. If they go with you, you will become dependent on them, and they will become your world and they will become your attachment. They cannot go with you. And it is inherently, intrinsically impossible for somebody else to take you to your center. He can indicate the way – buddhas only point the way; *you* have to move.

Suddenly there was darkness – the mind stopped. The mind could not conceive, the mind could not reconcile this inconsistent behavior. There was a gap, a discontinuity in the mind – and that gap becomes meditation. Suddenly his mind opened. When the mind cannot function, when the mind finds something impossible to reconcile, to solve, the mind drops.

If the mind can find the logic then it continues. So a master has to be illogical because of your mind; only then gaps are possible. This moment he behaves in a certain way, and the next moment he contradicts himself. This moment he says something, the next moment he says something quite the opposite. You cannot make a system out of it.

That's why when Buddha died many systems arose, because everybody started to create a system of his own. And he was an inconsistent man, he was not a system-maker, so there were millions of contradictions. So everybody – philosophers – started working, and now Buddhists have many philosophies. In those philosophies contradictions have been left out and they have made a consistent whole.

But when you leave the contradictions out, you have left Buddha himself out – because he was in his contradictions. He was in the gaps. He was giving shocks to your mind. This is a shock: Tokusan, at that moment, suddenly became alert. He could not have predicted it. If the mind can predict anything, there is no shock. If I repeat this story with you…if I give you a candle this night, you know the story well, and then I blow it out – nothing will happen, because you expect it.

So a device cannot be used again; it is impossible to use it again. That's why new buddhas are always needed, because old buddhas …your mind has absorbed them, it knows very well. So a new buddha may do exactly the opposite. He may give you the candle and will not blow it out, and you will go in the dark night with that candle thinking continuously, "What happened? The story seems incomplete." A new buddha has to create new devices, new methods, new techniques, because your mind is so cunning: once it knows, it makes everything part of it.

At that moment the mind of Tokusan was opened. And when the mind is opened you are enlightened. Mind is a closing, mind is a closed door. And being is an open door – that's the only difference. Mind open, you are a being; mind closed, you are just a past, a memory, not a living, alive force. Mind closed, you can look only outside, because how can you look inside? The mind is closed, the door is closed. Mind open, you can look inside.

Looking inside, you are totally transformed. Once there is a single glimpse of the inside, you will never be the same again. Then you can move, you can look outside, you can move in the world; you can be a shopkeeper, you can be a clerk, you can be a teacher in a school, you can be a butcher – you can be whatsoever you were before, but the quality has changed.

In Zen they say that before a man is enlightened, rivers are rivers, mountains are mountains. Then, when a man becomes a seeker, rivers are no longer rivers, mountains are no longer

mountains – everything is confused, a chaos. And when a man becomes enlightened, rivers are again rivers, mountains are again
mountains.

Zen people say that a man of enlightenment lives the same way
as any ordinary man – no difference on the outside. He eats when
he feels hungry, he sleeps when he feels tired – no difference on the
outside. Just the nature of being, the quality of being has changed:
now the mind is open. He can look outside, but he remains inside.
He can move in the world, but the world never moves in him. He
remains in the world, but the world is no more a part of his being.
He can do whatsoever is needed, but he is never attached. Not that
he is detached – no, he is neither attached nor detached. The world
has become a dream, the world has become a play, a game. It is no
more real, it is no more substantial. If he happens to be a butcher,
he will remain a butcher; he will carry it out to the very end.

Zen says that the ordinary mind is the enlightened mind – with
only one difference; the mind open, the door open, alert, awake.
The sleep has gone. You are no more in hypnosis, you are no more
in a drugged state. You are alert.

If you try too much to change the outside, that shows that you
are still attached. If a man tries to be detached, it shows attachment. Why bother about detachment if you are not attached? If a
man escapes from women, it shows that sex is still the obsession.
Otherwise, why escape from women if you are not obsessed?

If a man avoids the market, moves to the Himalayas, he is still
somehow in the market, or the market is in him. He is still afraid,
and fear always shows that you have not changed. Otherwise, a
man of enlightenment will be as ordinary as anybody else. More
ordinary than anybody else! Extraordinarily ordinary! Why? –
because he is not an exhibitionist. He may just be your next-door
neighbor and you may not know him ever, because you are after
extraordinary men.

If a man stands for years, you will go...many, many miles you
will travel. It will become a pilgrimage, because you are going to see
a man who has been standing for ten years. It may be a feat, but it

doesn't show anything. It again shows just an egoist standpoint, an exhibition. You may go and bow down to a man who has been fasting, because you cannot fast. This man has achieved the goal and you cannot achieve it. You feel inferior before this man. You bow down because deep down you also wanted to be like this: extraordinary. You wanted some powers, miracles, and this man has achieved.

A man is a *brahmachari*, a celibate: you feel awe, you feel very much influenced, impressed, because you cannot live without a woman, and this man has. He has achieved the desire that you also have deep down, a desire to live without a woman, because the woman is the bondage. You feel she creates a boundary around you, she possesses you. You cannot move beyond that boundary, you are afraid of women.

Somebody was asking Mulla Nasruddin, "Why, Nasruddin, are you leaving so early today?" – he was leaving the tavern.

He said, "Every day it is a problem. The wife!"

So the man said, "Are you afraid of your wife? Are you a man or a mouse?"

Nasruddin said, "I am a man."

And the man said, "Then why you are going so early if you are a man? And what certainty have you got that you are a man?"

Said Nasruddin, "I am certain, absolutely certain, because my wife is afraid of mice. I am certainly a man. I am afraid of her and she is afraid of mice. Had I been a mouse...!"

The wife, the husband, the family, the work, the responsibility, the world – everything becomes a burden, a boundary around you. You feel encaged, imprisoned. And a man who has left all, standing alone in his majesty, neither burdened by a wife nor children, neither worried, nor afraid – you bow down to him, because you feel, "This is the goal. This is what I would also like to achieve."

But this man is just the opposite pole of you. He may have become the mouse and you may still be the man, the wife may be afraid of him, but nothing has changed. He is just the opposite. He is also hiding the same fears. He is also hiding the same lust, but he has reversed the whole process. He is floating upstream, that's all – but the stream is the same, the fight continues. He may be a greater fighter than you, or may be a more stupid fighter than you – because stupid people are always courageous, and they can float upstream more easily than anybody else. Idiots can do things intelligent men ordinarily cannot do.

Fools can enter where even angels are afraid to go. So if you see in your monks in the monasteries, your sannyasins, your so-called *sadhus,* stupid people, that is natural. Look in their eyes, you will never see the look of intelligence, you will not see the clarity, you will not see the flame. You will just see stupid, idiotic people, dull – dullards! They can do such things more easily. They can stand on their heads, *shirshasan,* and they can do so for years, but *they* have not changed, the transformation has not happened.

Zen says the ordinary mind is the enlightened mind. You don't go anywhere; the ordinary world is the paradise. Here and now, everything is there. You need not go anywhere.

A man whose mind is open, the wife disappears. Not that he goes, escapes from the wife – simply the wife disappears and a beautiful being is there. When there is no wife, a beautiful being is there. When you make a being a wife, a husband, ugliness enters. Then there is a friend, a beautiful loving friend – because expectations bring enmity. It is your mind, a closed mind, which creates the problems, not the wife.

For the first time you become aware of the beauty of the world …everything is young and fresh and alive, and God is here! If you think your God is somewhere else you are still listening to the mind, because that is the language of the mind: "Somewhere else, somewhere else. *Never* here" – and he is always here.

Meditation reveals to you the here and now. And then the ordinary mind becomes the most extraordinary, and the ordinary life becomes the supreme, the ultimate. The only difference is of a closed or open mind.

When thoughts are there the mind is closed. When thoughts are not there, the clouds are not there and the mind is open. And when the mind is open the old pail has fallen, the water has flowed out, the reflection disappears – no water, no moon.

Enough for today.

black-nosed
buddha

BLACK-NOSED BUDDHA

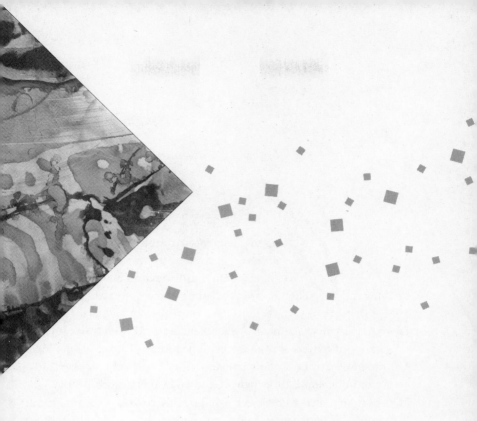

A *nun who was searching for enlightenment made
a wooden statue of Buddha and covered it with
gold leaf. It was very pretty and she carried it with
her wherever she went.*
*Years passed, and still carrying her Buddha, the
nun settled down in a small country temple where
there were many statues of Buddha each having
its own shrine.*
*The nun burned incense before her golden Buddha
each day, but not liking the idea of her perfume
straying to the other statues, she devised a funnel
through which the smoke would ascend to her
statue only.*
*This blackened the nose of the golden statue and
made it especially ugly.*

*O*ne of the greatest problems that is bound to face everybody who is traveling the path, is to make a clear-cut distinction between love and attachment. They appear the same – they are not. They look alike – they are not. Rather, on the contrary, even hate is more similar to love than attachment. Attachment is just the contrary; it hides the reality of hatred and gives the appearance of love, it kills love. Nothing else can be so poisonous as attachment, as possessiveness. So try to understand this, then we can enter this beautiful story.

It has happened to many, it is happening to you – because mind is so confused between love and attachment. And those who look at things from the outside, they always become victims. Attachment is taken as if it is love, and once you have taken attachment, possessiveness, as love, you will always go on missing the real thing. You have chosen a false coin. Now you will not look for the real coin because you think this is the real. You have been deceived.

Possessiveness, attachment, is the false love. Hatred is better, because at least it is true, at least it is a fact. And hatred can become love any day, but possessiveness can never become love. You simply have to drop it to grow into love. Why does attachment appear like love? And what is the difference? The mechanism is subtle.

Love means that you are ready to merge yourself into the other. It is a death, the deepest death possible, the deepest abyss possible in which you can fall, and go on falling and falling. And there is no end to it, there is no bottom to it, it is an eternal falling into the other. It never ends. To love means the other has become so significant that you can lose yourself. Love is surrender – unconditional;

because if there is even a single condition then you are important, not the other; then you are the center, not the other. And if you are the center, the other is just a means. You are using the other, exploiting the other, finding satisfaction, gratification through the other – but you are the goal. And love says, make the end the other, and dissolve, and merge. It is a dying phenomenon, a death-process. That's why people are afraid of love. You may talk about it, you may sing about it, but deep down you are afraid of love. You never enter into it.

All your poetries, all your songs about love, are just substitutes so that you can sing without entering into it, so that you can feel that you are loving without loving. And love is such a deep need that you cannot live without it; either the real or some substitute is needed. The substitute may be false, but at least for a time, for the time being, it gives you the feeling that you are in love. And even the false is enjoyed. Sooner or later you will realize that it is false; then you are not going to change the false love into real love – then you will change the lover or the beloved.

These are the two possibilities: when you come to know that this love is false you can change, you can drop this false love and become a real lover. The other possibility is to change the partner. And this is how your mind functions: whenever you feel, "This love has not given me the bliss it promised, rather on the contrary, I have become more miserable" – you think the other is deceiving, not that you are deceiving.

Nobody can deceive you except yourself...so you feel the other is deceiving, the other is responsible: change the wife, change the husband, change the master, change the god, move from Buddha's temple to Mahavira's temple, change your religion, change your prayer, don't go to the mosque, go to the church – change the other. Then again for a time you will have the feeling that you are in love, in prayer. But sooner or later again the false will be known – because it cannot satisfy. You can befool yourself, but how long can one befool oneself...? Then again you have to change – the other.

If you come to realize the other is not the problem, that your love is false...you have been talking about it, you have not been doing anything to enter into it – you are afraid and scared. Love is death-like, and if you are afraid of death you will also be afraid of love. In death only your body dies. The essential, the ego that looks essential to you, remains safe. The mind, that appears significant to you, is carried on further into another life. Your inner identity remains the same; only the outer garb, the clothes, change in death.

So death is never very deep, it is just superficial. And if you are afraid of death, how can you be ready to enter into love? Because in love not only the garb, not only the house, but *you* die – the mind, the ego dies. This fear of death becomes the fear of love, and the fear of love becomes the fear of prayer, meditation. These three things are similar: death, love, meditation. And the route is the same but you have to move on it. And if you have never loved you cannot pray, you cannot do meditation. And if you have never loved and meditated, you will miss the beautiful experience of death completely.

If you have loved, then death is such a beautiful and intense experience that you cannot compare it with anything in life. Life can never be so deep as death, because life is spread out over seventy, eighty years. Death is in a single moment – so intense; life can never be so intense. And death is the culmination, it is not the end. It is the culmination, the very peak; your whole life you have been making effort to reach it. And what stupidity – when you reach to the peak you are so afraid, you feel so dizzy, you close your eyes, you become so scared that you become unconscious. People die, they die in an unconscious state. They miss the experience.

So love can be helpful because love will prepare you for death, and love will prepare you for meditation also. In meditation you have to lose – the other is not there – you simply have to lose yourself. Love is deeper than death; meditation is even deeper than love, because the other is still there in love – you have something to cling to. And when you can cling, something of you survives.

But in meditation there is no other. That is why Buddha, Mahavira and Lao Tzu, they deny the existence of God. Why? They know very well God is, but they deny the existence so that you have no support left for meditation. If the other is there, your meditation can become at the most love, devotion, but the total death is still not experienced. Total death is possible only when there is no other and you simply dissolve, you simply evaporate; there is nobody to cling to – then the greatest ecstasy happens.

The word ecstasy is very meaningful. This English word ecstasy is so beautiful and so significant; no other language has such a word. Ecstasy means to stand outside. Ecstasy means you are completely dead, and you are standing outside yourself and looking at this death, as if your whole existence has become a corpse. You are out of it and looking at your own death; then the supreme bliss happens. If I say it to you, you will be scared. If I say to you that you are in search of the supreme death, you will be scared – but you *are* in search of it. The whole of religion is the art of learning how to die.

Love means death, but attachment is not death. Love means the other has become so significant that you can dissolve yourself; you trust the other so much that you need not have your own mind – you can put it aside.

This is why people say love is mad, and people say love is blind; it is. Not that your eyes go blind, but when you put your ego aside, your mind aside, to everybody else you will look blind and mad. This is the state of madness. You are not thinking on your own. You trust the other so much that now there is no need to think, because thinking is needed if there is doubt. Doubt creates thinking, doubt is the base of thinking. If you cannot doubt, thinking stops. If you cannot think, where is the ego, how can the ego stand? That is why ego always doubts things, never trusts.

If you trust, no ego appears – the ego is gone. Hence the insistence of all religions that only through faith and trust and love will you enter the temple of the divine – there is no other door to it. Through doubt you cannot enter, because through doubt *you* remain. In trust you are lost.

Love is a trust, a dissolving of the ego. The center moves to the other. The other becomes so significant – your very life, your very being. Not even a flicker of doubt comes to you. It is so peaceful, so beautiful, that not a flicker of doubt comes to you, not a ripple in the mind. Trust is complete, perfect. In that perfect trust there is a beatitude, a blessing. Even if you think about it you will have a small glimpse of it, what it can be. But if you feel it, it is tremendous, there is nothing like it.

But the ego creates a false trick. Instead of love it gives you attachment, possessiveness. Love says, be possessed by the other; ego says, possess the other. Love says, dissolve into the other; ego says, let the other yield to you, force the other to be yours, don't allow the other to move in freedom. Cut the other's freedom, let him become your periphery, your shadow.

Love gives life to the other; possessiveness, attachment, kills the other, takes the life of the other. That is why lovers, so-called lovers, always kill each other – they are poisonous. Look at a husband and a wife: once they were lovers – they thought they were lovers and then they started killing each other. Now they are two dead persons, they have become an imprisonment for each other. They are simply afraid and bored, scared of the other.

Once it happened: In a circus, there was a woman lion-tamer. And the fiercest lions were in her perfect control; she would order them and they would obey. And the greatest thing, when everybody's breathing would stop, was when the fiercest lion would be ordered to come near and he would come, and the lion-tamer, the woman, would have a piece of sugar on her tongue, and the lion would come and take the sugar from her mouth. Everybody would go mad – so much excitement, everybody would clap and show their appreciation.

One day Mulla Nasruddin was there. Everybody clapped but he was not moved at all. He said, "Nothing, anybody can do that."

The woman, the lion-tamer, looked scornfully at him and said, "Can you do it?"

He said, "Yes, anybody can do it – if the lion can do it."

Man is so afraid of woman – and this is through the experience of love. Love, the so-called love, kills the other. Otherwise, why is this world so ugly? So many lovers, everybody is a lover; the husband loving the wife, the wife loving the husband, the parents loving the children, the children loving the parents, and friends, and everybody, relatives, the whole world is in love…. So much love – and so much ugliness, so much misery?

Somewhere, something seems to have gone deeply wrong – in the very roots. This is not love; otherwise, fear disappears – the more you love, the less you fear. When love really comes to its totality there is no fear. But in possessiveness, fear goes on growing more and more, because when you possess a person you are always afraid he may leave you, he may go away – and the doubt is always there. The husband is always doubting that the wife may love somebody else. They become spies on each other, and they cut each other's freedom so there is no possibility.

But when you cut freedom, when you cut the possibility of the unknown, life becomes dead, stale. Everything becomes flat, meaningless, a boredom, a monotone. And the more it happens, the more you become possessive. When life is ebbing, when the love is going, when something is going out of your hands, you become more possessive, more clinging; you become more protective, you create more walls and more prisons. This is the vicious circle.

The more prisons, the less life there will be. You will be more afraid that something is happening – and love is disappearing so create a bigger prison. Then love will disappear more, then a still bigger prison will be needed. And there are many subtle methods how to do it: jealousy, continuous jealousy, and possessiveness, to such an extent that the other remains no longer a person. The other becomes just a thing, a commodity, because a thing can be possessed easier than a person, because a thing cannot rebel, cannot disobey, cannot go away without your permission, cannot fall in love with somebody else.

When love becomes a frustration – and it will become a frustration, because it is not love – then you by and by start loving things.

Look at people when they polish their cars, the way they look at their car – enchanted! Look at the romantic light that comes to their face when they look at their car; they are in love with their car.

In the West particularly, where love has been killed completely, people are in love with things or animals: dogs, cats, cars, houses. It is easier to love a thing or an animal; a dog is more faithful than a wife ever can be. You cannot find a more faithful animal than a dog – he remains faithful, there is no danger. A wife is dangerous. A husband is dangerous; any moment he can move away and you cannot do anything. And when he moves, your whole ego is shattered, you feel hurt. To protect from that hurt ever happening you start killing the husband or the wife, so they become just like cars and houses – dead things.

This is the misery though: that whenever you possess a person he becomes a thing – but you wanted to love a person, not a thing. Because a thing can be possessed, but a thing cannot be responsive. You may love a thing, but the thing cannot answer your love. You may hug your car, but the car cannot hug you. You may kiss your car, but the kiss cannot be returned.

I have heard about Picasso: A woman, a woman appreciator, a fan of Picasso's, once came to him and said, "I saw your self-portrait in an art gallery. It is so beautiful, and I became so possessed by it, that I forgot completely and kissed the portrait."

Picasso looked at the woman and said, "Did the portrait return the kiss?"

The woman said, "What are you asking? How can a portrait return the kiss?"

And Picasso said, "Then that is not my portrait!" How can a dead wife return the kiss? How can a dead husband return the kiss?

This is the misery: if you want to possess, you kill. And the moment you have succeeded the whole glory is lost, because now the other cannot respond. The other can respond only in freedom, but you cannot allow freedom because you are not in love.

Love is never possessive. It cannot be, by its very nature.

And not only loving a man or a woman: if you start loving a Buddha you will repeat this whole thing. You will do the same, you will be possessive there also. That is why so many temples have been created – possessiveness. Christians think Christ belongs to them. Christ cannot belong to anybody, but Christians think he belongs to them; they are the possessors. Mohammedans think Mohammed belongs to them. You cannot draw a picture of Mohammed – you will be dragged to the court. You cannot make a statue of Mohammed, because Mohammedans won't allow it. But who are these Mohammedans? How did they become the possessors? They have turned Mohammed into a dead thing.

Nobody can possess Mohammed, nobody can possess Christ – they are so big and your hands are so small. They cannot be possessed. Love can never be possessed; it is such a vital force, and such an infinite force, and you are so tiny and so small, you cannot possess it. But Christians have their Christ, Mohammedans have their Mohammed, Hindus their Krishna, Buddhists their Buddha.

Amongst Jainas, there are two communities – they have divided their Mahavira. There are a few temples in India which belong to both communities, so there is always fight and always cases in the courts, because a time division is there: in the morning the *swetambers* will worship; in the evening the *digambers,* the other community, will worship. And they change because swetambers put false, open eyes on the Mahavira's statue, and digambers worship Mahavira with closed eyes, so they cannot worship the same statue. First they have to close the eyes, or remove the false eyes, only then are they at ease; then it is *their* Mahavira. But how can it be yours or mine? Is Mahavira a thing, a house, a shop, a commodity? But lovers are false lovers – they are really possessors, not lovers.

This has happened in religions so deeply, that religion, rather than becoming a blessing to the world, has proved dangerous. Through this possessiveness religion becomes the sect – then you go on worshipping this dead thing and then nothing happens in your life; and then you think something is wrong with religion. Nothing is wrong with religion. Mahavira could have transformed you. Krishna could have given you the light that he had, but you didn't allow him. Christ certainly could have become the salvation, but you didn't allow. Jews crucified him, and you – you have mummified him in the churches. Now he is a dead thing – good to worship, good to possess, but how can a dead Christ transform you?

And the priest knows it very well. That is why I have never come across a priest who is a believer. Priests are deep down always non-believers, because they know the whole business, and they know this Christ is dead. When they worship it is just a gesture, for show.

It happened once, it is an historic fact, that in the year 999, on December 31st, there was a rumor all over the world, particularly in Christian communities, that the last day is coming on January 1st; in the year 1000, on January 1st, the last day of judgment is coming and the world is going to be dissolved and everybody is going to face the divine.

So, on December 31st, 999, all the Christians all over the world closed their shops, closed their offices – people even distributed their things, because on the morning of January 1st there was going to be no world. People kissed and hugged each other, even went to their enemies to be forgiven, and there was a totally different world that evening. Everything closed, because tomorrow there is going to be no future. So why be an enemy? And why not love? Why not enjoy? People were celebrating – the last day is coming.

All over the world, Christians closed everything. Only the offices of the Vatican in Rome were open – because the pope knows well, the priests know well, that this is not going to happen, this is just a superstition. And they created the whole thing! But not a single thing was distributed from the pope.

Priests are in the know. They know that Christ is dead – and you are a fool, you are praying to a dead thing. But they cannot say that to you, because that is a trade secret; and only through it is exploitation possible. And it is in their favor, because if Christ is alive they cannot become the agents in between. An alive Christ will come directly to you; he will not allow a mediator, a broker. He will not allow it. Christ will not allow a priest to come and stand in between the lovers and himself – he will face them, he will come to you directly. So for priests, a live Christ is dangerous, only a dead Christ is good.

Priests never like a Mahavira when he is alive, they never like a Buddha when he is alive – they are always against when he is alive. When he is dead, they immediately come and organize around him, make a temple and start exploiting you. Priests are against a Mahavira, a Buddha, a Krishna, but they know that when they are dead their names can be exploited.

But you have to remember well that with your love, your prayer, your worship – if it becomes possessive – you are killing. And if you kill Krishna how can he transform you? How can he bring you to Krishna consciousness? Impossible!

Now we should enter this story. It is beautiful.

> *A nun who was searching for enlightenment made*
> *a wooden statue of Buddha and covered it with*
> *gold leaf. It was very pretty, and she carried it*
> *with her wherever she went.*

Many things have to be understood – even word by word. *A nun*...because this is the heart of the woman – to possess. That's why not a monk, but a nun. And don't think that only women possess; men also possess, but then they have the heart of the woman, not of the man. Why is woman more possessive than man? – because possession is out of fear. Man is less afraid than woman, that's why – man is less afraid than woman. Because he is less afraid, he is less possessive. The feminine mind is more afraid, fear is natural to it, there is always a trembling. Because of that fear woman is more possessive. Unless she is completely satisfied that she possesses, she is not happy. And when she possesses completely she cannot be happy, because the man is dead. Only in freedom life exists.

Hence, in the story, a nun has been chosen. But remember well, it doesn't make any difference if you are a man – your mind can still be feminine. There are rarely men.... You may be a woman and still have a man's fearless mind. So the distinction is not through sex, it is through attitudes. A man can be a woman, a woman can be a man – the symbol is just to show the attitude. What attitude?

If you are a man and still possessive, you have a feminine mind. If you are a woman and not possessive, you have a male mind. It is said that Mahavira insisted that no woman can enter into enlightenment unless she becomes a man. People took it literally, and they missed the point. They thought that no woman can enter into enlightenment, so every woman who is striving will have to be born in the next life as a man, and then only can she enter. This is foolishness – but no feminine *mind* can enter into enlightenment, that is true, because the feminine mind means fear and possessiveness. And with fear and possessiveness, no love, no meditation is possible.

One woman became enlightened. Jainas – the followers of Mahavira and followers of the *tirthankaras* – were much disturbed. What to do? So they changed the name of the woman into the name of a man, and they simply forgot the whole thing. A woman named Mallibai became enlightened – what to do about the theory now? So they changed the name, they call Mallibai, Mallinath. They changed the statue, you will never find a woman's statue. And this Mallibai – or Mallinath – she was such a rare being that they had to concede tirthankarhood to her. So in twenty-four tirthankaras one is a woman, but you will never find her because the name given is Mallinath.

So one feels no woman has attained enlightenment. But it is true in a different, deeper sense; no feminine mind can enter – because fear cannot enter it, possessiveness cannot enter.

A nun who was searching for enlightenment made
a wooden statue of Buddha...

And it is very difficult for a mind which is feminine – man or woman. But the mind, if it is feminine, will create a statue; you will create the other. You cannot be alone.

A statue means the other has been created. There is no one, but you cannot be satisfied with nothingness; something has to be there to cling to. Hence so many temples and so many statues – they are created out of the feminine mind. That's why you will not find many men in the temples whenever you go, but many women will be there. And if some men have come, those are the henpecked husbands. They have come with their wives, they have not come directly; they had to come just because of the wife.

When Mahavira preached, forty thousand people took sannyas from him – thirty thousand were women, only ten thousand men. What is the matter? And this is the ratio – this is the ratio with me also. If four persons come – three women, one man. And the man comes with difficulty and goes very easily, and the woman comes very easily and it is very difficult for her to go. She clings; it is very difficult for her to go.

But a feminine mind can create difficulties, barriers. If you start becoming possessive, then you miss. You have to remember: the fear has to be left – only then love arises. The fear has to be dropped, because the fear is of the ego. And if fear exists, the ego will persist; then you can create a statue and cling to the statue. This statue is not going to lead you to the ultimate, because this is your creation. You may cover it with gold leaf, it may look pretty, but it is a dead thing. You may make a golden statue, but it is not going to help – it is a dead thing.

It was very pretty, and she carried it with her wherever she went.

It became a burden, it had to be carried, protected. She couldn't sleep well because somebody may steal it. She could not go without it, because somebody else may want to possess it, it may have been taken from her. Her whole mind became possessive around it. The statue became the center, the center of her possessiveness, fear, worship. But this is not love.

> *Years passed, and still carrying her Buddha, the*
> *nun settled down in a small country temple where*
> *there were many statues of Buddha each having*
> *its own shrine.*

Years passed, nothing happened. Carrying a Buddha nothing can happen, because how can you carry a Buddha? You can only carry a statue. Buddha has to be lived, not carried. Buddha has to be loved, not possessed. You have to dissolve yourself in the Buddha, not carry him as your possession.

Buddha is alive if you dissolve into him. But then Buddha is dangerous, because you will never come back. It is a point from where no one can come back. Once you have fallen, you have fallen into it; there is no returning. There is fear and trembling, you are afraid you may be lost. And your fear is true – you are going to be lost.

But with a statue there is no fear, you can carry it. The statue can be lost some day, but you will not be lost. You can create another, even a prettier one, there is no difficulty – it is your creation. Go to the temples: what has man done? – created statues, his own creations. Now he is bowing down before them, weeping and crying, and the whole thing is false, because the base is false. Your tears, your prayers – to whom are you addressing them? Before whom are you weeping and crying? – your own creations, your own toys. Howsoever beautiful and costly, it makes no difference. But you are the creator of your gods, and before them you cry and weep and you think something is going to happen. You are simply acting stupidly. Temples are filled with stupid people. They are not aware of what they are doing, bowing down before their own creations. Now, how can this help you?

She carried…many years passed, many lives may have passed – and still carrying her Buddha she was nowhere. Just wandering from one place to another, from one life to another, from one mood to another, from one mind to another – but just wandering, reaching nowhere! Then she got fed up with the journey; the goal seemed nowhere to be achieved, the goal seemed nowhere to be coming closer.

> So she…*settled down in a small country temple where there were many statues of Buddha each having its own shrine.*

But there were many statues of the Buddha. In China, in Japan, they have created very big temples for Buddha. In China there is one temple with ten thousand Buddhas, ten thousand shrines in one temple! Ten thousand statues! But even ten thousand statues are of no help. One Buddha is enough, ten thousand statues are not enough.

Why does the mind go on, working nonsense? – one statue is not doing it, so create two. This is the arithmetic; two are not doing it, so create three – ten thousand statues! One man wandering amongst ten thousand statues and nothing is happening. Nothing is going to happen, because life never arises out of a dead thing, a man is never transformed out of a dead statue.

Seek a living buddha. And if you cannot find a living buddha, close your eyes and seek there. If you cannot find him without, you will find him within, because Buddhas are never dead. They are there, just to be sought – and they are *always* there. They may be just by the corner of your house, but you have never looked. Or you are so acquainted with the neighbor, with the corner, that you feel you know. Nobody knows – you may meet the buddha in a beggar.

Just remain with open eyes. If you are carrying a statue, your eyes are closed. This woman may have missed many buddhas because of this statue – because she thinks she already possesses. She already has the Buddha, so what need is there to look elsewhere? Then she settled in a temple – people who live with statues will always settle in a temple. People who live with statues cannot reach to the ultimate goal; they have to settle somewhere on the way, by the side of the way – a shrine, a temple.

Many people have settled in temples. They wandered and they searched and then they found that nothing can be found, it is impossible. Not because the goal is very far away – the goal is very near, nearer than you can conceive – but because they are carrying statues. Those statues have become their blindness; their eyes are closed with their statues, their hearts are burdened with their statues, words, scriptures – dead things.

I have heard: Once it happened in ancient days, a king, a very scholarly man, wanted to marry a girl, but no ordinary girl would do. He wanted a perfect woman, astrologically perfect. So he consulted many astrologers. It was very difficult – many years passed, his youth was almost gone. He was no longer young – because these astrologers are difficult people, and mathematics takes time. And then one woman would be found and one attribute would still be lacking – not exactly perfect.

Really, you cannot find anyone perfect. It is impossible, because perfection always means death. If someone is alive, it means imperfect – that's why we say that whenever one is perfect, he is born no more. Because how can you be born if you are perfect? Then you have passed through this world, you have gained, grown, you cannot be allowed back.

Then the king said to his advisers, "It is enough; if not perfect, then approximately perfect will do. But my youth is passing, I am almost thirty-eight. Now find a woman!"

So a woman was found – not exactly one hundred percent, but ninety-nine percent. Then the search started for the right time when this king should make love to this woman, because he wanted a rare, extraordinary child. It was very, very difficult, many scriptures were consulted, the I Ching and others; many wise men were called from faraway countries, and they consulted and they discussed – and the king was almost forty-four.

Then one day he got fed up, and he turned them out. He burned all the scriptures and told to his wife, "Enough is enough! Now we must make love" – they had not made love up to now. But the woman was old, he was also old, and with love there is a problem. If you start making love early, you can go on making love to the very end of your life. If you don't start early, you cannot make love later on, because lovemaking is a mechanical thing. The mechanism needs efficiency.

So if a man starts making love when he is fourteen, he may go on making love up to eighty. And don't think that if you make love too much in your young age, then in your old age you will not be able. You are absolutely wrong. If you make love too much, only then you will be able to later on. And you cannot make love too much, remember that, because the body won't allow. Too much is impossible; there is a thermostat in the body – too much is not possible. Whatsoever you do, it is always within the limit. But by this time the king had become impotent – he couldn't make love, the wife was frigid. They had missed the right moment. The child was never born to them, then they had to adopt a child.

This is what is happening: you have to adopt a Buddha, you have to adopt a god. It is not born to you – and God *must* be born to you, otherwise it is a false god. But you have been missing because you are so occupied with scriptures, wise men, astrology, and all sorts of nonsense. You are so obsessed with words, statues, temples, rituals, formalities, that by the time formalities are fulfilled life has gone. By the time you conclude logically, life is no longer there to do it.

This woman finally settled in a temple, and I tell you: never settle in a temple, because a temple can only be a night's shelter, it cannot be a permanent settlement. Never settle in a temple, never settle in a sect, never settle with the Vatican or Puri Shankaracharya, never settle with a sectarian mind.

You can have a rest, that's okay. Stay there for a night, and by the morning, before they catch hold of you, move! Go on moving – unless you reach the ultimate; only that is the temple. But there you will not find any statues. There you will find the real – not the statue, not the portrait, but the real. Don't settle with a portrait, don't settle with the false, don't settle with the carbon copy. Search for the original, the very source.

The woman settled – she had to settle. When you carry a wooden Buddha, how can you attain enlightenment? If wooden Buddhas can give you enlightenment, then there will be no problem. A wooden Buddha is a wooden Buddha. You can carry it, you can play with it.

> *The nun burned incense before her golden Buddha*
> *each day.*

The Buddha was wooden, just covered with gold, but she used to call her Buddha, "Golden Buddha." The gold was just skin-deep; deep down there was just a wooden Buddha, nothing else. But you can hide things, and through gold you can hide anything. When there is not love, then there is much gold around the wife. A wooden Buddha under the gold leaf – and you think everything is okay. And the wife also thinks everything is okay, because the husband every time comes and brings more and more ornaments. When love is dead, ornaments become very much alive. When there is love there is no need for ornaments.

You never cover a real Buddha with gold, do you? The Buddha won't allow you, he will simply escape. He will say, "Wait! What are you doing? You will kill me." Gold kills. Life can never be covered with gold – only death. Only death will allow you to do something. Life won't allow you such nonsense. But she called her wooden Buddha, "Golden Buddha."

> *The nun burned incense before her golden Buddha*
> *each day, but not liking the idea of her perfume*
> *straying to the other statues, she devised a funnel*
> *through which the smoke would ascend to her*
> *statue only.*

This is the mind of a possessive person: not even the perfume, the incense, the smoke, is allowed to reach to other Buddhas – and others are also Buddhas. "But my Buddha is something else. Your Buddha is nothing." In the temple all the other statues were Buddhas. It was not that somebody was a Krishna, or somebody was a Rama – then the difference would have been too much. She would not have stayed in that temple. But it was a Buddhist temple, so she could stay. But this was her statue, and those were not hers.

When there is really love, it doesn't bother to whom it reaches. When there is love, you love your beloved person, but you cannot devise a funnel so that your love reaches only to your beloved. Love is such a phenomenon that when it happens it goes on beyond your beloved, always goes on and on and on. It spreads to everyone. It is just like a ripple on the lake.

If you throw a stone in the lake a ripple arises and then it goes on spreading and spreading to the very end. If you love a person, it is not linear, it is circular, a wave is created. When you love a person, you are throwing a stone in the lake of love. Now everybody will be benefited, not only the person you love. If you try to benefit only the person you love, you will simply do the thing this nun did. It is not possible. When there is someone who loves, his love goes on falling all around. You cannot channelize it, it is not such a thing – rivers can be channelized – it is oceanic, it cannot be channelized. Attachment can be channelized, not love.

When you throw a stone in the lake, it falls at a particular spot, that's okay, but then the love goes on spreading. When you fall in love, you fall at a particular spot, with a particular person; but that is only the beginning, not the end. Then love goes on spreading, then the whole world is benefited. Whenever there is a single person of love, the whole world is benefited. There will be a center where the stone fell, from where the waves will arise and go on to the very end. There will be a center – the beloved, the lover; but the love cannot be contained there. It is a growing thing, nobody can contain it. So the lover becomes just the door, just the opening – and then the whole universe is benefited by it.

But this poor nun was just like you. Just a human mind, working through human stupidities. She did not like the idea of her perfume straying to the other statues – and the other statues are also of Buddha.

When I love a person, I find the divine there. Love reveals the divine in a person. Once it is revealed, all the statues of all the Buddhas.... Then everybody is divine; the tree is divine, the cloud is divine, the beggar on the street is divine, then everybody is divine. If love has happened and you have looked into the original face of a person – which is revealed only in love – then Buddhas everywhere are Buddhas, all the statues are Buddhas; then the whole world has become a temple.

But then you are not worried. Then you are not worried that your perfume is reaching somebody. You are not worried that your lover's perfume is reaching to somebody else. You will be happy that through you the whole world is being benefited, through you the whole world is receiving the blessing. If you are afraid and you try to contain it, then it is possessiveness and it will kill. Don't try to contain it, don't try to possess it. Allow it to grow, help it to grow, help it to reach to everyone. Only then you will receive it, because you can receive only when the whole world receives it.

But this is the problem: whenever you love a person, you want him to be contained, confined. It is as if you are confining a tree in a pot; not only the roots but the whole tree – then you will kill it. The tree has to move into the sky, it has to spread into the sky. Its flowers will give perfume to many, its branches will give shadow to many; many will be benefited by its fruits. Of course the roots are contained in you, but the tree goes on growing. And love is the greatest tree possible; it can spread into the whole sky, it cannot be confined, cannot be contained. You cannot make it finite – the very nature of love is infinite.

But not liking the idea of her perfume straying to the other statues, she devised a funnel through which the smoke would ascend to her statue only.

Then what happened? It was bound to happen:

This blackened the nose of the golden Buddha and made it especially ugly.

This is happening to every lover and beloved, because then the perfume is not perfume, it becomes just smoke; perfume needs to spread. Then the nose is blackened, and all the Buddhas now have black noses.

Look at your Krishna, look at your Buddha, your Mahavira; all their noses are blackened – because of you, your possessiveness. Your prayer is possessiveness, it is not real. Jainas won't allow anybody to enter their temples if they are not a Jaina. Hindus won't allow the untouchables, because they are not a higher caste. All the temples are blackened because they are possessed: "My temple." The moment I assert 'my', it is no longer a temple, because how can a temple be mine or yours? A temple is simply a temple!

I was once dragged into court because I inaugurated a church. The church had been closed for at least twenty years. The worshippers of the church had moved, they were not in India – it was the possession of some English Christian sect – and there was nobody in the town, nobody even to take care of it. It was a beautiful church, but completely dilapidated. Then a few Christians came to me and they said, "We don't belong to that sect, but we don't have a church. So can you help us? Will you inaugurate this church and we will start worshipping."

I said, "Okay." So they broke the lock, they cleaned the church – they cleaned the blackened nose of Christ. And I opened it for all. So I said, "It is not a question of to whom a church belongs. Those who worship, theirs is the church."

But within two or three months the news reached to the owners. They appointed a lawyer; he dragged me to the court, because, "Why did you open this church?"

The magistrate asked me, "Why did you open this church? It

doesn't belong to these people. It is not their property."

I told him, "A church cannot be anybody's property. Those who worship – it is theirs. A church is not a property, it is not a legal question at all."

The magistrate said, "Don't lead us astray. We cannot go into philosophy. It is a legal question."

A church is a legal question? Yes, it has become a legal question. A temple is a legal question? If a temple is a legal question, then it belongs to this world, not to that. So I said, "Okay, you can close it, if it is a legal question. You can close it, but remember well, this is how religion is killed, murdered. It is not a property at all."

But all the churches, all the temples have become properties. They are mine or thine – then Buddha's nose is blackened, and it *...made it especially ugly.*

All the temples, all the churches, have become ugly. They have to be really destroyed, cleaned, so the earth is clean. And the real temple can exist only then – when these temples disappear. They have become part of your market, of your legal system. They are now no longer symbols of the beyond.

Mind is such a thing; it turns everything into a possession, because the ego can exist only if it possesses. And ego is the barrier. Ego is the water in which only reflections can be caught, the real can never be known. Now drop this pail! Why wait for an accident? Drop this old pail and let the water flow – no water, no moon.

Enough for today.

the giver should be thankful

THE GIVER SHOULD BE THANKFUL

The Master Seistsu required larger premises as the
building he was teaching in was very
overcrowded.
Umezu, a merchant, decided to donate five
hundred pieces of gold for the construction of a
new building.
Umezu took the money to the teacher and Seistsu
said, "Alright, I will take it."
Umezu gave the sack of gold to Seistsu, but he
was very dissatisfied with the attitude of the
teacher as the amount he had given was very great
– one could live for a whole year on three pieces
of gold, and the teacher had not even thanked
him.
"In that sack there are five hundred pieces of
gold," hinted Umezu.
"You told me that before," said Seistsu.
"Even if I am a wealthy merchant, five hundred
pieces of gold is a lot of money," said Umezu.
"Do you want me to thank you for it?" said
Seistsu.
"You ought to," said Umezu.
"Why should I?" said Seistsu, "The giver should
be thankful."

*t*here are only two ways to live your life, only two ways to be: one is the right way, the other is the wrong way. The right is to give, to share, to love. The wrong is to snatch, to exploit, to accumulate. Love and money are the symbols of these two ways. Love is the right way and money is the wrong way. Everybody is living the wrong way.

Why does it happen? What are the dynamics of it? Why does everybody go wrong? Where are the rules? So we will have to penetrate deeply, only then will you be able to understand this beautiful story. And if you cannot understand this story, you cannot understand Buddha, Jesus, Mahavira. No, it is impossible, because they moved on the path of love, you move on the path of money, and these two ways never meet. They cannot meet.

Sometimes, even if you try to understand Mahavira, Buddha, Jesus, you try to understand them in terms of money. Jainas go on relating how much Mahavira renounced – 'how much' is the point. If Mahavira had been the son of a beggar, no Jaina would worship him. He was the son of a great king. He had a big kingdom, much money, gold, diamonds – and he renounced them. Suddenly he becomes important to you. The importance is in the money that he renounced, not in him.

Even if you approach Mahavira, you approach him through money. What an absurdity. And then Jainas go on emphasizing the fact, exaggerating it, because the kingdom was really not so great. It was a small principality – because in India at that time there were two thousand kingdoms – it was just like a small district. And

Mahavira's father was also not very rich, but rich, of course. When first they looked at Mahavira because he had renounced the money, he became very important. Then they started to exaggerate the amount of money that he had renounced. And now they have gone to fantastic, absurd lengths; whatsoever they say is simply wrong. And then Mahavira becomes important through the money he renounces. What is really important in your eyes?

Why does it happen that not a single *tirthankara* of the Jainas comes from an ordinary family? – all the twenty-four are the sons of kings. Why does it happen that not a single poor man could become a Hindu *avatar*? Why only Rama, Krishna – the kings? Why does it happen that not a single poor man could become a Buddha – only Gautam Siddhartha, the prince? How does it happen?

All three religions were born in India, and they are the greatest! Not that a tirthankara is not born in a poor family, but you will not recognize him. Not that a buddha is not born in a beggar's house, but if he is, you will not recognize him. Your recognition can only be through the money he renounces. Buddha is worthless – the money he renounces is the real thing. That attracts you, that hypnotizes you.

A man on the path of money cannot understand the man on the path of love – it is impossible, they never meet. You can worship, but you will worship for the wrong reasons, because you cannot understand. Your worship is going to be based on something wrong. What is the mechanism?

First try to understand why love becomes so impossible, because that is the root – why you cannot love. If you can love, then money will never be the attachment, can never be. Why can't you love? From the very beginning, something goes wrong in the mind of a child so he can't love. One thing: love is a spontaneous phenomenon, you cannot manipulate it. If you start manipulating it you will miss it. This is the trouble with spontaneous things. Spontaneous things are beautiful, the most beautiful, but you cannot manipulate them. If you manipulate they become artificial, something goes wrong.

When a child is born you start manipulating his love, you say,

"I am your father, love me," as if love is a logical syllogism. "I am your father, therefore love me." "I am your mother, therefore love me." "He is your brother, therefore love him." And love knows no 'therefore', it is not a syllogism. We never wait for the child, so that love happens to him or her. We start manipulating, controlling, as if we are afraid that if he is left to his own spontaneity he may not love his mother – there is no necessity; he may not love his father – there is no inevitability. You cannot depend on it. He may, he may not.

So before the spontaneous happens, we start forcing the child. And the child has to yield, because he is helpless. He starts selling his love. Politics is born, he becomes a politician, he smiles, and deep down he is angry; he shows his love, and deep down there is no love – he hates the father. Every son hates, that's why every society starts forcing the child to respect the father, to love the father. Because every culture is aware that the son will hate the father, so "Create the opposite before the hatred explodes." Every daughter, every girl hates her mother, so "Love the mother, she is your mother. Respect her." We are so afraid that we create the opposite just as a protection.

Why does a son hate his father? Not because he is bound to hate – there is a vicious circle. First, conflict is necessary, it is a natural part of growth. A child has to fight with his parents, otherwise he will never grow. And the fight starts the very first moment a child is born, the fight starts with birth. The child wants to be born and the mother wants to hold, that's why there is so much pain.

Now physiologists say that the pain exists because of the conflict. The child wants to come out and the mother wants to hold him in – this is the conflict. That's why there is so much pain in birth. Otherwise, in animals there is not much pain; in primitive societies there is no pain. Why does the birth become more painful, the more a woman is civilized? Because the more you are civilized, the more ego is there; a stronger ego is there.

The mother wants to hold the child in...an unconscious fear that the child is leaving her. And this will possess the whole life: that the child is leaving her. And the child has to leave, otherwise he will be dead in the womb. He has to kick the womb behind, go away from the womb – that is natural. And once a mother understands it, there is no pain in birth; then she helps the child to move away.

And if you help the child to move away, he will never hate you. This is the problem: if you don't allow the child to move away, if you create barriers, because of those barriers he will hate you. And you are afraid of the hate, so you create the opposite. You force the child to love you and he is helpless, so he has to yield in his help-lessness; not willingly – unwillingly. He has to yield. Hate remains deep down, and love becomes just a mask, a façade. The child is born and then every day he will move away from the mother. He has to, otherwise he will never be independent, he will never be his own self. He has to move, every day in every way, and the mother will not allow it: "Don't go beyond this boundary. Don't go outside the house. Don't go on the street. Don't play with that boy. Don't move."

The mother will create more and more boundaries. And the more boundaries that are created, the more the freedom is killed; the child suffers – hatred is born. Now what to do with this hatred? – the mother creates the opposite. But whenever you create the op-posite, you have moved in the wrong direction.

This hatred has to be understood, accepted; not that the opposite has to be created. And you have to know that this is part of growth. The child has to move away, and you have to allow it more and more freedom. Of course you have to be very alert, because the child can harm himself.

So freedom should not become a chaos – and that is very deli-cate. But if you cut his whole freedom because the child may harm himself, then you are creating a hateful mind. And if a child starts hating his mother, he will not be able to love any woman ever, be-cause the first woman has become associated with hatred. That's why you hate your wife – because in the beginning you hated your mother, and you will never be at ease with a woman. A woman will always create an unease; she will attract you and she will repel you also. She will become the focus of your love but the love will be superficial, because if you couldn't love your mother deeply, how can you love any other woman? Impossible!

And behind every love, there will be a running current of hatred. Love becomes divided, the opposite is hidden there – then everything becomes poisonous. The child will move more and more, and one day he will fall in love with another woman. That is the last break. On that day, really, the child is born. The 'birthbreak' finished that day. It continues twenty years, twenty-five years; every day there is pain and conflict. Then the child as the final step falls in love with another woman – that is the breaking point. Now he has left the mother completely. Now another woman has entered. That's why mothers can never be at ease with daughters-in-law – impossible! That's why so many stories go around and around against the mother-in-law: they cannot be at ease. Impossible, because this is the enemy; this woman is the enemy, this man is the enemy, who has taken their child away completely.

There is a saying of Jesus – one of the most mysterious, impossible to reconcile with Jesus' mind, and very dangerous, and the wording is also dangerous. Jesus says to his disciples, "Unless you hate your father and mother, you cannot come to me." A man like Jesus, who says love is the path, who says God is love, who raises love to the highest possible peak and makes it equivalent to meditation, says, "Unless you hate your father and mother, you cannot come to me." He is right, because unless Jesus becomes your father and mother…. You cannot come to a master unless you leave your father and mother completely – that is your complete past, past associations, past relationships – completely, totally. How can you come to a Jesus, how can you come to a master…?

If you are still committed to the past, your present is burdened, your future is dark. You have to be uncommitted to the past, completely broken with the past, discontinued. Only then your present is light, and your future not a mechanical progression of the past.

Jesus is right: unless you hate your father and mother you cannot come to a master. That's why, whenever you go to a master, your father and mother are very disturbed – it has to be so. They are never so disturbed. You can go to a prostitute – they will not be so disturbed; you can become an alcoholic – they will not be so disturbed.

But going to a Buddha or a Jesus...to a master, they are absolutely disturbed. Something in the unconscious says, "Now this is the last break. Now, if this boy or this girl goes to a master, then 'father' and 'mother' are completely closed" – the fear! Even if a son moves with a woman, the mother can have some relationship, some sort of relationship. But if the son moves with a Jesus, then all relationship is broken; then there is no possibility; Jesus demands total surrender. No woman can demand it, no husband can demand it; only a master can demand total surrender, no holding back.

The child has to move, and when a child becomes enlightened, then he is completely broken, completely, absolutely broken with all the past, with the mother, the father – everything.

There is another saying which is also very mysterious, looks very hard on the part of Jesus. He was talking to a crowd and then somebody said, "Jesus, your mother is waiting outside, and the crowd is so large she cannot come in, and she wants to see you."

Jesus said, "No one is my mother. Tell that woman, no one is my mother" – looks very hard, rude. But Jesus cannot be rude and he cannot be hard. But sometimes truth is rude, truth is hard. And Jesus cannot lie, he is right: "No one is my mother."

Once it happened: Jesus was a small child and the father and mother had come to the great temple of the Jews for the annual festival. Jesus was lost somewhere in the crowd, so they tried and tried, and only by the evening – when they were very much disturbed, worried – only by the evening could they find him. He was sitting with some scholars, and he was just a child, and he was discussing things about the unknown with them. So his father said, "Jesus, what are you doing here? We have been worried about you the whole day."

Jesus said, "Don't be worried about me. I was looking after my father's business."

The father said, "I am your father – and what type of business are you looking after here? I am a carpenter."

And Jesus said, "My father is there, up in heaven. You are not my father."

Just as a child has to leave the body of the mother, otherwise he will be dead in the womb – he has to come out of the womb – the same happens mentally also. One day he has to come out of the father and mother's womb. Not only physically – mentally; not only mentally – spiritually. And when the spiritual child is born, is completely out of the past, has broken with it completely – only then for the first time does he become a self, an independent reality, standing on his own feet. He is! Before this he was just a part of the mother, or the father, or the family – but he was never himself.

From the very beginning the mother and father are trying not to give freedom to the child. And love is born only in freedom, because it is a spontaneous phenomenon, you cannot do anything about it. If you do, you will destroy the whole possibility. They try: "Love us" – and the child has to yield, he is helpless. Just to exist he has to bargain. This is a bargain when a child says, "Yes, I love you mother," and when he says, "I love no one else like you." When a child says, "I love you, father, and there is nobody else like you. You are unique, the best, the greatest father that ever was," he is just making a bargain, he is just playing politics, he has become part of a deceiving game.

In the beginning he is not aware that love is a spontaneous phenomenon. You have to be free, waiting, prayerful, for it to come. You cannot do anything about it, it is a happening. Now this happening will not happen his whole life. He will always manipulate, he will always try to control it, he will always be artificial.

Have you ever observed? – whenever you are in love you become two, one part manipulating. And deep down you always know you are manipulating; the man is trying to exploit the woman, the woman is trying to exploit the man. And once they are married – that is, once their love becomes a bond – the whole falsity by and by disappears. Then the authentic, the real person comes into being, and there is a clash. Then the whole love disappears, because that love was never there in the first place. Otherwise, how can love disappear?

Love is the most eternal thing in the world. The earth can disappear, the stars can disappear, the whole world can disappear – not love. Love is the eternal phenomenon, the most divine. How can it disappear so soon? The honeymoon is not even over and the love has disappeared; it was never there in the first place. You were just trying to fool the other and yourself also. How long can you fool yourself? And if you go on fooling yourself too long, it becomes such a burden, it becomes so heavy, that it becomes impossible to live. You cannot be an actor twenty-four hours a day. For a few minutes it is okay – on the beach, in the hills, it is very good; you can be romantic artificially.

For a few minutes it is okay. It is good, it is a game – but for twenty-four hours? If you have to be artificial for twenty-four hours it will become such a tense state of mind, it will create so much anxiety, because you will feel confined, imprisoned. And when you feel that you are confined, in prison, you feel the other person is responsible. Then you take revenge, you react; then whatsoever your wife says you are angry, whatsoever the husband says the wife is angry. Then silence becomes golden, the more you can keep quiet the better. But it happens because from the very beginning the real thing is not there.

Mulla Nasruddin was in love with a woman. The woman was very tall, and the woman lived far away, almost one mile from the tram terminus. So Nasruddin used to walk her to her home every evening.

One day, after just a few minutes' walk, Nasruddin said, "Give me a kiss." But she was so tall that Nasruddin needed a stool or something. So they looked around and saw a blacksmith's shop, abandoned. They found an anvil there, so he stood on the anvil, kissed the woman, and they started again towards home. After half a mile, Nasruddin said, "One more, darling."

The woman said, "No! I have given you one kiss and it is enough for tonight."

So Nasruddin said, "Then what is the use of carrying this damned anvil!" – he was carrying that anvil.

If you carry a burden, sooner or later...what is the use? If your love is just a means to something else and not the end, then it can be a game, but it cannot become a really meaningful existence. Then you play.

Nasruddin presented a wedding ring to this woman, a diamond ring. She looked at it and said, "Beautiful, but there is one flaw in the diamond."

Nasruddin said, "Honey, have you not heard that love is blind?"

The woman said, "Yes, I have heard, and I know love is blind, but not stone-blind."

The cunningness! The manipulating mind! You can even play that you are blind, but how can you be blind really? You can play, but play cannot become life. And deep down you are not related to it, and then you start hating.

Love can only be spontaneous. There is no other way to it. Whatsoever Dale Carnegie says, there is no other way to it. Love can only be spontaneous, you cannot be trained for it. Trained, you will miss forever. One has just to wait, wait prayerfully. The child should be allowed freedom, so that some day love arises. But a very daring mother and a very daring father are needed.

This is why I always say that to be a mother is one of the most difficult things in the world. Anybody can give birth to a child, but to be a mother or to be a father, very few are qualified, rarely, because to be a mother means to give the child so much freedom, with much love, that the spontaneous love in the child arises.

The child must fall in love with the mother, he should not be forced. It may happen, it may not happen. That is why it is a very courageous act; it may not happen. Nobody knows. Nobody can predict it, it is not mechanical. If it happens, it will be beautiful with the mother; otherwise, the mother can go on praying that this will happen with some other woman – but don't force it. If you force it, the child has learned a trick, he has learned a gimmick. Now he will go on playing the gimmick again and again – with this woman and that, with this man and that, and the whole life will become a gimmickry; it will not be real, it will become artificial.

When love becomes artificial, money becomes important. This is to be understood. Why does money become important when love is artificial? Because love gives you an inner security. When you are in love you are safe – no other safety is needed. When you are in love you are absolutely secure – no other security is needed. Love is enough, nothing else is needed. You can be a beggar on the street, but if you are in love no emperor can compete with you in your security; even Solomon is a poor man before you.

If you are in love you are the richest. Nothing is in any way comparable to the riches of love. You may not have anything but you have all. A single moment of love and the whole life is fulfilled. When you are in love you are never afraid of death, because you have known a death – the death of love. And it was so beautiful, it was so melodious, it was such a benediction, that now you can accept even the real death, the death of the body. You can accept it. Now there is no fear, because you have known that merging into one woman or one man was so beautiful – how much more beautiful will it not be when you merge with the whole of existence?

Death is a merger. If you know love, there is no fear in death. If you don't know love, then fear becomes the center of your life. How to protect yourself? So you make castles, then you make bank balances; these are just protections against death. And when you are afraid of death you are afraid to live, because to live is always dangerous. To live you have to move on unknown paths. And there is danger; on every corner death may be waiting.

A man who is afraid of death by and by shrinks and becomes afraid of life also. He cannot fly in an airplane, he cannot go in a train, because there are accidents. He cannot make a stranger a friend, because who knows...? He cannot fall in love with a woman, because who knows whether she is going to deceive or not? He cannot believe. If love has not happened, you can never be trusting. You are always doubtful, skeptical. And how can a relationship grow when you are in doubt?

And if love has not happened, you can never reach a master. Even if a Buddha comes to your town, you will miss him. You will not go there, because these people are dangerous. They can hypnotize you and they may lead you astray. They may disturb your routine world where you are earning, accumulating, and where you are getting more successful every day: the factory is growing bigger and bigger, and the bank balance is accumulating, and everything is going so good. Why become disturbed by a new, foreign element? So don't allow in any element from the outside. Live in your prison, sheltered, secure.

If you know love you are not afraid of death. And when you are not afraid of death, then only do you become capable of living – because if a man is afraid of death, how can he live? He is even afraid of taking a breath because germs are there.

I know one poet. He is a great poet, but I have always been wondering how he can be a great poet – he cannot even be a man. He must know the tricks of language, he must be a grammarian. He must be playing tricks with words, but cannot be a great poet, because great poetry comes out of life – and he is so afraid. Once he traveled with me. His wife had told me, "Don't take him with you because he will create trouble" – and trouble started, because he would not take the tea at the hotel.

He said, "Who knows? Somebody may have poisoned it."

So I said, "Who is against a poet? Who is going to poison you? Nobody bothers about you." But he would not take it.

He said, "I will bring a stove and prepare tea." He would not take the food in the hotel, because who knows...? He was so afraid of everything. How can this man live? As if the only point is, not to die.

But life brings death, death is the culmination. If you don't want to die, don't live – that is the only way. There is no other way, because if you live you are moving towards death. Life brings death. So the logical way is not to live. The less you live, the less the possibility of death. If you don't live completely, if you commit suicide, you will never be dead again, you have finished. There is no life, now you cannot die. So such a man becomes already a dead man. You will find these corpses moving in the markets, universities, working, doing things – but they are corpses.

Life needs expansion. Fear does not allow you, then security becomes the whole thing – how to be secure. How not to die becomes the whole art of life. And I tell you, the whole art of life is how to die joyfully, how to die blissfully, how to allow death – because if you are ready to die, you are ready to live. If you are ready to die, you are ready to love. If you are ready to die, you are ready to meet the divine. There is no other way, death is the door.

What do I mean when I say death is the door? You have to not be there, you have to dissolve, you have to lose yourself. What does security mean? Whatsoever happens, you have to be, you have to persist in your ego. That's why money is so meaningful, because money helps you not to live. A poor man has to live, a rich man need not.

I have heard about one very rich man: he would travel in his car...even from the porch to the room he would be carried on a stretcher. He had come to a new town, to a new hotel where he had never been, and when he was being carried in on the stretcher, the manager thought that he was paralyzed or something. So he asked his wife, "What is the matter?" – he felt very sorry – "Your husband looked quite okay. Is he paralyzed, or is something wrong with his legs?"

The wife said, "No. His legs are absolutely okay. But he need not walk – he is a rich man."

A rich man need not live, he can afford it! A poor man has to live. A poor man has to go on the street, move in danger, in crowds. A poor man cannot afford not to live. That is why a rich man, by and by, becomes encaged in his richness, isolated. Then he lives alone, then he cannot even allow his wife in the room. He may find an explanation: "We are not poor, so why should my wife and I live in one room? We are rich. We can afford two separate rooms" – but the real thing is something else.

Hitler never allowed anybody to live in his room because he was afraid. Who knows? – the wife may be a spy. He never got married. He got married only just before he committed suicide – three hours before, because then there was no fear. When death was certain he got married, never before – because a wife is a dangerous thing. Who knows? – she may be in association with some foreign power, or she may be a communist; in the night she may kill him.

He loved many women, but never allowed any woman to live with him, never allowed any woman to be in his room in the night. Just three hours before, when he had decided that now there was no way to escape – death is certain, the enemy is bombing Berlin – he called in a priest in the night. The priest was awakened from his sleep; immediately he was brought to the underground cell where Hitler was, and Hitler told him, "Now perform the marriage ceremony." And when the ceremony was finished, they went into the room and both took poison and were dead.

What manner of man is this? But this manner of man you will find everywhere. When there is fear, nobody can be a friend. Then everybody is the enemy and you have to protect yourself. A rich man can protect himself more; that's why there is so much emphasis on money, so much madness! You cannot even understand what is happening. Why this neurosis about money?

Mulla Nasruddin was dying. He opened his eyes, he looked at his wife. His wife said, "We are here, Mulla. You go to the divine silently, in peace and prayer. We are all here."

Mulla Nasruddin looked at the faces – his eyes were dim, he was almost gone, it was difficult to see.

He asked, "Where is Rehman?" – his eldest son.

His wife said, "He is standing by your right side."

Then he asked, "Where is Rahim?" – another son.

And his wife said, "He is there, standing by your feet."

"And where is Abdul, and where is Farid?" he asked.

All were there, so his wife said, "You rest, we are all here."

Nasruddin immediately became worried and said, "Then who is minding the store? If everybody is here then who is minding the store?" And he was on his deathbed; just a moment later he died. No, neither life is meaningful nor death...the store, "Who is minding the store?" Even at the last moment, no temple is there in the mind – just the store, the market, the money.

Why is money so important? It is your protection against love, against life, against death, against God. Hence, Mahavira and Buddha renounced it. The renouncement is simply coming to understand that this whole arrangement is against life, against love, against God. They simply renounce! It is not because of money that they are renouncing it, but just because they have come to understand that through this protection they have been killing themselves, this was poison. So they simply escaped from the palaces.

Then a new life starts when you understand that money is neurosis. Security, the hankering after security and safety, shows that you are already dead, that life has left you. Continuous effort to be secure means you have not yet been able to love; otherwise, love is enough security, no other security is needed. One moment of love is eternity – no fear of death, a lover can die easily, lovingly. He has known life, he is thankful. Even for a single moment love happened...he has known the glory of it, the benediction, all blessings have been on him. He can thank God for this single moment that has been given to him – and he was not worthy.

Who is worthy? Nobody is worthy. Have you ever thought about it – that you are alive? Are you worthy to be alive? How have you earned it? You have known the flowers and the trees and the birds on the wing and the sun rising, so many mornings, so many evenings, and the stars. How have you earned to be alive? It is simple grace. You are not worthy, you have not earned it in any way. It is simply God's grace that you are.

But when somebody comes to know a single moment of love, this whole life becomes nothing. Then all the birds that you have seen, and all the songs that you have heard, and all the musicians of the world – nothing! Then all this greenery of the trees is nothing. Then there is no radiance in the sun and there is no music in the stars. If you have known a single moment of love, then this whole world is just dim and a shadow; it is just a reflection, not the real.

If you have known a single moment of love, for eternity and eternity you will be thankful and singing songs of gratitude to the divine. Then there is no death – love knows no death, love knows only life. You know only death. Love...you have bypassed it, somehow you have not been through it; you have bypassed it, and now money has become significant. Money is symbolic of a dead man, money is the love of a dead man.

So look at a miser. It is not simply money when he takes notes in his hands. I have seen one miser – so much romance in his eyes when he would look at the notes; never so lovingly has a lover looked all over the beloved. He would feel and touch...and look at his eyes! The radiance that came to his eyes, the poetry that took over his being. He became a completely transformed man. No, Majnu was not so happy when he looked at Laila. No, Shiri was not so happy when she looked at Farhad.

This man was a relative, so I had many chances to see him and understand him. He was the perfect man of money, a buddha on that path. He never got married; he would always say, "It is so expensive and I cannot afford it. Some day I will get married." He is now dead. He never got married – he remained a bachelor. But he would rationalize it; he would say, "This is *brahmacharya*"; he would say, "This is celibacy. In the scriptures, in the Vedas, the life of a celibate is the highest life." But he was simply a miser, even a miser about semen. That was his celibacy – he was not a *brahmachari*.

So when you find celibates, ninety-nine out of a hundred will just be misers about semen. They are afraid to let go: if the semen goes out of their body, their bank balances.... Their brahmacharya is a sort of constipation. They stink! You can never have any fragrance coming out of them. They are misers – but they rationalize. And they always live through reason, never through the heart – because heart is a dangerous thing.

Reason always grabs things and the heart always wants to give. The heart is the giver and the heart is never a miser, so a miser can never believe the heart. By and by he will kill the heart, he becomes just the head. There is no feeling in him – feeling is dangerous. He doesn't feel, he becomes insensitive. He doesn't allow any sensitivity in his being, because a beggar comes and he asks...if you have feeling, it will be difficult to say no. But if you have only the head, you will rationalize and you will say, "I don't believe in beggary; this is bad for the economy, this is not good for the culture – and you look perfectly healthy, so go and work." You will rationalize, and these reasons you also know are just superficial; deep down you don't want to give – that is the basis. But you cannot accept the fact that you are not a giver.

You live in words, reasons, rationalizations, and go on hiding the basic fact that you are killing your feeling. If you are on the path of money – and almost everybody is, more or less – then see the whole phenomenon of what is happening within you; you are killing yourself. And life cannot be prevented from moving, life will reach up to death. You cannot withhold it, it is not in your control. It has to go – as it has come, it has to go. Before it leaves you, you can only create anxiety, that is all.

If you accept the ebb and flow of life, the birth and death of life; if you accept, you need not create any anxiety. You can love. While dying is there, love. And allow love to happen. Don't try for security and don't be afraid of death. Death will come. Give a chance to life to flower. If life really flowers, death will be the culmination, not the end. It will be the climax, the crescendo. It will be the highest peak, the Everest, not the end.

And at the moment of death, a man who has lived rightly, through love – and that is the only right way to live – for him death comes as the most beautiful ecstasy. He dies with a song in the heart. He dies with ecstasy all over the body, throbbing. He is going to meet the divine beloved. He has learned how to love and how to give. So in the moment of death also he can give. He gives his whole being back to nature; the body, the air goes to the air, the fire goes to the fire, the earth goes to the earth, the sky goes to the sky. He gives, he is a giver, and the being goes to the source, to the *Brahma;* he does not cling.

But you cannot do it if you have been a clinger your whole life. At the moment of death, if you cling everything becomes ugly. If you have been clinging and clinging and clinging, and always afraid and in fear and have never allowed love, then at the moment of death you will miss the highest peak that is possible, that was possible. These are the two paths; one is right, the other is wrong.

Now we will try to go into this story. You will be able to understand – but understand through the heart:

> *The Master Seistsu required larger premises as the*
> *building he was teaching in was very overcrowded*
> – he must have been in the same situation as I am.
> *Umezu, a merchant...*he has not yet come to me...
> *Umezu, a merchant, decided to donate*
> *five hundred pieces of gold for the construction*
> *of a new building –*
> five hundred pieces of gold is real money.
> *Umezu took the money to the teacher*
> *and Seistsu said, "All right, I will take it" –*
> but this is no way, from a miser.

The man must have been a miser, otherwise how can you accumulate five hundred pieces of gold? And this was not all; this must have been just a small part, a hundredth part of his accumulations. But why, if he is a miser, has he come to give to this master? Looks contradictory: if he is a miser and a man of money, he should not go. But I know the reason – that too is part of fear, that too is making security in the other world.

He must have been nearing death, he must have become an old man. And people of money are always old, they are never young – because death is always near and they are trembling. He must have been feeling any day death can come; he has to make arrangements for the other world also. He must have had millions of gold pieces. Just five hundred pieces...this is just to be safe: "Give it to this master; people say he is enlightened. Give these five hundred pieces to this man, he will take care of the other world, he may give a certificate. People say that he is on good terms with God, his name is in the good books; he will be helpful somehow."

It is groping in the dark. A man who has missed life is thinking of some other life. Remember, only people who have missed this life think of that. And if you can miss this you will miss that also, because you will remain the same. Even if you are forced to enter into heaven, you will make a hell out of it, because you will take your habits, your mechanism of the mind, your working – your whole past you will take with you. You will make a hell out of it.

Can you be in heaven? I don't see any way; you cannot be. Wherever you go you will carry your hell with you. It is a part of you. So those who know say that hell and heaven are not without – they are within you, they are qualities of your being. On this earth people have lived in heaven; on this earth you are in hell. Remember well, wherever you go you will provide your own hell there. Immediately you reach there you will create your hell all around. You cannot do anything new. The mind is old, it goes on in a pattern, moving in a circle.

This Umezu must have been a miser. But now death is coming near and he must think of the other world also. This world he has lost, now the other cannot be lost. Something has to be done, but that too has to be done through money. See the mind: he thought that through money life can be purchased, now he thinks through money God can be purchased. He thought through money love can be purchased. Now he thinks that through money heaven can be purchased. But his mind remains focused in the neurosis of money. He is still mad, money still remains the means. Anything that he is going to do is to be done through money.

That's why the master behaved in such a way. He said, "All right, I will take it," as if it was nothing. That is the meaning of it; as if it was nothing, five hundred pieces of gold – just dirt.

The master said, *"All right, I will take it,"* as if it is a burden and he was obliging this Umezu. Always remember that if you go to a master with money, this is going to be the treatment. It is very easy to understand in the story. It is very difficult when the treatment is given to you.

Just a few days ago somebody phoned; he used to give some money for the ashram. Then he said, "Now I will stop, because there seems to be no gratefulness about it. I am not even allowed a special interview with Osho so I am not going to give it." He is here, he should try to understand this story well, because it is easier to understand a story when you are not part of it. It is very easy. But when you are part of it, then it becomes very difficult. Five hundred pieces of gold that man should bring to me, right? And then I will tell him, *"All right, I will take it!"*

> Umezu gave the sack of gold to Seistsu,
> but he was very dissatisfied with the attitude
> of the teacher as the amount he had given was
> very great – one could live for a whole year on
> three pieces of gold, and the teacher had not
> even thanked him.

Look at the mind, the mind which is neurotic about money. What he is saying? He is saying, "This sack of gold I have given – a man can live on three pieces of gold for one year." He thinks life is through money. Money may be needed, but nobody can live through money. Money may be necessary; it is not enough. And if there is only money and nothing else, it is better you die, the sooner the better. Because you are living unnecessarily, you are just passing the days – it is not life.

Jesus is reported to have said: "Man cannot live by bread alone." He also knows that bread is needed – nobody can live without bread, that's right. But there is a higher dimension of life where nobody can live by bread alone. If there is only bread, commit suicide! – because eating the same bread again and again is useless.

But the man who lives through money thinks that a man can live for a whole year on three pieces of gold, and these are five hundred pieces – a man can live forever and forever! Eternal life is possible through five hundred pieces of gold. And what type of man is this? – he has not even thanked me. He was very dissatisfied.

Whenever you give with a condition you will always be dissatisfied, because the condition cannot be fulfilled. Whenever you give without a condition you will feel a deep contentment, because there is no reason to be dissatisfied. Whenever you give and enjoy it, whenever giving is an end unto itself...this man would have been dancing because the master had accepted – enough! He should have thanked the master that, "I was worried whether you are going to accept it or not. Because I know you well: this is just dirt for you and you have accepted. You are so kind, your compassion is so deep." He would have danced and thanked him. He would have gone deeply happy and blissful. But no, it was not possible because it was not the end, it was a means. He wanted the master to be obliged to him.

If this man reaches to God, he will give him a sack of gold and wait for the thank you. What can you give to God who has given all to you? And a master is nothing but a representative of the divine, of the same quality. That is why we call Mahavira 'Bhagwan', why we call Buddha 'Bhagwan' – because of that same quality. What can you give to him? All comes to you through him. At the most you are returning back...at the most. You should be thankful that you have been accepted.

But a money-mad man cannot understand this. He wanted the master to be obliged because he had done this, and this is so much.

For him it was so much. As far as his attitude was concerned, it was such a great amount – five hundred pieces of gold; one man can live for one year on three pieces – because mind thinks in relativity. It does not know anything of the absolute. It knows only of relativity. It is his mind!

I have heard: Mulla Nasruddin died and went immediately, or was sent immediately, to hell. There he reached Satan who had been waiting for him for a long time – he was a man long awaited there. Satan received him, welcomed him, and Mulla Nasruddin said to the devil, "Boy, am I happy being here in heaven."

The devil said, "Nasruddin, you are mistaken. This is no heaven."

Nasruddin said, "That may be your attitude. I am coming from India – to me it looks like heaven."

Mind is relative. Five hundred pieces of gold! He was giving his very life; his very heart was there in that sack of gold. Those five hundred pieces were not of gold, they were of his heart. He has sold his life and bargained for this gold. He had died for this sack of gold – and not even a thank you. It was too much. The master is not behaving rightly; he was dissatisfied.

If you think about any master, you will always come to the conclusion that he is not behaving rightly. Remember this: if you *think* – I repeat – then you will always come to the conclusion that he is not behaving rightly. If you look, not think, then you will know that he is always behaving rightly.

He thought, calculated. It was so plain to him; five hundred pieces of gold – his whole life in that sack. And this man simply says, *"All right, I will take it."*

> *"In that sack there are five hundred pieces of gold," hinted Umezu.*

He thought, "Maybe he has missed. Maybe he is in meditation

or somewhere else, because how can it happen that five hundred pieces of gold and all he says is, 'All right, I will take it'? He is not in his senses." So he hinted.

> *"In that sack there are five hundred pieces of gold," hinted Umezu.*
> *"You told me that before," said the master.*

He said, "It is unnecessary, why repeat it? I have heard it."
This was even worse, no thank you coming from the man. Rather, he would not even take the hint, and he felt a little angry it seems, because he said, "You have told me that before. No need...."

> *"Even if I am a wealthy merchant, five hundred pieces of gold is a lot of money," said Umezu.*

This is the problem of the mind. He says, *"Even if I am a wealthy merchant...I* have enough money with me, but even then... *five hundred pieces of gold is a lot of money.* So to you, just a beggar, it is the whole world. To me it is a lot of money, and you are treating it as if it is nothing. You are insulting me."
A man who is focused on money cannot understand a man of love. The man of love will always appear like a beggar, a madman, not of this world – he doesn't understand. He is behaving in a crazy way. Howsoever you may worship Buddha and Mahavira, if you meet them somehow, somewhere, you will think they are mad. Even if you don't say it, because it will be so impolite...but you understand well that this man has wasted his life sitting under a tree. He could have earned a lot of money – this was said to Buddha many times.
Buddha left his home and went to another kingdom, just to get rid of the relatives and the family, because they would bother him there and they would go on coming, trying to persuade him to come back. So he left the kingdom and went to another kingdom,

then he became aware that those people are everywhere – you cannot escape.

There was a rumor that a prince had left a neighboring kingdom and had come there. So even the king of the neighboring kingdom came, and he said, "My son, you are young and you don't know the ways of the world. You are immature, I am experienced. I say to you through my experience, go back to your home. This is foolish. At this age such foolish ideas catch hold of the mind. One has to resist. At this age, when one is young, one is prone to, tends to be idealistic. But later on experience proves it is wrong. Don't be a hippy, go back!"

Buddha listened and he said, "You may be right as far as your own experience is concerned, but I have lived in that world for many lives, and nothing, nothing was ever attained. Now it is enough. It is through experience that I have left, not through some romantic idealism of a young man."

The old man would not listen. He said, "If you don't want to go back, I understand – there may be some trouble. You may not be feeling good with your father, or with your family, or something has gone wrong. Then don't go back, come to me. I have got a beautiful daughter; get married to her and this kingdom is yours."

Buddha said, "I am married and I have left a very beautiful woman. It is impossible to find another like her. But even that beautiful woman will not give me the ultimate – and I am in search of the ultimate."

The old king left, he said, "You are mad, incurably mad."

This happened wherever Buddha would go. And he was so young and so beautiful...he had never walked on the streets. Wherever he would go, anybody would know that he was a prince, he was not a beggar – and then everybody would give him advice to go back.

Mind lives through its own ideas, thinks through its own ideas. You cannot put the mind aside and then look. This old man who came to Buddha missed an opportunity. It may not happen again for millions of lives. But he was teaching the greatest teacher, he was trying to teach him something; he wanted that Buddha should learn something from him. And he has not gained anything himself, he has not reached anywhere.

This man says, *"In that sack there are five hundred pieces of gold. Even if I am a wealthy merchant, five hundred pieces of gold is a lot of money"* – and you are just a beggar; it is not said, it is implied. "You should know the meaning of it, what I am doing. Such a great donation and you simply say, 'Okay, I will take it.'"

"Do you want me to thank you for it?" said the master – because masters never answer what you ask. They answer what you mean to ask. They never answer your question, because that is irrelevant. They always answer what is hidden behind the question – why you are hinting at these things.

You are not interested in proving that gold is significant, you are not interested in proving that five hundred pieces of gold is a large sum – those are just rationalizations. You are hinting at something else. The master caught him immediately, and said *"Do you want me to thank you for it?"* – he hit the nail, he hit right at the heart.

"You ought to," said Umezu. Not that, "I expect and want," but *"You ought to."*

This man is not a giver, he has never been a giver. Even when he is giving, he is not giving. Even when he is donating, it is a bargain. He says, *"You ought to.* I have done such a great thing, now this is your duty, not my desire or my request."

"Why should I?" said Seistsu. *"The giver should be thankful."*

This is impossible to understand for the mind, for the money-oriented mind; the giver should be the thankful one. But this is the peak on the path of love.

Those who love, they come to know that the giving is so beautiful and so blissful; they come to know that the more you give, the more you have of it – the more love you give, the more love you have there inside; the more you go on throwing, sharing, the more it bubbles up – it is an eternal spring. And once you come to know that the more you give, the more you have, you have learned the basic arithmetic of spirituality. Then you never hold back, then you are always in search of someone who can take it. Then you are always in search of someone who can share it, because he will make you fresh. The old is gone, the new arises; it is always coming there.

You are like a well which has gone rotten, because you have not given anybody anything. You have never shared your water; the water has become rotten. Give it! Let people come and let them drink out of you, and then fresh sources are always available. The moment the old water is removed, fresh is coming in. Your well is joined to the infinite ocean deep down. Your well is just a door to the ocean. The giver comes to know, the sharer comes to know, then he feels thankful. Whenever somebody takes something from you, something new has come into being in you. Your being is renewed through it. You are being made young again and again, the more you give. The giver remains always young. The non-giver is always old, dead, rotten.

The master says, *"The giver should be thankful. You should be thankful to me that I accept – and that I accept a thing like money. You should be thankful, because money means nothing to me."* It may be necessary in the world, because a master has also to live in the world; it may be the means of exchange in this mad world, because a master has to live in this mad world – but it is nothing. It is just an invented means, agreed upon by all, so that we can exchange things.

The society can live without money; for thousands of years society lived without money. And sooner or later a day will come when society will again live without money, because living through money is so burdensome and so useless and so unnecessary. But because the world was poor up to now, that's why money has had to be used; but the more affluence grows....

America will be the first to drop money. When there is enough money, there is no need to carry it – why carry it? Then it is foolish, then it is burdensome. Soon the earth will not need money. But masters have always known it, always, that this is just a market device; but a master has to live with you.

If you go to a madhouse, it is better to pretend that you are also mad, otherwise you will be in difficulty. If you try to prove that you are a sane man, the madmen will kill you. They did this with Jesus, they did this with Socrates, they did this with Mansoor. These were very innocent people. They tried to live in a madhouse as they were – not mad. They were innocent, but they did not know that the rule of the madhouse is: even if you are not mad, pretend that you are mad, because madness is the coin prevalent there, it is the currency there. Don't be an outsider in a madhouse, otherwise madmen will collect together and kill you. If you say that you are not mad, that means you are trying to say to them that, "You are mad!" – that cannot be tolerated.

An enlightened person also has to live in this world with you. He has to use your techniques, your tricks.

It happened once: it was found in Japan that one enlightened man was always caught – sometimes stealing, sometimes something else, a criminal act, small things. He would steal just a small amount of money, and then he was to be sent to the jail – and he was an enlightened man! Twenty-six times in his whole life he was jailed, but those who were his disciples, they knew him. The last time he came out of jail he was seventy-eight, and the disciples said, "Now don't do such a thing...and why do you go on doing such things?"

He said, "Then who will go inside the jail and try to make those jailors meditative, those jailbirds? Who will go there? I have to steal, that is the only way to reach those people. And it is nothing to me. I have been helping and there is real disease. I am needed there. But that is the only way I can get in, otherwise they won't allow me. That is the only currency that is required." An enlightened man has to live with you jailbirds!

But if you are ready to understand the neurosis of money and the ecstasy of love, then you will be able to understand this: the giver should be thankful. Give and be thankful – because the other could have refused. That possibility does not exist for this miser. He cannot conceive of anybody refusing five hundred pieces of gold. He does not know he could have been refused. The master may have thrown the sack out of the temple and said, "Don't bring this rubbish here."

It happened: One man came – he also came with five hundred pieces of gold. These misers also have their mathematics; five hundred seems to be the highest, the limit; they cannot go beyond it – he came to Ramakrishna. Ramakrishna was even more dangerous. He not only said, "All right, I will take it," he behaved even more rudely. He said, "So okay, go to the Ganges and throw it all in."

The man could not do anything, because Ramakrishna has said so – he became afraid. It was impossible for him to go to the Ganges and throw in five hundred pieces of gold. But when Ramakrishna says.... Still he hesitated. Ramakrishna said, "Why are you hesitating? Haven't you given the money to me? Then it is my money. Just go and throw it into the Ganges, because right now I don't need it, and the Ganges needs it."

So the man went, very slowly of course, and he didn't come back. One hour passed, two hours passed, and Ramakrishna sent some disciples to see what had happened to that man. Had he drowned himself and saved the money? Misers are doing that. So the disciples went to see what he was doing. There was a big crowd, he had made it into a great show. He would bring one gold coin, throw it on a stone – khannnng! The sound! And many people were there. Then he would count: "One hundred and one, one hundred and two, one hundred and three..." and then throw it into the Ganges.

So the disciples reported: "That man is a perfect exhibitionist. He has gathered a big crowd and he is throwing each single coin, counting, and doing the whole thing very slowly."

So Ramakrishna went, slapped that man and told him, "When one accumulates, counting is needed, but when one renounces....

What are you doing? When one has to throw the coins, one can throw the whole bag!"

But people renounce and still count – they have not renounced.

Givers should be thankful; give and be thankful. If you can follow this rule the old pail will fall down, the water will flow out. The whole maya, illusion, disappears. No water, no moon. Then you can look at the sky, at the real moon. It is always there, but you are caught in the reflection.

Love is the real moon; money is the reflection.

Enough for today.

a philosopher asks buddha

A philosopher came to Buddha one day and
asked, "Without words, without the wordless,
will you tell me the truth?"
The Buddha kept silence.
The philosopher bowed and thanked Buddha,
saying, "With your loving kindness I have cleared
away my delusions and entered the true path."
After the philosopher had gone Ananda asked
Buddha what the philosopher had attained.
The Buddha replied, "A good horse runs even at
the shadow of the whip."

A PHILOSOPHER ASKS BUDDHA

A philosopher came to Buddha one day and asked, "Without words, without the wordless, will you tell me the truth?"

It is very rarely that a philosopher comes to a buddha. It is almost impossible. But whenever it happens, it can become a revolution, it can become a transformation in the philosopher. Why is it so impossible that a philosopher comes to Buddha? Because philosophy and religion are very antagonistic; their approach is totally opposite, diametrically opposite.

Philosophy believes in thinking and religion believes in trust. A thinker doubts easily, but cannot trust so easily. A doubting mind is needed to be a philosopher, a very skeptical mind. To be religious deep trust is needed – not at all skeptical, not doubting at all. The philosopher lives through logic; the religious man lives through love, and there is no way to help love and logic meet. There is no way; they never meet, their paths never cross each other. They may run parallel – just like the railway tracks – but they never meet. They may be very close, but they always run parallel. Even if you think they meet somewhere, it is an illusion.

Just stand at a railway track and see the rails running parallel: on the faraway distant horizon you will think they are meeting. They are not meeting, that is an illusion. Go to that point and you will find they are still parallel. Two parallel lines can never meet. Heart and head are parallel lines, they never meet. You can take a jump, from one line you can go to the other – that's possible. You can take a jump from the head to the heart, but there is no continuity; it is a jump.

If you believe in the head too much – that means believing in doubting – this jump becomes impossible. There have been great philosophers; they thought and thought, and they pondered and contemplated, and they have created big systems, miracles of words, but they are not nearer to the truth than any ignorant man. Rather, on the contrary, the ignorant man may be nearer, because at least he is humble in his ignorance, at least he is not egoist, at least he can listen to the other. At least if a buddha comes to the town the ignorant man can go to him, because he knows he does not know – that much humility is there. A philosopher cannot go because he already knows. That is the problem: without knowing anything, he thinks he knows.

This is happening with me every day. If a philosopher comes, a psychiatrist comes – a man who has studied psychology, philosophy and religion in some university – it is difficult, almost impossible to have any communion with him. You can discuss, but you cannot meet – you will move parallel. You may appear close because you use the same words, but that is just appearance.

Why is it so difficult for logic to love? – because love needs a very courageous act, and that courageous act is to move into the unknown. Logic is always a coward, it never moves into the unknown. Logic says, "First I must know. When the territory is well known, then I will move."

Logic has no adventure in it. Love is absolutely adventurous; sometimes it even looks foolish. To the logical mind it always looks foolish: "What are you doing, moving into the unknown without knowing where you are going? What you are doing? And leaving the territory that was known, secure, safe, becoming unnecessarily homeless. Don't lose that which you have got, first be sure of that which you are going to gain." This is the problem. Logic says, "First know the further step well; only then leave the step you are standing on." Then you can never leave this step, because there is no way of knowing the further step unless you reach to it. Logic is...

I have heard: It once happened, Mulla Nasruddin wanted to learn swimming. He went to a teacher and the teacher said, "Come along with me, I am going to the river. It is not difficult, you will learn. It is simple, even children can learn."

But accidentally, when Nasruddin came near the bank, he slipped. It was muddy and he fell down, and he became very afraid. He ran to the farthest point of the bank, under a tree. The teacher followed. He said, "Why are you escaping? Where are you going?"

Nasruddin said, "Listen: first teach me swimming, only then will I come closer. This is dangerous! If something goes wrong, who will be responsible? So I will come near the river only when I have learned swimming."

But is there any way to learn swimming without going to the river? So, Mulla Nasruddin remained without even learning to swim.

It is too dangerous, the step is too foolish. A man, a learned man, a man of logic, cannot take that step. Logic becomes a grave. You become more and more confined because life *is* danger. There is no way to avoid it, it is always moving into the unknown. The river is always going towards the sea. This is how life progresses: it always leaves the known, moves into the unknown. That's the way life is. Nothing can be done about it. If you try to do something – then the Ganges should be flowing towards the source, the Gangotri, because that is the known thing; not towards Ganga Sagar, not towards the ocean.

In African mythology there is a bird: the name is woofle-woofle – African. The bird is one of the most mythical of all the mythologies of the world. That bird has only one peculiarity: it is not interested in where it is going, it is only interested in where it is coming from – so it goes backwards. It never reaches anywhere because it is always interested in where it is coming from. It is interested in the past. That is as if you are old and going towards the womb. This is impossible – but this is how human mind functions.

With logic you move towards the source; with love you move

towards the ultimate flowering – the dimensions are different. Logic asks, "Who created the world?" It is interested in the creator, in the past, the original source – the Gangotri, from where the Ganges flows. Love never asks who created the world. It is already there, so why bother? Whosoever created ABC makes no difference. How is it going to affect you, whoever created the world? Whether it was a Hindu god, a Brahma, or a Christian trinity – what difference does it make?

Love is interested in what the ultimate flowering is going to be. Love is interested in buddhahood. Love is interested what is going to happen to me, to my seed, how it will flower. Note the difference: logic is always interested in the known, in the past, the path that you have already traveled; love is always interested in the unknown, in the ultimate flowering, the path that you have not traveled – not only not traveled, the path that you have not even imagined, not even dreamed of.

That's why a philosopher rarely comes to a buddha. They are moving in diametrically opposite directions; a philosopher going to the past, a buddha moving to the future. Their departing point may be the same, but there is no meeting point. But when a philosopher comes to a buddha...rarely it happens, but whenever it happens there is immediate transformation.

Why? Because if a philosopher comes to a buddha, it means deep down he has understood the failure of philosophy. Otherwise, why would he have come? Deep down he has felt the failure of logic. He has made every effort to know truth through it: arguing about and about, for, in favor, against. He has been arguing and arguing and has now come to the point where he knows the whole thing is futile; nothing can be known through it. This failure gives him the deepest humility possible in the world. Even an ignorant man is not so humble, because he is not such a deep failure. He has not come to know the suffering of failure. He has not been thrown from the peak to the valley.

This philosopher was thinking that he was at the peak. Suddenly he became aware that he had been standing in the valley and dreaming about the peak. There had never been a peak: he had not moved a single inch. The truth had remained as unknown as ever. His whole life had been a waste. When somebody comes to feel this, suddenly the ego disappears, one becomes humble. And unless you are humble, you cannot come to a buddha. Only humbleness, deep humility, can bring you to a buddha – now you are ready to learn, because you don't know anything.

So there are two types of ignorance: ordinary ignorance is when a man is ignorant but is not aware that he is ignorant. When a philosopher becomes aware that he is ignorant – this is the second type of ignorance, very deep: he has come to realize that he is ignorant, he is fully aware that he is ignorant – when ignorance is aware of itself, that becomes the first step of wisdom.

So the first thing to understand:

> *A philosopher came to Buddha one day, and asked…*

There were many philosophers in Buddha's time. Really, there has never been such a flowering of intellect as happened at that time – not only in India, all over the world. Buddha was there; Mahavira was there; Prabuddha Katyayan, a great logician; Ajit Keshakambal, a great philosopher; Makkhali Goshal, a rare intellect; Sanjay Vilethiputta and many others were there in Bihar. Now their names are not well known because they never created any following. Exactly at the same time in Greece there was Socrates, Plato, Aristotle – the three who created the whole Western mind. Exactly at the same time in China there was Confucius, Lao Tzu, Chuang Tzu, Mencius. It seems at that peak, all over the world, mind was at its Everest.

There are only three cultures: one is Chinese, another is Indian, and the other is Greek. Only three cultures exist, all the others are just byproducts. The whole West originated with the Greek mind in Athens. The whole Chinese civilization, a totally different type of civilization, arose out of Confucius' and Lao Tzu's confrontation, and all that is beautiful in India came out of Buddha, Mahavira. And all these people existed at a single moment of history.

Historians say that history moves like a wheel: there are moments when intelligence is at its peak, there are moments when intelligence goes down. These were the times when intelligence was at its peak. Many were the philosophers, particularly in India; the whole country was philosophic. People moved from this corner to that corner seeking for truth – millions of seekers!

Only when there are millions of seekers, then a few can become enlightened, because it is a pyramid-like thing. A pyramid is very broad at the base, and then, by and by, comes the peak. A Buddha exists only when at the broad base millions of people are seeking truth; otherwise he cannot exist. There is no possibility, he cannot stand. Where will he stand? He needs millions, millions of seekers; they become the base.

And in those days when systems were being created everywhere, and such complicated, complex systems that there has never been anything to compare with them.... Historians of philosophy and religion say that at that time India knew all that has been known in philosophy – every shade and nuance of thought, every approach. India has looked at all the paths and possibilities, and every possibility has been finished. Now, since that time, there has been nothing new in philosophy; and if you think there is something new, it only means that you are not well acquainted with India. There has been nothing new since Buddha, because at that time everything was searched, almost every possibility finished.

And if you think... In the West many people come to realize something and think that they are giving something new. It looks new because they are unacquainted with it, they don't know it. And now the whole of this treasure is hidden in Pali, in Prakrit and in Sanskrit, languages not spoken, not used. But every nuance of thought...

For example, when Sigmund Freud said for the first time that, "I suspect that the conscious mind is not the whole mind. Deep down below the conscious there is a subconscious layer. And even beyond that, I suspect an unconscious layer," it was thought that it was a very revolutionary discovery. But in Buddha's time this was known; not only this – Buddha talks about still further layers. He talks about seven layers of the mind. These three are there, as Freud says – but four more...and if he is right up to the third, there is every possibility he will be right beyond them, because he is on the right track.

Then Jung suggested that beyond the unconscious there seems to be a collective unconscious – that is the fourth layer of Buddha. Now the whole of psychology has come to this fourth layer. All four are suggested by Buddha – but three more are there; sooner or later we will discover them.

Since then there has never been such appreciation for thinking, logic. And the hair-splitting went to its very extreme. Buddha talks about seven layers of mind and Prabuddha Katyayan talks about seven hundred layers of mind. Incomprehensible, but very logical... and the possibility is that the mind *can* be divided into seven hundred layers. Nothing is impossible.

At that time a philosopher came to Buddha. First try to understand the situation of Buddha; Buddha's situation is as anti-metaphysical as possible, he is not a philosopher. Really, you cannot find a man who is more anti-philosophical than Buddha, because he says all philosophical questions are nonsense. This is the standpoint now in the West – Bertrand Russell, Wittgenstein. The latest discovery in the West is Wittgenstein, and this is the standpoint of Wittgenstein: that all philosophical questions, answers, are nonsense. Still, if you ask a question, a philosophical question, Bertrand Russell answers it yes or no. Buddha never answered, because if it is nonsense, why answer? Buddha would keep silent.

So it was the routine, whenever Buddha would come to any town, that Buddha's *bhikkhus* would go into the town and inform people: "Please don't ask these eleven questions." They had a list of eleven questions; in those eleven questions all metaphysics is finished, you cannot ask anything beyond those eleven. They are the whole expanse of all philosophical inquiry.

So beforehand, before Buddha would reach a town, the bhikkhus would go and spread the news: "Please don't ask about these eleven questions, because he is not going to answer. If you have something beyond these eleven you can come, you are invited." But there is nothing beyond those eleven, so what to do?

This man was not a philosopher, he was not skeptical, he didn't believe in doubt. And he disbelieved in doubt so much that he never talked about trust. This has to be understood, because trust is needed only if you are in doubt. If you are not in doubt, why talk about trust? All talk about faith means doubt has entered. He never said, "Believe!" because, he said, there is no question of believing or not believing; one has to *be*. It is not an intellectual question – because faith and doubt both remain intellectual. From where do you doubt? From the mind. From where will you believe? From the mind.

So your belief will also be from the same root. It will already be poisoned. Who will believe? And who will doubt? You will remain the same, and *you* are the problem. So Buddha hits at the root; he says, "No need to trust, no need to doubt. You simply come to me and be. Don't move to this extreme, don't move to the other. Don't take any standpoint, simply be in the middle." That's why his path is known as the middle path – *majjhim nikaya*: never move to the extreme. This is one of the most original discoveries about human mind and its functioning, because the mind always likes to move to the opposite.

You love a person. Through love you magnify the person, he becomes a god. Then love disappears; immediately you start hating. You then do exactly the opposite – nobody stops in the middle. Then the person shrinks under your hate, becomes a devil. Is there any way to stand between God and the Devil and not move to the opposite? Mind feels very easy moving from one thing to the contrary. There is no problem, you have been doing that: you doubt a person, then you can believe; you believe a person, then you can doubt.

Buddha says to stop in the middle, because in the middle there is no mind; mind exists only on the extremes. Love? Mind is there. Hate? Mind is there. For? Mind is there. Against? Mind is there. In the middle, mind cannot exist. In the middle there is no possibility of any thought, because either the thought will be of doubt or of trust, of love or hate, enmity or friendship. And you know well that in every friend the enemy is hidden, in every enemy the friend is possible.

One of the most cunning minds of the world, Machiavelli, has written in his book The Prince, "Don't say anything, even to a friend, which you would not like to say to an enemy, because a friend is a potential enemy any day. And don't say anything against an enemy which you would not like to say against a friend, because then you will be in trouble any day. If the enemy becomes the friend, then you will be embarrassed."

And this is a suggestion from one politician to princes, to other politicians. So politicians remain alert; the more they become seasoned, the less you can find in their words, statements, who they are talking against, who they are talking for. Their words become more and more elusive, so it is possible that if the friend turns into an enemy, they will not be in trouble. If an enemy turns into a friend... And politics changes every day; it is just like the climate, and you never know....

I have heard: Two politicians were talking about a third fellow traveler. One said, "This man is so dishonest, so cunning, so crude, that I have never known anybody like that. This is the most dishonest man here." And he said, "And I feel that you don't know him as well as I know him."

The other man said, "No, you are wrong. I also know him very well."

The first said, "How can you know him very well? I am his best friend!"

Only friends know each other very well. And he is saying that he is the most dishonest, the greatest rascal around. And he says,

"How can you know him very well? I am his best friend."

Friendship and enmity are the two faces of one mind. Stop in the middle! And Buddha stopped in the middle...and he helped many people to stop in the middle. It is just like walking on a tightrope. Have you observed a tightrope walker, what he is doing? One of the deepest truths of life is revealed there. Whenever he feels that he will fall to the left, he immediately moves to the right. It may not be so visible to you, because you think he is moving to the right, leaning to the right. But whenever he leans to the right, he knows that he was going to fall towards the left. Just to balance, when he feels he is going to fall to the right, he immediately leans towards the left; the opposite has to be chosen to get balance.

When you love a person too much in the morning, in the evening you have to hate him, otherwise you will fall down from the rope – it is tightrope walking. If you love a person too much, you have leaned too much to the left; now you will fall. To gain balance you have to lean to the right. Lovers are always fighting; that's just a sort of balancing, nothing else, nothing serious. It is natural – unless you get down off the rope, that's another thing.

That's what Buddha says: he says, "Don't lean to the right, don't lean to the left." Then what will happen? You will fall down from the rope. And that rope is the mind, that rope is the ego; you have to balance it, continuously balance it. So...it looks so paradoxical.

Whenever you hate your beloved, your wife, your friend, really you are trying to get balance so that you can love again. Otherwise, you will fall down from the mind. And without mind there is no love, no hate – at least, the hate that you know, the love that you know; they are not there. A different kind of compassion arises which is beyond the duality, but that arises only when you have lost the rope, lost the effort to balance on the rope. When you are lost, your ego is lost – ego is a subtle balance.

A philosopher came to Buddha one day and asked, "Without words, without the wordless, will you tell me the truth?"

He is asking something impossible; but near a buddha the impossible becomes possible – and only near a buddha the impossible become possible. There all laws, all ordinary laws, are broken.

What is he asking? He is asking: *"Without words and without the wordless, will you tell me the truth?"* This has happened many times. It also happened once before with Buddha: another man came, but the man must have been totally different qualitatively, because Buddha behaved differently.

A buddha has no fixed answers. He has no obsession, because he has no-mind. Whenever a person comes before him, he is just like a mirror – he reflects the person. Another man asks the same question – the man came and asked, "Sir, can you tell me something about the truth without using words?"

Buddha said, "Then you will have to ask without using words. You ask, and I will tell. If you can't ask without using words, how do you expect...? So go, train yourself! Be ready to ask it without using words, then come."

But to this philosopher, Buddha didn't reply in that way. And really this man was asking a different question, because this man was different. The question carries the meaning of the person. The question has no meaning in the words. It carries you, your quality. You can ask the same question, but it cannot mean the same. If you are different the question will be different. A word carries meaning from the person. A word in itself is meaningless. You may consult dictionaries, and you may come to know the meaning of the words, but that is not a real, live meaning, it is dead. When a person uses a word he gives it a live meaning, a real meaning. The significance comes from the person.

This man asked...what had he asked? A very subtle question. He said, *"Without words, and without the wordless, will you tell me the truth?"*

Without words, it is easy – you can remain silent. But without the wordless it becomes impossible, because if you remain silent you are using the wordless. And the man has asked, "Don't use words, don't use no-words, and tell me the truth." Silence won't help, words won't help. Language will not be of much use, and silence also is not of much use. Then what is Buddha going to do?

The Buddha kept silence – but this silence is different.

There are two types of silence. When you keep silence, it is a forced stillness. Words are there within you, noise is there; silence is just on the surface. You look silent; you are not silent. This is one type of silence that you know. There is another type of silence – that on the surface you are also silent, and you can be forced inside also to be silent. If you are in danger – somebody threatens you, that he is going to kill you – then you will become silent inside also, but this silence will be wordless. The first silence, when on the surface you were silent – inside there were words and chattering – was silence with word. This second silence will be wordless silence, there will be no noise within – because in a dangerous situation, in a shock, the noise has stopped.

But still it is not a buddha's silence. A buddha's silence is a third type of silence which you have not known. It is neither with noise nor with no-noise. Buddha is silent; not that he has forced his words to be silent – it is not a stillness with effort – he is simply silent because there is nothing else to do. This silence is positive, not the opposite of words. This silence is in the middle, not on the other extreme. One extreme is words, the other extreme is wordlessness. This silence is just in the middle: there is no word, there is no wordlessness. He is simply silent – not against noise.

If you are against noise, then your silence can be disturbed very easily. You know many people who are praying or meditating, and a child starts laughing and giggling and they are disturbed. There is some noise on the street, traffic noise; there is somebody honking the horn, and they are disturbed. A silence that is forced can be disturbed very easily. Only a silence that is forced can be disturbed. But if you are really silent in the sense of a Buddha, a child starts giggling, a bird starts singing, somebody honks the horn – the noise will be there, but you are not disturbed. The noise will come and pass, just as in an empty room: the noise comes from this door and goes from that door. There is nobody inside who can be disturbed.

But if you have a forced silence, then you are there, the ego is there – just riding on the mind, just forcing the mind, just making every effort to be silent. This is a constrained, strained silence. It can be disturbed very easily, even a child can disturb it. Then what type of buddhahood is this? This is no buddhahood, this is just a false coin.

Remember, while meditating this will be your deepest problem. Ordinarily you are chattering. You can move to the opposite end easily; you can force the chattering not to be there. It is just like a child playing, running around, doing many things uselessly, and you threaten him that he will be punished: "Sit in that corner!" And you are strong and the child is helpless, so he sits in the corner, looks very buddhalike – but bubbling, exploding within, just getting ready to get any chance when he can start running again.

Look at a child when you have forced him to be silent, that will be the second type of silence. He is not moving; if you force him too much he will not even move the body, he will close his eyes – but what is he doing? Forcing himself, fighting with himself; constant effort. He is pushing himself down, sitting on his own chest. He will not be able to breathe because he is afraid – because if you breathe then movement starts.

That's why nobody breathes, really. You have lost the dimension of breathing from your childhood when you were forced. Everybody breathes just from the upper lungs. The breath cannot go deep because you are afraid. From your very childhood, you have been forced....

Look at a child sleeping. See what is happening: his chest remains unmoving, his belly moves. His breath goes to the deepest, to the very bottom. His belly moves, his chest is unmoving. This child is still not part of society, he is not a citizen, he is still wild. You will have to train him, then you will have to use force.

And whenever you say to a child, "Don't do this!" how can he manipulate himself? The first thing is not to breathe. Whenever you suppress something you start shallow breathing. Suppression and shallow breathing are synonymous. Whenever you throw your suppression, you express; breathing goes deep. Only while you are fast asleep the breathing goes deep, because in sleep you cannot suppress, the ego has fallen unconscious. So in sleep you breathe from the belly; that is the right sort of breathing. Or while making love your breathing goes deep; it has to go, because all suppressions are around sex, and if you are making love, if you allow sex, then all suppressions are thrown away. Then the breath goes deep, it goes to the belly; you again breathe like a child, you again become wild, you again become natural, you again become spontaneous.

Look at a child when you have threatened him – and look at your monks in the monasteries. You have threatened them also. Afraid of hell, in greed for heaven, they are sitting there, suppressed. Their silence is of the other pole, the other extreme; they are wordless, they have forced the word to disappear, but they are not beyond the two.

Buddha remained silent. Buddha is of the third dimension. He would not say anything – words are not allowed. He would not suppress the word, because the wordlessness was not allowed. He simply remained there, not thinking, not meditating – simply there like a tree.

For five hundred years after Buddha, his statue was not made. For five hundred years there was no picture of Buddha; and whenever Buddha was to be represented, people just drew the bodhi tree. That was beautiful, because he was just like a tree. Can you say this tree is silent? You cannot say that, because this tree is never noisy so how can it be silent? Can you say this tree is meditating? How can it meditate? It has never thought, there has been no thinking, so how can it meditate? Then where is this tree? This tree is in the third dimension where no chattering exists and no non-chattering exists. This tree is in the middle, exactly in the middle.

You may not be a buddha, but this tree is a bodhi tree. And if you can sit under a tree, just like the tree, you will become a buddha. And any tree could become a bodhi tree, all trees are; just buddhas are needed to discover which tree is a bodhi tree. Sit under any tree, and if you are in the middle, the tree becomes the bodhi tree. All trees

are, only somebody is needed to reveal the fact, because trees don't
believe in advertisement – otherwise, they will reveal.

> *The Buddha kept silence.*
> *The philosopher bowed and thanked Buddha,*
> *saying, "With your loving kindness, I have cleared*
> *away my delusions and entered the true path."*

Seems to be miraculous, or absurd, because Buddha has not said
anything and he has understood – and I have been saying things
and you have not understood. There were many with Buddha
also with whom he was talking and talking, and they did not
understand – and this man understood without words, without
wordlessness. What happened? What type of communication happened in that moment when Buddha kept silent?

No knowledge was transferred, obviously – because you cannot
transfer knowledge without words, you cannot transfer knowledge
without wordlessness. There are two types of knowledge: one, ordinary knowledge which can be transferred through words. There is
another kind of knowledge, occult, which can be transferred
through wordlessness – occult, telepathic. You need not say it, but it
can be transferred. Both were not allowed.

That philosopher said, "Don't use words and don't use no-words.
I am fed up with both. I am fed up with all extreme polarities. I have
moved into logic too much – from this to that. I have lived all the
possibilities of logic...and enough! You simply give me the truth
without word and without wordlessness."

And what happened, what type of transfer? What communion
happened in this moment? In a single moment it happened. And
the philosopher bowed and thanked Buddha and said, "With your
loving kindness, I have cleared away my delusions and entered the
true path."

When a Buddha is silent, and if you also can be silent, then *being*
is transferred, not knowledge; not what Buddha knows, but what
Buddha is. Being is transferred. Suddenly he enters you, if you are

silent. And this man who was genuinely asking about the true path, and who was asking not to use words and not to use wordlessness, who was denying all duality, was ready. Buddha kept silent. The philosopher looked at Buddha – the look was there. He was attentive, he gave his total attention. What was happening?

He was not thinking – he had finished that, he had thought enough. That is why I say that whenever a philosopher comes, it is a transformation. He was fed up with it. You are still not fed up with it. You still cling to it, because you have not thought to the very end. You still hope that some day, through thinking, you may come to a conclusion, because you have not gone to the very end. If you go to the very end you will know that thinking never gives any conclusions, it is never conclusive. It only gives you the feeling that soon the door is to open. The door opens, of course, but only opens into another room.

Then there is another door. It also opens, but into another room. You are never out of it; the house seems to be infinite, millions of rooms. From one room you enter another, from another you enter another, and you go on moving and always hoping, "This door will lead me out." It leads only again into a room.

If you have gone to the very end, as this man had gone, then you can listen in silence. He was not waiting for any answer, because he knows answers cannot be given without words, answers cannot be given without wordlessness – all answers will be either this or that.

Buddha kept silent. That man looked at Buddha. In that look the two personalities dissolved. They were not two – in that moment there was one; two bodies, two hearts throbbing, but one being, all the boundaries transcended. Buddha trespassed him, he entered. It is a transfer of being. The man tasted what Buddha is, not what he knows. He does not know much – you can defeat Buddha very easily. You can easily know more, now more knowledge is available; that is not the question. But Buddha has more being.

Gurdjieff used to ask every seeker, whosoever would come to him...the first question Gurdjieff used to ask was whether you are in search of knowledge or of being. "You want to know more, or do you want to *be* more?" These are basically different dimensions. And if somebody would say, "I want to know more," Gurdjieff would say, "This door is closed. I am not here to impart knowledge to you. You go...there are many departments, universities, colleges; they are imparting knowledge – you go there. When you are fed up with knowledge, then come and knock. If I am alive, this door is open, but this door is open only for those who are in search of being."

What are you going...? Even if you come to know, how is it going to help? A man can know everything about water, but how is it going to satisfy the thirst? It is so patently foolish! You may know that H_2O is the basis of all water, and a man is dying of thirst in a desert and you write the formula on paper that this is the secret of water. He will say, "Okay, this is the secret. But what about my thirst?"

A man is dying without love and you go on feeding him knowledge about love. How is it going to help? There are millions of books about love, but not even a single lover can be satisfied by them. How is it going to help? A man is dying; he is dying and you talk about immortality. This is not going to feed him. This is not going to create immortality for him.

Being is needed; somebody to impart being, not knowledge. Knowledge is about and about; being is at the center, knowledge is at the periphery. You have come to me...have you come to gather more knowledge? Then you have come to a wrong person; then you are wasting your time. But if you are in search of being, then something is possible.

At that moment this miracle happened, the mystery of Buddha opened. It always opens in silence, just like a flower opens at midnight. Nobody knows: it opens in silence. If somebody is there who can wait patiently, then the flower can impart, share his being. Buddha entered in that moment.

Ananda, who was Buddha's chief disciple, couldn't understand what was happening, because he was after knowledge. He was needed in a way, but he was not the right seeker, and it is because of Ananda that we know all that Buddha said. He collected – he was the tape recorder. But now tape recorders are available, so I don't need any Ananda. And that was not good – a thing that can be done by a mechanical device should not be done by a man, because doing it he becomes mechanical.

Ananda could repeat every single word Buddha used in forty years. His was one of these rare memories. When Buddha died he repeated the whole forty years – thousands of pages, and he recorded them. He was needed, but he was not the real seeker – a recorder, and a good recorder, but for himself he was missing something.

If you are recording what I am saying, you are missing something. Don't be a memory before me, don't record – understand! Because when you are in the effort to record, you misunderstand. And there are many people who think, "First record it, then we will try and understand it."

I have seen many people who take notes. Here I am talking and they are taking notes. Here they are missing me, and at home they will look at their notes and then try to understand them. There are people who will go to the Himalayas, and then what they will do there? They will just hunt for good scenery and pictures and take photographs. There the Himalayas don't exist, only the camera. Then back home they will look at the album and enjoy them. You could have bought pictures, there was no need to go to the Himalayas. Professional photographers are doing that – there is no need for you to go – and you cannot do better than the professionals, your photographs will be amateurish. But then, sitting at home, you will enjoy them. You missed the Himalayas and you have brought only secondhand photographs.

Try to understand what I am saying. Try to be! Don't record it, there is no need. Just forget what I said. If you have really understood, it will follow you like a fragrance. No need to carry it in the memory, it will be part of your being.

In that moment, the philosopher understood. He bowed down in deep gratitude. And what did he say? The words are very significant. He said: *"With your loving kindness..."* Not, "With your great wisdom..." No! Not, "You know so much, you are all-knowing. Your wisdom, your knowledge..." No, that was not the point – *"With your loving kindness..."*

Buddha says that when one becomes enlightened, he has two things in him – they flower simultaneously. One is *karuna* – kindness, loving kindness – the other is wisdom, *prajna:* these two things flower in him. So if you are a seeker after knowledge, he will talk to you through his wisdom, but that is secondary. But if you are a seeker of being, he will talk to you through his loving kindness – through his karuna. Wisdom can miss the target, but karuna never misses, loving kindness never misses.

When this man said, "Without words and without no-words, will you tell me the truth?" he was saying, "I am not here to know more. I have already done too much of that; I have gathered much knowledge but it never gives you freedom. Rather, on the contrary, it becomes an imprisonment. Now I am here to know something about being, to be myself. I want the taste not the words. I want to enter."

Buddha remained silent, looked from his whole being at the man with a deep-flowing love and kindness. Whenever you look towards somebody with deep love something flows from you to the other person, just like a river flows to the ocean. But the other person needs to be just like a valley, only then it can flow; otherwise it cannot flow.

Just the other day somebody asked me, "I have come to see you; you are sitting on the chair and I am sitting down. Why? Why not another chair for me?"

I said, "It is possible and I am not losing anything in it. You can have an even taller chair than me, or you can just go on the roof and sit there; but I am not losing anything. You will lose much because it is simply symbolic."

You have to be a valley, only then the river can flow, just like the water flows towards the valley. You have to be a valley – a deep humbleness, a receptivity, a womb – so that you can receive.

This man remained silent before Buddha – humble, ready to receive. And Buddha looked at him with a deep love, infinite love, he flowed into him...he got the taste. He lived Buddha for a moment. He had the glimpse, as if for a single moment the darkness disappeared and there was lightning. For a single moment, when Buddha's being touched this man, there was lightning – everything changed.

He bowed down in deep gratitude and said, "*With your loving kindness, I have cleared away my delusions...*" Delusions cannot be cleared away through theories. No philosophy can help. Delusions are very real; they need something more real than they are, only then can they be dispelled.

If you are in the delusion of sex, no theories will be of any help. Only a love flowing towards you will dispel them, because love is a higher reality than sex. If you are in delusions about the world, only a buddha can dispel them. If he flows in you, for that moment there is no world. For that moment only Buddha existed, there was no world. For that moment, even the seeker was not there. He said:

> "*I have cleared away my delusions and entered
> the true path.*"
> *After the philosopher had gone Ananda asked
> Buddha...*

He must have been puzzled, "What is happening?" Buddha has not said anything. If he had, Ananda would have recorded it. If I keep silence, this tape recorder will miss. The tape recorder, if it can ask, will ask, "What happened?" – because the tape recorder can only record the visible, the sound, the physical. The spiritual is completely beyond it.

Ananda was deeply puzzled – "What is happening?" He must have been ready: "This man has raised a great question. Now what is Buddha going to say?" And then Buddha said nothing. Not only that – it happened many times that Buddha would not say anything, that was not new – but this man bowed down as if he had received something. And he said, "I have entered the true path." And he said, "Through your loving kindness, all my delusions are cleared away."

Ananda was present and he missed. How will *you* be able to understand what happened? Why had Ananda missed? He was not humble; that remained the whole problem for him. He was a cousin-brother of Buddha, an elder cousin-brother – that created the whole trouble. He always deep down believed that he was older than Buddha – and he knows this man from his very childhood: "He may have become wise in some ways, he may be a little further ahead than me, but I am his elder brother." That continued in his unconscious, created the barrier.

It is very difficult...if a Jesus is born to your family, it is very difficult for the mother, for the father, for the brothers, sisters, for the family, for the town, to recognize him. Impossible! – because how can you believe that a miracle can happen in *your* family? How can you believe that a miracle has happened to this person, and has not happened to you? No, it is impossible. You know yourself well, you know others also. Then either this man is deceiving, or something of minor importance has happened which can happen to you also – a little effort is needed, no other problem is there.

This remained the barrier, and Ananda remained blind. He asked after the philosopher had gone what the philosopher had attained, "Because I don't see anything being communicated. I don't see anything happening, and this man says he has attained the path, he has entered. What has happened?"

The Buddha replied – and the reply is beautiful. He said, *"A good horse runs even at the shadow of the whip."*

There are three types of horses – all the three types are here! First type: unless you beat him, he will not budge. You beat him and he will somehow carry the burden a little. You stop beating and he stops. You have to be constantly on him, beating, whipping – only then a little progress is made.

Then there is another type of horse: so much beating is not

needed. Just once you threaten him or you are going to beat him, and he will move.

And then there is a third type of horse, the best. Just the shadow of the whip, not even the whip, just the shadow of the whip – you need not even raise the whip, just the possibility, and he will run. This third type of horse attains enlightenment, in a single moment.

Buddha did nothing. He neither whipped this man, nor threatened him with hell and heaven. He didn't even say anything, he remained silent. And in this silence the shadow was seen. It was enough.

It happened once: Three ministers of Akbar, the great Moghul, did something wrong. It was a crime, so he asked the one, "What should I do? What punishment?"

The man said, "It is enough that you asked." He went home and committed suicide. The second man was sent to the jail for two years, and the third man was sent to the gallows.

Other ministers became very puzzled because the crime was the same; they were all partners in one crime and all three had confessed. So they asked, "What type of justice is this, that one man is not even told anything, he is left to go home? Another has been sentenced for two years, and the third to the gallows?"

Akbar said, "They are three different types of horses. For the first, just the shadow of the whip was enough. I asked him what type of punishment he would like, and he said this is enough. He went home, committed suicide. This was too much! Enough punishment had been given.

"The second man has been sent to jail for two years because less than that won't do. Now he is continuously thinking: 'It was bad that I did it, and as soon as I am out of the jail I will do some good deeds so the balance is regained.' He is not feeling any guilt, just missed, and he will regain. He is thinking and planning how to come out and how....

"The third man – even life imprisonment would not be enough, because he doesn't feel at all that any crime has been done. Rather, on the contrary, he thinks it was because he was not clever enough, that's why he has been caught. Next time he will be more clever, he will learn the secrets, he will learn the tricks – more and better – that's all. He feels no guilt. No punishment can help this man, this man has to be removed from society. And the first man has removed himself because this was too much."

> Said Buddha: *"A good horse runs even at the shadow of the whip."*

If you are understanding, the shadow is enough; no hell is needed for you. Those are created for the third type of horse: those who will not listen. No heaven is needed for you, for your greed and gratification; life is enough if you understand.

And if you feel, you will start changing through your feeling. A mutation happens if you become more and more sensitive towards life. The very sensitivity gives you awareness, alertness. Otherwise, even a Buddha cannot help.

I have heard: Mulla Nasruddin fingered a banker who was coming out of his office and said, "What about two *annas* for a cup of coffee?"

The Mulla was looking so distraught, so sad, that the man felt for him, and he said, "Here is one rupee. Take it and have eight cups of coffee." So Mulla went.

Next day he was again there on the steps of the office, and as the banker came out, he punched his face, on the nose.

The man said, "Hey, what are you doing? And this is after I gave you one rupee just yesterday? What type of thankfulness is this?"

Mulla said, "You and your lousy eight cups of coffee." And he punched him again on his nose and said, "They kept me awake the whole night!"

Nobody has said to him, "Go and take eight cups of coffee right now!" Don't take even a buddha in too much of a dose, it will keep you awake the whole night – and you may like to punch my nose! Be understanding, sensitive. Move according to your understanding, your possibility, your capacity. Look always at the shadow of the whip, and move according to the shadow. Be more alert, more and more alert, otherwise even religion can be poison; otherwise you can fall into hell because of a buddha.

Buddha is not the certainty, he is not the guarantee. Finally your own awareness... If you are aware, by and by, you will see that less and less thoughts come to the mind. The old pail breaks. The water flows out. It makes no reflection of the moon, and only when the reflection is gone can you look at the sky, at the real moon. No water, no moon.

Enough for today.

ninakawa smiles

NINAKAWA SMILES

Just before Ninakawa passed away the Zen Master Ikkyu visited him. "Shall I lead you on?" Ikkyu asked.

Ninakawa replied, "I came here alone, and I go alone. What help could you be to me?"

Ikkyu answered, "If you think you really come and go, that is your delusion. Let me show you the path in which there is no coming and going." With his words, Ikkyu had revealed the path so clearly that Ninakawa smiled and passed away.

*d*eath is the crescendo, the highest peak that life can attain. In the moment of death much is possible. If you have been preparing and preparing, meditating and waiting, then at the moment of death enlightenment is very easily possible – because death and enlightenment are similar. A master, one who is enlightened, can easily make you enlightened at the moment of death. Even before, whenever it happens, you have to be ready to die.

What happens in death? Suddenly you are losing your body, suddenly you are losing your mind. Suddenly you feel you are going away from yourself – all that you believe to be yourself. It is painful, because you feel you are going to be drowned into emptiness. You will be nowhere now, because you were always identified with the body and the mind, and you never knew the beyond; you never knew yourself beyond the body and the mind. You got so fixed and obsessed with the periphery that the center was completely forgotten.

In death you have to encounter this fact: that the body is going, now it cannot be retained any more. The mind is leaving you – now you are no more in control of the mind. The ego is dissolving – you cannot even say 'I'. You tremble with fear, on the verge of nothingness. You will be no more.

But if you have been preparing, if you have been meditating – and preparation means if you have been making all efforts to use death, to use this abyss of nothingness – rather than being pulled into it you have been getting ready to jump into it, it makes a lot of difference. If you are being pulled into it, grudgingly – you don't want to go into it and you have been snatched – then it is painful. Much anguish! And the anguish is so intense that you will become unconscious in the moment of death. Then you miss.

But if you are ready to jump there is no anguish. If you accept and welcome it, and there is no complaint – rather, you are happy and celebrating that the moment has come, and now I can jump out of this body which is a limitation, can jump out of this body which is a confinement, can jump out of this ego which has always been a suffering – if you can welcome, then there is no need to become unconscious. If you can become accepting, welcoming – what Buddhists call *tathata,* to accept it, and not only to accept, because the word accept is not very good, deep down some nonacceptance is hidden in it – no, if you welcome, if it is such a celebration, an ecstasy, if it is a benediction, then you need not become unconscious.

If it is a benediction, you will become perfectly conscious in that moment. Remember these two things: if you reject, if you say no, you will become totally unconscious; if you accept, welcome, and say yes with your full heart, you will become perfectly conscious. Yes to death makes you perfectly conscious; no to death makes you perfectly unconscious – and these are the two ways of dying.

A Buddha dies totally accepting. There is no resistance, no fight between him and death. Death is divine; *you* die fighting.

If a man has been preparing, getting ready, at the moment of death the master can be miraculously helpful. Just a word at the right moment and the flame inside suddenly explodes, you become enlightened – because the moment is such, so intense, you are so concentrated at one point.

This is happening in this story. Ikkyu is one of the greatest masters, a very rare, revolutionary, nonconformist. Once he stayed in a temple. The night was very cold and there were three wooden Buddhas in the temple, so he burned one Buddha to warm himself. The priest became aware – he was fast asleep, it was in the middle of the night and the night was very cold – he became aware that something was going on, so he looked.

Buddha was burning! – and this man Ikkyu was sitting, happy, warming his hands. The priest became mad; he said, "What are you doing? Are you a madman? – and I thought you to be a Buddhist monk, that's why I allowed you to stay in the temple. And you have done the most sacrilegious act."

Ikkyu looked at the priest and said, "But the buddha within me was feeling very cold. So it was a question whether to sacrifice the living Buddha to the wooden one, or to sacrifice the wooden one to the living one. And I decided for life."

But the priest was so mad with anger, he couldn't listen to what Ikkyu was saying. He said, "You are a madman. You simply get out of here! You have burned Buddha."

So Ikkyu started to poke the burned Buddha – ashes were there, the statue was almost completely finished. He started to poke with a stick. The priest asked, "What are you doing?"

He said, "I am trying to find the bones of Buddha."

So the priest laughed, he said, "You are either a fool or a madman. And you are absolutely mad! You cannot find bones there, because it is just a wooden Buddha."

Ikkyu laughed, he said, "Then bring the other two. The night is still very cold and the morning is still far away."

This Ikkyu was a very rare man. He was turned out immediately, out of the temple. In the morning he was sitting just on the side of the street outside the temple – worshipping a milestone, putting flowers, doing his prayers. So the priest said, "You fool! In the night you misbehaved with Buddha. What have you done? You have committed a sin, and now what are you doing with this milestone? This is not a statue."

Ikkyu said, "When you want to pray, everything is a statue. At that time the buddha within was feeling very cold. At this time the buddha within is feeling very prayerful."

This man Ikkyu had thousands of disciples all over the country, and he used to wander from one place to another to help disciples. This story is about one of his disciples, Ninakawa. He was just on the verge, almost enlightened. But 'almost enlightened' means nothing; you can move back, from the last point also you can fall.

Unless it has happened, it has not happened. From the very last moment, when only one step remains and you will become an enlightened one, you can come back. This Ninakawa was almost enlightened but still in the grip of the scriptures, because unless you reach to the truth, it is very difficult to get out of the grip of the scriptures.

It is very difficult to get out of the prison of words. It happens only when you are really enlightened. Then you can see that words are just words: nothing is there, they are not substantial, they are made of the stuff dreams are made of. They are just ripples in the mind, nothing else; sounds in the mind. And the meaning? Meaning is given by us; it is not there, no word is meaningful. And any word can become meaningful by common agreement.

So it is just a social phenomenon, not concerned with truth at all. But people live by words: if someone says something against Jesus and you are a Christian you will be ready to kill him, or be ready to be killed – it is a question of life and death. Someone says something against Mohammed, a Mohammedan gets mad. Just a word – 'Mohammed' is just a word, 'Jesus' is just a word – but people live by words.

I have heard: Once Mulla Nasruddin caught hold of a man on the street and said, "I am in a very difficult situation: my wife is hungry, my children are ill. Will you help me a little?"

The man looked at Nasruddin; he was really in a sad plight. He asked, "Why should I help you? But one thing I would like to ask: what brought you to this sad plight? How did you become so miserable? What has happened to you?"

Nasruddin said, "It is a long story. But to say it in short: just a few years ago I was also a businessman like you, and beggars used to catch hold of me on the street. Everything was going wonderfully. Then a catastrophe...."

The man became interested. He said, "Then what happened?"

Mulla Nasruddin said, "My business was very good, money was pouring in continuously. I was a very industrious worker, totally absorbed in my business. And I had a motto on my table: 'Think constructively! Act decisively!' and money continued pouring in. And then..." Mulla Nasruddin's frame started convulsing and he said, "then my wife burned the motto. That motto, 'Think constructively! Act decisively!' – the whole thing depended on that motto. And my wife burned it! That was the greatest catastrophe, and that has led me to this sad plight."

Have you ever thought, if your scriptures are burned, what will happen to you? If your mottos are burned, what will happen to you? If your words are burned, what will happen to you? You will be in a very sad plight. That's why, if someone says anything against the Bible, you become mad. It is not because he is saying something against the Bible – he is burning your motto. You depend on the word. And you depend on the word because you don't know what truth is. If you come to know what truth is you will throw all the words, you will burn all the mottos.

Mulla Nasruddin seems to be foolish – he is not. He is just a representative human being, the most representative, the normal. He is you, in all your absurdities – but magnified, of course.

This Ninakawa was struggling his whole life, meditating, sitting, using many techniques, trying in every way to become calm and quiet and still; but he was still in the grip of scripture. The day he was dying Ikkyu visited him. That was the moment now to push this man into the infinite abyss. He may miss, because at the time of death, if scripture is there, you will miss.

You need to be totally vacant, you need to be totally empty; only then can you meet death, because death is emptiness. And only the alike can know the alike, the same can understand the same. If you are filled, even with a single word, you will miss, because then the mind is there – and death has no mind, death has no thought; death is simply falling into emptiness.

So Ikkyu came to push this disciple at the last moment. He had been missing his whole life – he should not miss this last moment.

And I also tell you: if you miss your whole life, then there is only one possibility and only one hope – at the moment of death. But no need to wait for it, it can happen right now. If it is not happening right now, then go on trying. But get ready for death. If you are ready, I will be there to push you. If you are ready, then it is very easy: just a little jerk, and the mind blows.

> *Just before Ninakawa passed away the Zen Master Ikkyu visited him.*

Masters have been visiting always. It may not have actually happened, remember that; it may not have actually happened. It may be, it is possible, that nobody else than Ninakawa saw the master visiting him. It may have actually happened, but that is irrelevant. One thing is certain: that while Ninakawa was dying, just at the last moment the master was there. This dialogue happened with Ninakawa and Ikkyu. There may have been many others there, they may not have heard it at all; they may not have seen Ikkyu coming at all. It was or it was not a physical visit. But it happened, and it did...whatsoever was needed was done.

> *"Shall I lead you on?" Ikkyu asked. Ninakawa replied...*

A man of scripture, particularly Buddhist, because in Buddhism the guru is not accepted. Buddha is the greatest guru, but in Buddhism the guru is not accepted. They have a reason for it. Because the human mind is so complex, it creates trouble everywhere: the guru is to liberate you, but you can make a bondage out of him. Hindus have been teaching that without the guru, without the master, there is no liberation. And this is true, absolutely true, but by the time of Buddha it became a bondage.

Without the guru, without the master, there is no liberation. So people started becoming slaves of masters, because without them there is no liberation. Look at the human mind and the stupidity: a master is to liberate, but you can become a slave to the master because only *he* can liberate; then you can become just docile. Much slavery was created; nobody else on this earth has created such a deep slavery as Hindus. You cannot come across a single revolution in the whole history of Hinduism against the priest. No – the whole thing was so settled and so fixed and systematized, and everybody was aware that if you rebel against the priest there is no liberation – he is the guru, he is the master.

The untouchables – the *sudras* – have existed in the most miserable condition. They are the greatest of slaves and they have the longest history of slavery, but never have they revolted against it, because it was not possible. The guru, the master, the *brahmin* – he is the door to the divine. You have missed this life, and if you rebel you miss the other also – so remain a slave.

Then came Buddha, and he said, "No need for the guru" – not because there is no need for the guru: he said no need for the guru, and he meant no need to become a slave – but that was the only way to say it. So Buddha says, "Be a light unto yourself. Nobody is needed to lead you. Nobody is needed to guide you. You are enough unto yourself."

This is the greatest possibility of being free, of freedom. But you can misuse this also, this is the problem. Then you think that if there is no need for a master, then why listen to the Buddha? If there is no need for the master, then why go to the Buddha? If I am totally independent, then I am Buddha myself. That happened through Buddhism: slavery didn't happen, but deep egoism happened. But both are the two extremes: either you become an egoist – because no guru, no master, nobody to follow – or you become a slave, because without the guru there is no liberation.

Can't you be in the middle? Can't you just stand in the middle without moving to the extreme? If you can be in the middle, the mind disappears.

Ikkyu came, and he said, "Shall I lead you?"

Ikkyu asked the basic Buddhist question, and Ikkyu knows that if he is still burdened with the scripture he will say, "No, who can lead anybody? Nobody is a guru. Every soul is absolutely independent. I am a light unto myself." If he is burdened with the scripture, this will be the response. If he is not burdened with the scripture, then the response can be any – infinite possibilities open.

Ninakawa replied, "I came here alone..."
This is what Buddha says
"...I go alone. What help could you be to me?"

Everybody is born alone, goes alone; and in the middle of these two, coming and going, you may delude yourself that you are with somebody, but you still remain alone. Because if you are in the beginning alone and in the end alone, how in the middle can you be with somebody? The wife, the husband, the friend, the society, are all illusions. You remain alone, aloneness is your nature. You can be deluded, that's all. You can have dreams, that's all, but the other remains always the other and there is no meeting point. This is the basic Buddhist teaching to make man free.

That's why Buddha even denied God, because if there is God how can you be alone? He is always there. Even when you are in your bathroom he is there – because he is omnipotent, omnipresent. You cannot escape him; wherever you go he will be there. He is the cosmic eye, the cosmic spy, following you. Whatsoever you do, he will be looking! It is very difficult to escape God; if he is, then he is everywhere. You cannot hide – this is beautiful if you can understand – and religious people used it to help.

Hindus, Mohammedans, Christians, they have all used the omnipresence of God. It is a great help, because if you can really feel God following you like a shadow everywhere, you will become very, very much alert and aware – because he is there. You are not alone, you cannot relax into sin, you cannot relax into ignorance, sleepiness – he is there. The presence will make you alert.

This is the right use. But otherwise the presence can become a bondage, a heavy burden, anxiety.

I have heard about a Christian nun who would not even take her bath in the nude. No, she would continue to have her clothes on even under the shower, so somebody asked, "What are you doing?"

She said, "How I can be naked? – because God is everywhere." But if God is everywhere – in the bathroom – he is inside the clothes also, you cannot escape him. He is inside you. He is everywhere.

This can become a deep anxiety, just like when you are taking your bath, and you become aware that somebody is peeping through the keyhole – you become anxious. And God is the cosmic Peeping Tom – he is sitting at every keyhole; you cannot do anything without his knowing it; you make love and he is there. Whatsoever you do he knows, and everything is recorded.

This can become a deep anxiety, a neurosis; this can create guilt, and then you have missed. And remember: every key that can open a door can destroy the lock also if you use it wrongly. There is a way, a right way to use a key; only then it opens the lock. If you use it wrongly, the lock may be destroyed. And as the mind is, it always uses keys in a wrong way. Then somebody is needed who must say to you, "Throw this key, because this key is now useless. This is only destroying the lock, not helping you in any way."

Buddha said no guru is needed – because in his time the guru meant the brahmin. Krishnamurti is saying the same thing: no guru is needed. But there is another possibility – it may give you freedom. If it gives you freedom it is perfectly okay. But it may give you egoism and that's the problem, there is the rub. If it gives you egoism, you may not become a slave to somebody else, but you have become a slave to your own ego. And remember, nobody can be such a dangerous master as your ego can be. Nobody can make you so blind as your ego can make you. Nobody can lead you to such hells as your ego can lead you.

Ikkyu just wanted to know whether this man is still clinging to the scriptures, or he has come to understand Buddha. Understanding is different, clinging is different. Clinging is to the dead letter. If he has understood, then Buddha is the greatest master. If he has not understood, then he will not allow; even at the point of death, he will cling to the scriptures.

Ikkyu was standing there, and was asking, "Can I lead you? Shall I lead you on? ...Because the path is unknown. You have never been through it, I have been along it. I know how to die, I know how to celebrate death. I know how to lose yourself into death, and then you never lose; then the real self is born for the first time. I know the secret of dying and rebirth. Can I lead you on?"

> *Ninakawa replied* – he refused – he said: *"I came here alone, and I go alone. What help could you be to me?"*

And he was in need of help. If he was not in need of help he would have simply laughed, smiled; he would have said, "Thank you." There was no need to use these words from the scriptures. Why do you use scriptures? They are rationalizations. Whenever you are uncertain you use the scripture, because the scripture is very certain. Whenever you are in doubt, you use Buddha, Krishna, Christ, because they can hide your hesitation, they can hide your reality, they can give you a false confidence.

Whenever you are using others' words you are hiding your ignorance. This man was not saying, *"I came here alone"* – this was not his experience. He was not saying *"...and I go alone."* He was repeating words, and you cannot deceive a master with words.

> *Ikkyu answered, "If you think you really come and go..."*

These are the most beautiful words ever uttered – the essence of all the Upanishads, the essence of all Buddhas and Mahaviras, just in one sentence.

> *"If you think you really come and go, that is your*

delusion. Let me show you the path on which
there is no coming and no going."

This is really very difficult and subtle.

Says Ikkyu, "If *you* think you really come and go, then the ego is there. Who comes? Who goes? If you think you come and go, you don't know; then you are simply repeating Buddha's words" – there is the catch.

If you have come to know that, "I come alone, and I go alone," then there is no coming and no going, because the soul is never born, never dies. Life is an eternal continuum. It continues. It never comes, never goes. This body may have been born, this body may die – but that life, the energy, the self, the soul, or whatsoever you call the consciousness that exists in this body, has never been born and will not die. That consciousness is continuous. There has never been any break in it.

If you really know, then you know that there is no coming, no going. Who comes? Who goes? If you don't understand, if you have not realized this, then you will say, "I come alone." But then this 'I' is the ego; then this 'I' is not the self. When you say, "I go alone," the emphasis is on 'I' – and the 'I' is the bondage. If there is no 'I', suddenly you will see that you have never been born, and are never going to die; then there is no beginning and no end.

Says Jesus...somebody asked Jesus, "Are you the messiah we have been waiting for? Who are you? Tell us about you."

Jesus said, "Before Abraham was, I am."

Abraham must have been thousands of years before, and Jesus says, "Before Abraham was, I am." The sentence is really very absurd, logically absurd, grammatically wrong: "Before Abraham was, I am." Abraham is in the past; Jesus says, "Before he was..." and Abraham is the first prophet. There is every possibility that Abraham is just a changed name of Ram, because in old Hebrew it is not Abraham, it is Abram. And Ab simply means respect, just like Shree Ram; it is just to pay respect. There is every possibility that Abraham is no one else than Ram.

Says Jesus, "Before Abraham was, I am." For Abraham he uses the past tense: he has been and is no more; the manifestation was there and now is no more. But "I am," because "I am always: I was, I am here, I will be."

The innermost consciousness knows no birth, no death; knows no past, no present, no future; knows no time. It is eternal, and eternity is not part of time.

> Said Ikkyu, *"If you think you really come and go*
> – if you think that there is a coming and going –
> *you are in delusion. Let me show you the path on*
> *which there is no coming and going."*

What have buddhas been doing? They have simply been showing you that you are perfect – as you are. No change is needed. You have not to go anywhere, you have not to move a single inch. As you are, you are in your perfect glory, here and now. There is no coming and no going. Just become aware of the phenomenon that you are. Just become aware who you are! Just be alert! And then nothing is to be achieved, no effort is to be made, because from the very beginning, before Abraham was, you are. You have seen the creation of the world, you will see the end of the world, but there is no beginning to you and no end to you.

You are the witness, and the witness cannot have any beginning and cannot have any end. If you had been alert you would have seen your own birth. If you can die consciously, you will see that death is happening in the body and you are just an onlooker. So the body dies, and you are just the witness. And if you can be a witness in the death, then in the next life, in the birth, you will be a witness. You will see that the mind is choosing a womb: hovering all around the earth, finding a woman, a couple, making love – you will see it.

Just as if you are hungry: you go to the market, and you can be a witness that your eyes, your mind is looking at the hotels, restaurants, to find the right place where you can have your food. You are hungry, but if you get too identified with the hunger then you cannot be a witness. Otherwise, hunger is there, but you are not the hunger. How can you be the hunger? – otherwise who will know that you are hungry?

Hunger, to be known, needs someone else beyond the hunger who can look and see, who can become alert. If you can become alert in hunger, then you can see how your mind is searching for a right place to have your food. The same happens after death: your mind is in search of a right womb. You choose, you see what is happening.

If you are in search of a particular womb, if you are a very good soul or a very bad soul, then you may take many years to find a right womb – very difficult. If you are just an ordinary person, just normal, nothing special good or bad, neither a Hitler nor a Gandhi, then you can be born immediately; there is no need, because everywhere ordinary, normal, standard wombs are available. Then, this moment you die and the next moment you are born – not even a single moment is lost.

But for a Hitler it may take many, many years – and it is good, we are fortunate, because he is a very perverted soul, very perverted. You cannot imagine his perversion, he perverted everything. And whenever a man becomes perverted, the first thing to be perverted is his love, because sex remains the root of your being. The first thing to be perverted is sex. When sex goes wrong, everything goes wrong; when sex is natural, everything remains natural.

Study Hitler's sexual life and you will be simply amazed; you cannot believe what he was doing. He would find beautiful women, but would never make love to them. What would he do? You cannot imagine! He would force those beautiful women... he would sit down and he would force them that they should urinate on his head. What type of man...? What is he doing? And he enjoyed it very much: not only urination, they should also defecate on him. And the women felt very guilty – what is he doing? – but he was such a powerful man: if you don't follow him...he killed many. All his beloveds were either killed by him or they committed suicide –

because this is such a perversion! But he felt very good. What was the matter?

He was so guilty he wanted to punish himself; even through love he was punishing. He was so guilty, and the guilt was so strong...if you are so guilty you cannot love, because love can only come of the heart of one who is not guilty, who doesn't feel any guilt, who is just a child, innocent. Then love flows, then it becomes a celebration. But if you are guilty, then through love you start punishing yourself, or you start punishing the other. You cannot enjoy love, because you feel you are so guilty, so bad – how you can enjoy love? You create a hell out of love. This seems impossible, because outside his room Hitler is almost a god, people worship him. And inside his room he feels himself so inferior, guilty, condemned, that he wants to punish himself, even through love.

This type of man will not easily find a womb – almost impossible. For centuries he will have to wait, only then he can find such a womb, such a man and such a woman making love, who are so guilt-ridden, so condemned in themselves, only then can he choose the womb. But this happens unconsciously, so you need not worry much about it. You die unconsciously, unconsciously you are born – it happens automatically. The mind moves, just gropes in the dark and enters a womb. But if you die consciously, then the next birth is going to be conscious.

If you die consciously and are born consciously you will know that there is no birth and no death, only a body has been chosen. You remain the same, only the house changes. If you change your old clothes, do you say this is a new birth, I am born? No, because you have only changed the clothes; you remain the same.

This is how one who becomes alert comes to know that all changes are just changes of dresses and houses and places, situations, circumstances, but you remain the same; the center never changes, it is eternal.

Says Ikkyu, *"If you think you really come and go*
that is your delusion. Let me show you the path

on which there is no coming and going."

What is that path? Is there really a path? Because we have to use language, that's why he says 'path'. Otherwise there is no path, because a path always leads somewhere. No path can lead to you because you are already there. If you want to come to me there is a path, has to be. If you come to somebody you have to follow a path, go through a passage, a bridge, something or other – because you are moving outward. But if you want to go inward there is no path. You are already there. A sudden jerk is needed and you simply feel that you are there.

It is just like when you dream in the night: you fall into sleep in Poona, and in the dream you are back at your London home, or in New York, or in Calcutta, or in Tokyo, and in the dream you completely forget that you are in Poona. Then what is needed? Just a jerk. Somebody comes and wakes you up. Will you wake up in London, Tokyo, New York, or in Poona? It would have been very difficult, it will create a very absurd world, if you are dreaming of New York and suddenly somebody wakes you and you wake up in New York! Then this world would have been a nightmare. But you wake up in Poona; the dream disappears.

Buddhas have been teaching this: that there is no need to go anywhere, because you are already there where you want to go; but you are in a dream. Only in a dream have you moved from the center – you cannot move from there. You *are* there. For millions of lives you may have been dreaming, but you have not moved from the center where you are. Nobody can move. Just a jerk, just somebody to shock you...you become alert and suddenly the dream disappears. The dreamland and New York and London, they disappear, and you are here and now.

This jerk, this shock can be given very easily at the moment of death – because the whole body-mind is going through a great change. Everything is in chaos. In a chaos you can be made alert more easily because everything is uncomfortable. When everything is comfortable it is difficult to bring a man out of the dream – nobody really wants to come out of a comfortable dream. Only when the dream becomes a nightmare, then you scream.

I have heard: One night Mulla Nasruddin screamed so loudly that even the neighbors came to ask what has happened. Mulla Nasruddin was sitting on his bed weeping, tears flowing down, and his wife was consoling him, saying, "It was just a dream Nasruddin. Why are you creating so much nuisance? – the neighbors have come, there is a crowd."

Nasruddin said, "But the dream was such...let me first tell you the dream. In the dream I went to a wife auction – such beautiful women. One woman fetched ten thousand rupees, another five thousand, and many for thousands.

"I had no money. I tried and tried but there was no money. I looked in all my pockets" – and he had one pocket, he would never look in it – he said, "I even looked in that pocket."

There was a special pocket he would never look in. And if something was lost people would ask, "Have you looked in all the pockets? Why not in this one?"

He would say, "Because that still gives me hope. If I look in that pocket also, hope is gone, because I think there maybe still is a possibility...but I never look in it because I know well it is not there."

He said, "I looked even in that special pocket – and no money. I was weeping and crying."

But his wife was not interested in this. She asked, "Nasruddin, and were there wives there like me also?" She asked foolishly, as any woman will ask, because no woman is interested in other beautiful women; rather, she felt jealous. She asked, "What about wives like me? How much were they fetching?"

Nasruddin said, "That's why I screamed. Wives like you those people had put in bundles. One dozen, two dozen – they were selling wives like you at one rupee a bunch. That's why I screamed: no money to purchase, and that was what was happening to my wife!"

But he was crying and weeping even out of the dream.

Dreams are effective, they go deep, because in an unconscious mind the distinction is really very vague; what is dream and what is real is very vague. They are mixed, the boundaries are not so clear-cut, the boundaries are blurred.

Have you seen a child waking, and weeping because he has lost a toy he saw in the dream? "I am looking around for the toy – where has the toy disappeared to?"

But this child never dies in you. It dies only when you make much effort to become alert; only then the dream and the reality become clear-cut distinctions. And once the vagueness is lost, once the boundaries are not blurred, once you become aware what is dream, what is reality, the dream stops – because then the dream cannot continue. If you have become aware the dream cannot continue. Even in a dream, if you become aware that this is a dream, the dream will stop immediately.

So you never become aware in a dream that this is a dream, you always feel this is real. For anything to continue, your feeling is needed that this is real. You give reality through the feeling. If you withdraw the feeling, the dream disappears and only the reality remains.

It is a dream that you are in this world, and it is the reality that you exist in the divine. It is a dream that you are in the market; it is the reality that you have never moved from the very center of existence, from God. It is a dream you have moved in the market – and a dream can continue, there is no time limit. If you think you are the body, this is a dream – you have never been a body. If you think you are born and you die, this is a dream – you have never been born and you can never die; that is impossible.

Said Ikkyu, "This is your delusion if you say, 'I come and I go.' There is no one to come and no one to go. And there is no place to come to and no place to go to. Let me show you the pathless path. Because then there can be no path – because if there is no one to come and no one to go, no place to come to and no place to go to, then how can the path exist? So let me show you the pathless path on which there is no coming and no going."

*With his words, Ikkyu had revealed the path so
clearly that Ninakawa smiled and passed away.*

It happened! You have heard the words – but you are not
Ninakawa, you are not that ready, you are not on your deathbed –
that's the problem. You are still hoping for something in life, your
dream still has much meaning for you, you have investments in
your dream. You may have a desire to come out of the dream, but
this desire is only half-hearted. The other part goes on saying,
"Dream it a little more, it is so beautiful."

One night Mulla Nasruddin called his wife and said, "Bring my
specs, because I have been seeing a beautiful dream and much more
is promised to me. Bring my specs, because the place is not so well
lighted, and I cannot see clearly."

You may be having nightmares; in those moments you feel,
"How to drop out of the dream?" – but you have beautiful dreams
also; not only hellish dreams, you have heavenly dreams. And that's
the problem: unless you become aware that even a heavenly dream
is a dream and useless, you are not on the deathbed. Your desire
continues, you go on watering the world of dreams, feeding it,
helping it to grow.

Ninakawa was on his deathbed, he was dying, there was no
future left. He was in a chaos. The whole system, the whole adjustment of body, mind and soul was getting looser and looser. Things
were falling apart, he was not together. The nightmare was intense,
because it is most intense in death. He was simply miserable in that
moment: death and no future.

If there is no future you cannot dream, because dreams need
space, time to move. That's why death looks so dangerous, because
it allows no time to think. You cannot hope, because there is no tomorrow. Death does not kill you, it simply kills the tomorrow, and
tomorrow has been your very existence. You have never lived
today, you have been always postponing for tomorrow. And death

kills the tomorrow, it simply burns your calendar – suddenly the clock stops, time doesn't move.

Without time what can you do? How can the mind think, desire, dream? Death closes the door – that is the fear.

Why does death make you so afraid and trembling and scared? Because there seems to be no beyond, no possibility to escape from it. You ca..not do anything because you cannot think, and you know only one thing: thinking, nothing else. Your whole life has been a thinking. Now, death allows no thinking. Only a man who has been meditating and has realized no-thinking before death will not be afraid – because he knows that thinking is not life.

And he knows a different plenum of existence. He knows the depth, not the length of existence. He is not moving from this moment to that, he is not moving from today to tomorrow. He is moving in this moment, deeper and deeper and deeper; in today, deeper and deeper and deeper. He is moving here and now, in the depth.

You touch this moment and you move to another moment; you have a horizontal movement: from A to B, from B to C, from C to D. And a man who meditates goes on moving from A1 to A2 to A3 – in the depth – not to B. He has no tomorrow. This here and now is the only existence, then how can there be death for him? This moment you are alive; only in the next moment can you die. This moment no one has ever died. This moment you are alive, and this man who meditates moves into this moment – how can he die?

Death will happen on the periphery; he will come to know about it. It will be just as you come to know about a neighbor who is dead: he will come to know about it, that the body is dead – this will be news. He may even feel sorry for the body, but *he* is not dying.

Ninakawa was a meditator just on the verge of enlightenment, still clinging. You can take a jump into the abyss, but still you can cling to a creeper – and you can go on clinging, afraid. You are almost in the abyss, sooner or later you will fall, but still for a moment more the mind says, "Cling!" He was clinging to the scriptures, to the buddhas, to the words, the doctrines. He was still repeating knowledge. Just a creeper – sooner or later he will have to leave this, because when life leaves you, how can words be retained? They will leave you.

With this, Ikkyu's revelation, he understood, he left the clinging. He smiled and passed away.

You never smile. Either you weep or you laugh, but you never smile. A smile is just in the middle, it is difficult for you. Either you weep or you laugh – they are the possibilities, the two extremes. Try to find out what this phenomenon of a smile is.

Only a buddha smiles, because it is just in the middle. A smile has both a sadness in it, the sadness of the tears, and the happiness of laughter. A smile has both. Smiling is never simple laughter: it has the expansion of laughter and the depth of sadness – it is both. Look at Buddha, meditate on him, and you will see in his face both a sadness and a happiness; a blissful flowing of his being and still a deep sadness.

With these two chemicals, so to say, a smile is created. When you feel sad for everybody, when you feel sad for the whole existence because they are unnecessarily suffering…. You cannot imagine the sadness of a buddha, it is difficult for you. You only think that a buddha is happy. He is happy as far as he himself is concerned, but for you? You cannot conceive his difficulty – because he sees you, and you are unnecessarily suffering, and nothing can be done, you cannot be helped. A disease that is not there – and incurable! And he knows that just by the corner, just a turn of your being, and everything will be solved. But you will not take that turn. You will jump and you will do many things, but you will always miss that turn. You will grope in the dark, but somehow, miraculously, you always miss the door. You know how to miss the door, you are perfect in that: how to miss the door and always go on groping.

A buddha is in difficulty because he has realized something which is there with you already. The same blissful existence, the same beauty, the same ecstasy that he has, you have. And you go on crying, and you go on beating your chest, and you are in such a suffering – and nothing can be done. A sadness...

It is said about Buddha that when he reached the door – the final door beyond which there is no door, and you cannot come back; that is the ultimate – when he reached the door of nirvana, the door was opened for him and there was welcome. Because once in millions of years somebody reaches to the ultimate. But he turned his back towards the door and looked at the world – and they say he is still standing there, he has not entered.

The doorkeeper asked, "What are you doing? You have been endeavoring for this for many, many lives. Now the door is open, come in."

And Buddha said, "Unless everybody who is suffering out there enters, I cannot enter. I will be the last to enter." This is the sadness.

The story is really beautiful. Nobody can stand at that ultimate door, that's true; there is no door like that and no doorkeeper. You fall, and there is no way to stop yourself. The story is beautiful; that shows in a symbolic way the consciousness of a buddha – the trouble, his anguish, his suffering. It is not *his* suffering now, it is the suffering of others that makes him sad.

It is as if you have awakened but everybody else is fast asleep, and they are dreaming and dreaming nightmares – screaming, jumping, crying, weeping, and you know that these are just nightmares, but these people are so drunk and so fast asleep, you cannot help. If you try to wake them up they become angry. They say, "Why are you disturbing our sleep? Who are you?" You cannot wake them, and you have to see their suffering, and suffer it.

Buddha is sad – for you. Buddha laughs deeply, his whole being is filled with laughter – just like a tree has come to flower, everything has become a dance. And these both meet in him: the laughter that bubbles and goes on coming out – and still he cannot laugh because of you – and the sadness that you create. They both meet and the meeting creates a smile. A smile is both laughter and tears.

You cannot smile – you can laugh, you can weep. When you

weep, how can you laugh? Because in weeping it is always for yourself; it is a single element. When you laugh, you laugh; how can you weep? – because laughing is for yourself. In Buddha, the ego has disappeared, now he is no more, the meeting has happened with the all. Two elements meet: his consciousness which has become perfect, and all around millions of consciousnesses which *are* perfect, suffering – unnecessarily suffering, suffering without any cause – these two meet, and a sad and yet happy smile comes to his face.

He cannot weep because what you are doing is so foolish. He cannot laugh because that will be too hard on you. At the most he can smile. This happened, so a smile has become a symbol of one who has become enlightened.

> *With his words, Ikkyu had revealed the path so*
> *clearly that Ninakawa smiled and passed away.*

Then it was not a death, but just a passing – passing to another world, a passing to another birth; then nobody was dying. And if you can die with a smile you know the art of dying, and the whole of religion consists in the art of dying, nothing else than that.

Now I will repeat the first story we started, so that you don't forget it: forgetfulness is a trick.

These ten days we have been talking about No Water, No Moon. It will remain just a talk – words and words and words – if you are not ready to die. Be on your deathbed! Be a Ninakawa! Then these words are so clear, as Ikkyu's never were. I tell you: these words are as clear as Ikkyu's never were. You can also smile and pass away – remember:

> *The nun Chiyono studied for years, but was*
> *unable to find enlightenment.*
> *One night, she was carrying an old pail filled with*
> *water. As she was walking along, she was watching*

the full moon reflected in the pail of water.
Suddenly, the bamboo strips that held the pail
together, broke, and the pail fell apart. The water
rushed out; the moon's reflection disappeared –
and Chiyono became enlightened.
Afterwards, she wrote this poem:

This way and that way,
I tried to keep the pail together,
hoping the weak bamboo
would never break.

Suddenly the bottom fell out.
No more water;
no more reflection of the full moon
in the water –
emptiness in my hand.

Go with emptiness in your hand, because that's all...that's all I can offer to you, and nothing is greater than that. This is my gift: go with emptiness in your hand. If you can carry emptiness in your hand, then everything becomes possible. Don't carry possessions, don't carry knowledge, don't carry anything that fills the pot and becomes the water, because then you will be seeing only the reflection. In wealth, in possessions, in houses, in cars, in prestige, you will see only the reflection of the full moon. And the full moon is there waiting for you.

Let the bottom drop! Don't try this way and that way to protect the old pail. It is not worth it. Don't protect yourself, it is not worth it. Let the pail break down, let the water flow, let the moon in the water disappear, because only then will you be able to raise your eyes towards the real moon. It is always there in the sky – but emptiness in the hand is needed. Remain more and more empty, think yourself more and more empty, behave more and more as if you are empty. By and by, by and by, you will have the taste of it.

And once the taste comes, it is so beautiful.

Once you know the taste of emptiness, you have known the very meaning of life. Carry emptiness, drop the pail of water which is your ego, your mind and your thoughts, and remember: no water, no moon – emptiness in the hand.

Enough for today.

ABOUT THE AUTHOR

Most of us live out our lives in the world of time, in memories of the past and anticipation of the future. Only rarely do we touch the timeless dimension of the present – in moments of sudden beauty, or sudden danger, in meeting with a lover or with the surprise of the unexpected. Very few people step out of the world of time and mind, its ambitions and competitiveness, and begin to live in the world of the timeless. And of those who do, only a few have attempted to share their experience. Lao Tzu, Gautam Buddha, Bodhidharma…or more recently, George Gurdjieff, Ramana Maharshi, J. Krishnamurti – they are thought by their contemporaries to be eccentrics or madmen; after their death they are called "philosophers." And in time they become legends – not flesh-and-blood human beings, but perhaps mythological representations of our collective wish to grow beyond the smallness and trivia, the meaninglessness of our everyday lives.

Osho is one who has discovered the door to living his life in the timeless dimension of the present – he has called himself a "true existentialist" – and he has devoted his life to provoking others to seek this same door, to step out of the world of past and future and discover for themselves the world of eternity.

Osho was born in Kuchwada, Madhya Pradesh, India, on December 11, 1931. From his earliest childhood, his was a rebellious and independent spirit, insisting on experiencing the truth for himself rather than acquiring knowledge and beliefs given by others.

After his enlightenment at the age of twenty-one, Osho completed his academic studies and spent several years teaching philosophy at the University of Jabalpur. Meanwhile, he traveled throughout India giving talks, challenging orthodox religious leaders in public debate, questioning traditional beliefs, and meeting people from all walks of life. He read extensively, everything he could find to broaden his understanding of the belief systems and psychology of contemporary man. By the late 1960s Osho had begun to develop his unique dynamic meditation techniques. Modern man, he says, is so burdened with the outmoded traditions of the past and the anxieties of modern-day living that he must go through a deep cleansing process before he can hope to discover the thought-less, relaxed state of meditation.

In the early 1970s the first Westerners began to hear of Osho. By 1974 a commune had been established around him in Poona, India, and the trickle of visitors from the West was soon to become a flood. In the course of his work, Osho has spoken on virtually every aspect of the development of human consciousness. He has distilled the essence of what is significant to the spiritual quest of contemporary man, based not on intellectual understanding but tested against his own existential experience.

He belongs to no tradition – "I am the beginning of a totally new religious consciousness," he says. "Please don't connect me with the past – it is not even worth remembering."

His talks to disciples and seekers from all over the world have been published in more than six hundred volumes, and translated into over thirty languages. And he says, "My message is not a doctrine, not a philosophy. My message is a certain alchemy, a science of transformation, so only those who are willing to die as they are and be born again into something so new that they cannot even imagine it right now...only those few courageous people will be ready to listen, because listening is going to be risky.

"Listening, you have taken the first step towards being reborn. So it is not a philosophy that you can just make an overcoat of and go bragging about. It is not a doctrine where you can find consolation for harassing questions. No, my message is not some verbal communication. It is far more risky. It is nothing less than death and rebirth."

Osho left his body on January 19, 1990. His huge commune in India continues to be the largest spiritual growth center in the world attracting thousands of international visitors who come to participate in its meditation, therapy, bodywork and creative programs, or just to experience being in a buddhafield.

OSHO COMMUNE INTERNATIONAL

The Osho Commune International in Poona, India, guided by the vision of the enlightened master Osho, might be described as a laboratory, an experiment in creating the "New Man" – a human being who lives in harmony with himself and his environment, and who is free from all ideologies and belief systems which now divide humanity.

The Commune's Osho Multiversity offers hundreds of workshops, groups and trainings, presented by its nine different faculties:

Osho School for Centering and Zen Martial Arts
Osho School of Creative Arts
Osho International Academy of Healing Arts
Osho Meditation Academy
Osho School for Love and Consciousness
Osho School of Mysticism
Osho Institute of Tibetan Pulsing
Osho Center for Transformation
Osho Academy of Zen Sports and Fitness

All these programs are designed to help people to find the knack of meditation: the passive witnessing of thoughts, emotions, and actions, without judgment or identification. Unlike many traditional Eastern disciplines, meditation at Osho Commune is an inseparable part of everyday life – working, relating or just being. The result is that people do not renounce the world but bring to it a spirit of awareness and celebration, in a deep reverence for life.

The highlight of the day at the Commune is the meeting of the White Robe Brotherhood. This two-hour celebration of music, dance and silence, with a discourse from Osho, is unique – a complete meditation in itself where thousands of seekers, in Osho's words, "dissolve into a sea of consciousness."

SUGGESTED FURTHER READING

THE HEART SUTRA

Discourses on the Prajnaparamita Hridayam Sutra of Gautama the Buddha reveal his essential teachings: the merging of negative and positive, the non-existence of the ego and the buddha-nature of mankind. In addition, Osho speaks on the seven *chakras* and the corresponding facets in man – the physical, psychosomatic, psychological, psycho-spiritual, spiritual, spiritual-transcendental and transcendental.

HEARTBEAT OF THE ABSOLUTE
DISCOURSES ON THE ISHAVASYA UPANISHAD

In these discourses Osho gave during an early meditation camp, sutras from ancient Hindu scriptures are transmuted into stunning insights that can open the reader's eyes to his own inner reality. Osho speaks on issues that touch the heart of every intelligent individual – on karma, death, love, possessiveness, God as another name for existence, the nature of mind, and meditation. In addition, he gives practical suggestions about how to prepare for meditation and how to get the most from his meditation techniques.

THE MUSTARD SEED
COMMENTARIES ON THE FIFTH GOSPEL OF SAINT THOMAS

Osho brings to life excerpts from a scroll found at Nag Hammadi, Egypt, contributing a new understanding to these little-known sayings of Jesus – the man he calls "a revolutionary of the inner world."

THE EMPTY BOAT
TALKS ON THE STORIES OF CHUANG TZU

Osho revitalizes the 3000-year-old Taoist message of self realization through the stories of the Chinese mystic Chuang Tzu. He speaks about the state of egolessness, "the empty boat"; about spontaneity, dreams and wholeness; about living life choicelessly and meeting death with the same equanimity. This series overflows with the wisdom of one who is an empty boat himself.

FOR FURTHER INFORMATION

Many of Osho's books have been translated and published in a variety of languages worldwide. For information about Osho, his meditations, books, audio and video tapes, and the address of an Osho meditation/ information center near you, contact:

Osho International
P.O. Box 2976, London NW5 2PZ, U.K.

Osho Commune International
17 Koregaon Park, Poona 411001, India

Chidvilas Inc.
P.O. Box 17550, Boulder, Colorado 80308, U.S.A.